MW00562545

Fishes of the Texas Laguna Madre

Number Fourteen:
GULF COAST STUDIES

SPONSORED BY

Texas A&M University–Corpus Christi
John W. Tunnell Jr., General Editor

TEXAS A&M UNIVERSITY PRESS

COLLEGE STATION

ATM nature guides

fishes

of the Texas Laguna Madre

a guide for anglers & naturalists

David A. McKee

Illustrations by Henry Compton & Janice D. Fechhelm

Manufactured in China by
Everbest Printing Co. through
Four Colour Imports

First edition

This paper meets the requirements of
ANSI/NISO Z39.48-1992 (Permanence of Paper).
Binding materials have been chosen for durability.

Fish illustrations are by Henry Compton unless otherwise noted.

Illustrations by Janice D. Fechhelm are from *Fishes of the Gulf of Mexico,* by John D. McEachran and Janice D. Fechhelm. From vol. 1*:* palespotted eel, finescale menhaden, mosquito fish, tidewater silverside, gulf pipefish, and fringed pipefish. From vol. 2*:* slender searobin, leopard searobin, barred searobin, northern kingfish, banded drum, highfin goby, southern puffer.

Library of Congress Cataloging-in-Publication Data

McKee, David A., 1947–
Fishes of the Texas Laguna Madre : a guide for anglers and naturalists / by David A. McKee ; illustrations by Henry Compton and Janice D. Fechhelm. — 1st ed.
p. cm. — (Gulf Coast studies ; no. 14)
Includes bibliographical references and index.
ISBN-13: 978-1-60344-028-8 (flexbound with flaps : alk. paper)
ISBN-10: 1-60344-028-3 (flexbound with flaps : alk. paper)
1. Fishes—Texas—Laguna Madre. 2. Fishing—Texas—Laguna Madre. 3. Laguna Madre (Tex.) I. Title.
QL628.T4M43 2008
597.177'364—dc22 2007037951

Contents

Foreword

The Laguna Madre, or Mother Lagoon, is arguably the most famous and productive hypersaline lagoon in the world. One of only five such places, this legendary lagoon is steeped in both South Texas history and natural history. Vast seagrass beds, extensive wind-tidal flats, huge numbers of redhead ducks, large nesting groups of colonial seabirds, and famous recreational fishing are just some of its highlights. Extending north and south—between Padre Island National Seashore, the first U.S. national seashore, to the east and the marvelous, very large King and Kenedy ranches to the west—the lagoon has drawn naturalists, fishers, hunters, and scientists for decades.

My first visit to Laguna Madre was with my college professor and mentor Allan Chaney while I was an undergraduate student at Texas A&I University (now Texas A&M University–Kingsville). We collected brine shrimp eggs from windrows along the eastern Laguna Madre shore in Tamaulipas, Mexico, more than one hundred miles south of the Rio Grande. Later, when I was a graduate student, we visited the Texas Laguna Madre again to count and study colonial waterbirds on spoil islands near the mouth of Baffin Bay in the upper Laguna Madre of Texas.

These two experiences stand out vividly in my mind as though they occurred yesterday, and they are partly responsible for helping me choose a career in field-oriented marine science. The excitement that came with scientific adventure and discovery had me hooked. Several decades later, I had the opportunity to work with The Nature Conservancy and other colleagues on compiling all known information about the Laguna Madre, which resulted in the scientific volume *The Laguna Madre of Texas and Tamaulipas* (Tunnell and Judd 2002), and gave me an even greater appreciation of this natural wonder.

Now, thanks to a series of intriguing circumstances, which David McKee very ably describes in the Preface, a much wider audience can learn about and enjoy the magnificent Laguna Madre. Too few people in the Texas Coastal Bend realize what an international treasure lies at our front door.

After the death of marine researcher Henry Hildebrand, his wife told me that he wanted me to have his library. Among many other valuable items, I found an incomplete, buried manuscript of what appeared to be a book Hildebrand had begun about the fishes of the Laguna Madre, which was to be illustrated by his colleague Hank Compton. After discovering this partial manuscript, I immediately thought of David McKee as the perfect person to complete it.

Raised in Sinton, Texas, David received his bachelor's degree in Biology at Texas A&I, as I did. He then taught high school for a while before continuing his education, this time at Corpus Christi State University (now Texas A&M University–Corpus Christi), to earn his master's degree. After a stint with the Texas Parks and Wildlife Department, he headed off to Texas A&M University to get his Ph.D. in wildlife and fisheries science. After his graduation in the late 1980s, we were in need of a marine ecologist and someone to help develop our new mariculture master's degree program. David was the man for the job.

All of this academic and practical knowledge, coupled with his love of fishing and the fact he owned a cabin on the Laguna Madre, made David the right person to transform the old Hildebrand manuscript into a wonderful book for students, fishers, and naturalists to enjoy.

I regarded Hildebrand as a "walking encyclopedia" when I was a student; he was kind of like Neptune of the Sea. As McKee so vividly describes, Hildebrand would drop in unannounced at any time. When I was living on the Yucatan Peninsula, about 1600 miles from Hildebrand's home in Corpus Christi, he once appeared at our house, stayed for a couple of hours, and then disappeared again.

Although I didn't know Hank Compton that well, I knew of his great ability in fish and marine art. In fact, I have several original, color paintings in my office that he painted from Alacran Reef, Campeche Bank, Mexico, in the late 1950s or early 1960s. Little did I know when I obtained those in the 1970s that I would later coedit a book on the *Coral Reefs of the Southern Gulf of Mexico,* including Alacran Reef. It is interesting how we have all connected.

A great big thank you goes to David McKee for putting this all together for everyone to enjoy. We should all become better stewards of this great Mother Lagoon, and this book should help inspire us to do just that.

—John W. Tunnell Jr.

Preface

Rarely is a significant work in progress discovered posthumously. Such was the case when a partially completed manuscript titled "Coastal Fishes of South Texas," written by Dr. Henry H. Hildebrand, was found among his extensive personal library holdings following his death on August 14, 2001. His friends, family, and colleagues knew nothing about this document or when he worked on it. Accompanying the manuscript were 164 exquisite illustrations of fishes drawn by his close friend, the late Henry (Hank) Compton. As with the manuscript, there is no indication of when the drawings were made, but the 1960s and 1970s seem likely. John W. (Wes) Tunnell Jr. asked me to review a copy of the manuscript for inclusion in the Center for Coastal Studies' Gulf Coast Series. After several discussions about how to approach publication of the incomplete manuscript, I decided that the best approach was to rewrite all of the fish descriptions and accompanying text to support and showcase Compton's artwork and to add chapters on the Laguna Madre, its fishes, serpulid worm reefs, fish kills, gulf passes, and issues and concerns along with text on the fishes and updated fish taxonomy. "Fishes of the Texas Laguna Madre" appeared to be the best title.

I have also added a concluding chapter about the Summer House, now a well-known landmark in the upper lagoon. In the 1950s Louis Turcotte, a cowboy working on the Kenedy Ranch, had helped build the Summer House, and I was fortunate to have interviewed Turcotte before his death.

For whom and how Hildebrand and Compton intended to make this material available is also unknown. It is intended to appeal to artists, anglers, naturalists, students, and fishery scientists. It should serve as a general field guide while providing information on the life history, ecology, and biology of the fishes of the Texas Laguna Madre, although it should not be used as an identification guide as the artwork is not always anatomically correct. Anyone living near the lagoon or those with an interest in this unique and expansive body of water and its fishes should derive benefit. It is my hope that the comments, personal observations, and both the empirical and anecdotal tidbits I have provided will be informative and entertaining.

In both work and play, I am deeply involved with the Laguna Madre on an almost weekly basis and have been for more than thirty years. I have "lived and breathed" this water for most of my life, continue to do so, and will for the rest of my life. After many years spent on and around the upper lagoon in the roles of both scientist and angler, I have encountered many people, places, and things in the Coastal Bend and wish to share some of these experiences and observations. Most of my time on the water there has been spent in the upper lagoon. I hope that no one on the lower lagoon takes offense because all my comments and stories pertain to the northern part of the bay.

Various sources were used to compile information on the Laguna Madre and its fishes. In addition to the species selected by Hildebrand and Compton, surveys, reports, and species lists were reviewed to develop as complete a list as possible of all the fishes reported from the Texas Laguna Madre. None were selected that are solely inhabitants of the Gulf of Mexico or that are resident species of the gulf passes and jetties. The taxonomy has been brought up to date as much as possible, but fish classification is ever changing, so staying current is difficult at best. Of the 164 fishes illustrated by Compton, 92 were selected for inclusion in this book. Other species have been reported from the Laguna Madre since Hildebrand compiled his list; thus another 13 have been included. The artwork for the additional fishes is by Janice Fechhelm, who provided the drawings for John McEachran and Fechhelm's two-volume *Fishes of the Gulf of Mexico* (1998). Many thanks to Jan for allowing the use of her work.

For those wanting additional information on the Texas "lagoon," a comprehensive bibliography is included. Notable extensive and highly informative ecological surveys of the Laguna Madre include those by Ernest Simmons on the upper Laguna Madre (1957) and Joseph Breuer on Baffin and Alazan Bays (1957) and the lower Laguna Madre (1962). The all-inclusive and thorough compendium edited by Wes Tunnell and Frank Judd on the Laguna Madre of Texas and Tamaulipas (2002) is highly recommended to anyone with an interest in this body of water. They provide more than 1,250 entries in their bibliography on the Texas and Mexico lagoons.

The format of this book is fairly standard for one reporting on a collective group of animals. The fishes are organized and discussed taxonomically, beginning with the more primitive cartilaginous fishes and progressing to the more recent or advanced bony fishes. All are grouped by order, and within each family the species are listed and text is provided. Common name(s), descriptions and characteristics, ecological range and distribution, feeding habits, and reproduction are provided. For certain economically important species, and especially the "Big 5" coastal sport fish (spotted seatrout, red drum, black drum, sheepshead, and southern flounder), additional notes on angling techniques, personal observations, record catches, and regulations are included. Varied sources along with personal experiences from a lifetime of fishing were used to develop the text on angling. Some species are more commonly encountered and some are more economically important; thus more text has been provided for those species. I have reported this information as succinctly and accurately as possible, and any errors, omissions, or inconsistencies are certainly not intentional.

Acknowledgments

This book is dedicated to Henry Hildebrand and Hank Compton. It would not have even been an idea without their text and artwork. Ernest Simmons and Joe Breuer (both former longtime biologists with the Texas Parks and Wildlife Department [TPWD]) were among the early pioneers in documenting the lagoon's fishes. They shared a deep love and respect for this unique and remote body of salty water. I cannot mention the lagoon without acknowledging Chatter Allen, Smiley Davis, Dr. Ford Allen, and Dick McCracken (all deceased) and the other founding members of the Ananias Fishing Club who were among the early fishermen that discovered the serenity of the "Mother Lagoon" in the early 1940s and the bounty of fish to be had with a rod and reel and a handful of plugs and spoons. I am proud to be included in the club membership of this prestigious group of anglers and characters. The Coastal Conservation Association must also be acknowledged because, along with TPWD, they are largely responsible for the great fishing available on the Texas coast today.

Much use was made of the individual chapters provided by Wes Tunnell and Kim Withers in Tunnell and Judd's book on the Laguna Madre of Texas and Tamaulipas. The task of gathering information on the lagoon was made much easier with the publication of that book. Significant and valuable contributions were made by the "laguna crew" with the Coastal Fisheries Division of the Texas Parks and Wildlife Department. A big thank you goes to Kyle Spiller, Randy Blankinship, Perry Trial, and Art Morris. Thanks also go to Robert Vega and his hatchery staff for their success in putting fish "back where they used to be." My hat is forever off to this great bunch of dedicated folks who work long and hard to ensure that the fishery resources in the Laguna Madre are well managed.

I owe a lot to my mother (Janie), my grandfather Frank Hunt (sheriff of San Patricio County), and my uncle Sam Hunt II, cousin Sam Hunt III, Bobby Hunt, and Robert (Doc) Johnson for teaching me not only how to fish but also, more importantly, why to fish. A special thanks to my wife (Jane) and my three children (Laura, Hunt, and Helen) for their love and support.

Assisting me with the compilation and organization of this book (and always with smiles and laughs and a can-do attitude) were Ashlie Simmons, Brenda Catlin, Nicole Ekstrom, Laura Heil, and Ken Rainer. Ashlie especially deserves much credit for the completion of this big project. I couldn't have done this without her. I must also thank all of my teaching assistants who have helped me with my marine science classes over the years. In chronological order they are: Paul Choucair, Beau Hardegree, Carl Beaver, Jim Tolan, Chris Stahl, Scott Fagan, Jim Giesen, Jace Tunnell, David Newstead, Jeff Landgraff, Jackie Staggs, and Aaron Baxter. I know this "team" has made a difference in the lives of many fledgling marine science students and helped them gain an appreciation and better understanding of the marine environment. I must also thank the hundreds of students whom I have had the pleasure to teach over the last twenty plus years. Many of the best years of my life have been spent in the classroom. As a result, I have been blessed with having one of the best and most rewarding jobs possible. Thank you all.

I owe a lot to Kyle Spiller and David Sikes for their reviews of the manuscript in its early phase of development. Their comments were most helpful. I thank artist Hank Compton's sister-in-law Helen Compton for providing background information on Hank and his life. I must also recognize my dear friend Captain Billy Sandifer. Few people of my generation have more passion about life and about the career they were chosen to undertake.

The Scientist and the Artist

THE SCIENTIST: Henry Hildebrand was born landlocked in Fowler, Kansas, in 1922 and developed an early interest in zoology and fisheries, in large part as a result of the influence of his uncle, Samuel Hildebrand, a renowned ichthyologist. Following his graduation from a public high school, Hildebrand attended the University of Kansas, where he received a bachelor of science degree in zoology in 1946. After a stint in the U.S. Navy he earned a master of science degree in fisheries at McGill University (Montreal) in 1948. After one year at the University of Washington, he traveled to South Texas and enrolled at the University of Texas Marine Science Institute in Port Aransas. Under the direction of Gordon Gunter he completed his Ph.D. in fisheries in 1954. Shortly after arriving at UT, he and several graduate students decided to travel to Veracruz, Mexico, to help the local commercial fishermen establish a fishery for pompano. Before they arrived, word was received that a red tide had devastated most of the local marine organisms so they returned to Texas. Hildebrand took a teaching position at the University of Corpus Christi (UCC, now Texas A&M University–Corpus Christi) in 1957 and, as a one-person faculty, began developing the marine science program at that Baptist institution. He remained there until 1973, when he accepted a faculty position at Texas A&I University (now Texas A&M University–Kingsville). Hildebrand loathed the necessary evil of the paperwork required in academia and retired in 1979. He then became a private consultant for the Texas commercial fishing and shrimping industries until fully retiring in 1985. Until his death he continued to visit TAMU–CC colleagues weekly to discuss and gather information on many different kinds of marine issues.

Most of the major achievements in his fifty-year career were made while at UCC, and several involved work done outside of Texas and the United States. Aside from starting the field-based, hands-on marine science program that became the model for the program in place today at TAMU–CC, he also discovered and mapped the nesting grounds of the endangered Kemp's ridley sea turtle in the Mexican Gulf of Mexico. He performed ground-breaking field research on the Laguna Madre of both Texas and Mexico and did extensive studies of the brown and pink shrimp grounds in the gulf. He reported on freeze-caused fish kills, harmful algal blooms, oil and tar on gulf beaches, brine discharges into Texas streams and rivers, and the dredging of oyster shell from Texas bays. He even reported on shrews, the birds and the cod fishery of Ungava Bay, Quebec, and the king crab fishery of the Bering Sea. While his publication record spanned from 1943 to 1978, he rarely published his results in scholarly journals. He was content to submit final reports to funding organizations, and rarely did he write anything more on the subject. Although extremely broad in his interests, he was considered an authority on most all of them.

In the late 1950s and early 1960s, Hildebrand began taking UCC students to Mexico and British Honduras (now Belize) to study coral reefs, local fisheries, and the general ecology of the areas visited. Always included were visits to historic ruins and commercial fishing villages. This practice continues today at TAMU–CC; the coral reef ecology class has been visiting that area annually for the past thirty years. Hildebrand influenced the lives of numerous students, many developing careers in the sciences with the foundation he provided them. His educational philosophy was simple and mirrored that of the nineteenth-century Swiss naturalist Louis Agassiz: "Study nature, not books."

Throughout his life, Hildebrand read newspapers daily and was well versed in current issues at all levels of government. He regularly wrote letters to the editor of the *Corpus Christi Caller-Times* newspaper, and these generally pertained to his opposition to Texas commercial shrimping regulations. His interests in fishery-related issues were largely based on his genuine concern for the economic well-being of those making their living in the fishing industry. He felt deeply for those whose lives were affected by fishery regulations, especially when he considered the regulations to be scientifically unfounded. Even in his final years, if one pushed one of his hot buttons (like commercial fishing regulations in Texas) his eyes would take on a sparkle and his voice would break up as he began a long discourse on the topic. One of his least favorite regulations was the Texas shrimp boat buy-back program.

At his memorial service, family, friends, past students, and colleagues told of the Henry Hildebrand they remembered. Terms used to describe him were "all business, he played no games," "modest, low-profile, and he always did his own thing," "a walking encyclopedia," and "a certifiable genius." Hildebrand was an individualist in the truest sense. He didn't care what others thought of him or his opinions. He was generally quite disheveled in appearance and gave little thought to the way he dressed. Garments making up his daily attire in his later years were likely purchased in the 1960s. He was often mistaken for a janitor when visitors encountered him in the hallway. When he had something on his mind and wanted to talk, he got right to it with absolutely no small talk beforehand. More than once he walked uninvited into private meetings, sat down, and waited impatiently for it to adjourn so that he could ask questions, gather information, and discuss at length some topic that was under his skin. He generally had questions compiled on a small notepad, and he often began a session with the question "What do you know about so and so?" He was famous for never knocking before entering an office, even when there was no meeting in progress.

In 2001, the Texas Shrimp Association presented Hildebrand with its Lifetime Achievement Award for his many years of service to that industry. In 2002 Wes Tunnell and Frank Judd dedicated their book on the Laguna Madre of Texas and Tamaulipas to him for his early and tireless investigations of this extensive, remote body of water that few had even considered studying in the 1950s and 1960s.

As a friend, a former student, and one whom Hildebrand would visit on his weekly rounds to campus, I continue the tradition of teaching marine science with an applied, hands-on, field-based approach, which Hildebrand thought was so essential for anyone attempting to understand and interpret nature.

THE ARTIST: Henry (Hank) Compton was born on April 10, 1928, in San Angelo, Texas, where his father worked as an accountant and his mother as a schoolteacher. Later the family moved to Snyder, Texas, where his father was able to find work. Hank Compton was always fond of animals and liked to draw and paint them, especially birds and fish. Following graduation from high school, he joined the air force at age eighteen. He was stationed in Maine and was a pilot with the rank of captain. Following his military service, he was hired by TPWD and worked out of the Rockport Marine Laboratory. While there, he participated in some of the first research in the Gulf of Mexico, working aboard the R/V *Western Gulf.* He retired from TPWD in 1969.

Compton assisted Hildebrand in his classic survey of the brown and pink shrimp grounds in the Gulf of Mexico. He also accompanied him on several trips to the Yucatan Peninsula in Mexico in the early 1960s and was an author of the work completed there.

Because of his talent as an artist, Hank Compton provided the fish illustrations for several TPWD bulletins, including the color illustrations used in *Saltwater Fishes of Texas* and *Freshwater Fishes of Texas.* Surprisingly, he had no formal training as an artist. He could paint what the eye could see with great accuracy and attention to detail. The artwork used in this book is evidence of his talent as an artist. Although he painted and drew many fish and birds during his lifetime, little is known about the whereabouts of that art today.

Many folks (especially fishery biologists) who have examined his art have commented on the "abstract" nature of his drawings. I liken his work to that of John Audubon, one of the foremost American bird illustrators. While the drawings may not always be useful to one trying to identify an unknown fish, one cannot deny that the art is simply splendid.

In his later years, Compton worked for Jack Maddux as manager of the Oso Pier on Corpus Christi Bay, a longtime hangout for many of the local fishing enthusiasts and characters around town. He died at the age of seventy-seven on October 20, 2005. Unfortunately, Hank Compton died the week I was to meet and interview him, but I am elated that he is finally getting the long overdue recognition for his artistic skill and the superb biological illustrations that he left behind.

Fishes of the Texas Laguna Madre

An Introduction to the Laguna Madre

About 18,000 years before the present (YBP) near the end of the last glaciation period (known as the Wisconsin period), sea level was three hundred to five hundred feet lower than it is today, and the Texas gulf shoreline was about fifty miles east of its present position. By 5,000 YBP, sea level had risen to fifteen feet below its present level, and by this time geologic processes, such as sand-bar formation parallel to the coast-line, were active. By the time sea level had reached its present level (2,500 YBP), these sandbars had combined to form Padre Island and the other barrier islands along the Texas coast. In short, the origin of the Laguna Madre is directly attributable to the formation of Padre Island.

Baffin Bay in the upper Laguna Madre is thought to have become hypersaline prior to the rest of the Laguna Madre, perhaps 4,500 YBP. Over the last several thousand years, hurricanes and tropical storms, in conjunction with wind patterns, have continually transported sediments from Padre Island into the Laguna Madre. This deposition has led to the formation of extensive tidal flats in the lagoon from southern Padre Island northward. In the Land Cut area, just south of Baffin Bay, these processes resulted in a slow but continuous infilling with sediment, eventually resulting in the formation of a land bridge connecting Padre Island to the mainland. It has long been proposed that this infilling was the result of a major hurricane in 1919, but indications are that the process was more gradual, with final closure completed only a few hundred years ago. Even at the northern end of Padre Island, the island has slowly migrated into the lagoon, likely because of extended periods of drought and overgrazing, both of which exposed bare sand to the prevailing southeasterly winds. Today sands are more common in the shallow eastern side of the lagoon, where storm surges and southeasterly winds continue to fill in the lagoon. Clays and silts are more common along the mainland (western) shore and in the west-central basins.

Geography

The Laguna Madre is a bar-built coastal lagoon bordered by barrier islands and peninsulas to the east and by the mainland on the west. Bar-built lagoons are water bodies that have been isolated by the formation of a barrier island or sand spit. Physically, the Laguna Madre is divided into two separate lagoons by the Rio Grande delta: the Laguna Madre of Texas, in the United States to the north, and the Laguna Madre de Tamaulipas, in Mexico to the south (Fig. 1). These two coastal ecosystems are similar in size (approximately 600 square miles each), share various characteristics, and together form the largest of only five hypersaline ecosystems in the world. The Laguna Madre extends 277 miles from Corpus Christi, Texas (27° 40.5' N), to Río Soto la Marina, Mexico, on the southern end (23° 47' N). Each of the lagoons are approximately 115 miles in length but vary in average width (in Texas averaging 4.3 miles and in Mexico, 7.5 miles).

The Laguna Madre of Texas extends from Corpus Christi to just south of Port Isabel (26° 0' N) and is the largest of seven estuarine systems on the Texas coast. It is divided into two subunits: the upper Laguna Madre (Fig. 2) and lower Laguna Madre (Fig. 3). The two Texas lagoons are physically divided by a sand sheet or land bridge (Land Cut) connecting Padre Island with the mainland. The Gulf Intracoastal Waterway (GIWW) bisects this extensive sand flat, thus connecting the two lagoons via the Land Cut. Both the upper and lower lagoons are similar in length, 47 and 57 miles long, respectively. The upper lagoon is slightly narrower in average width (3.7 miles versus 5.0 miles). Average depth for the upper lagoon is slightly shallower (2.6 feet deep) than the lower lagoon (4.6 feet deep).

The upper lagoon totals approximately 101,150 surface acres comprising Baffin Bay (33,560 acres), Alazan Bay (14,630 acres), Cayo del Grullo (7,500 acres), Laguna de los Olmos or Laguna Salada (3,675 acres), and Cayo del Infiernillo or Three Sloughs (1,423 acres). The remaining 40,370 acres, including the 16,500 acres of Nine Mile Hole, is simply referred to as the upper Laguna Madre. How Baffin Bay got its name is mostly unclear, but the most popular story indicates that Captain Mifflin Kenedy is responsible. Having visited Baffin Bay in the Arctic Ocean as a young seagoing man, he is said to have named the Texas bay in a tongue-in-cheek fashion because it was such a direct contrast to the one near the North Pole. Nevertheless, the name stuck. In the upper lagoon, names for areas like Dead Man's Hole, Bad Lands, and Starvation Point indicate that early

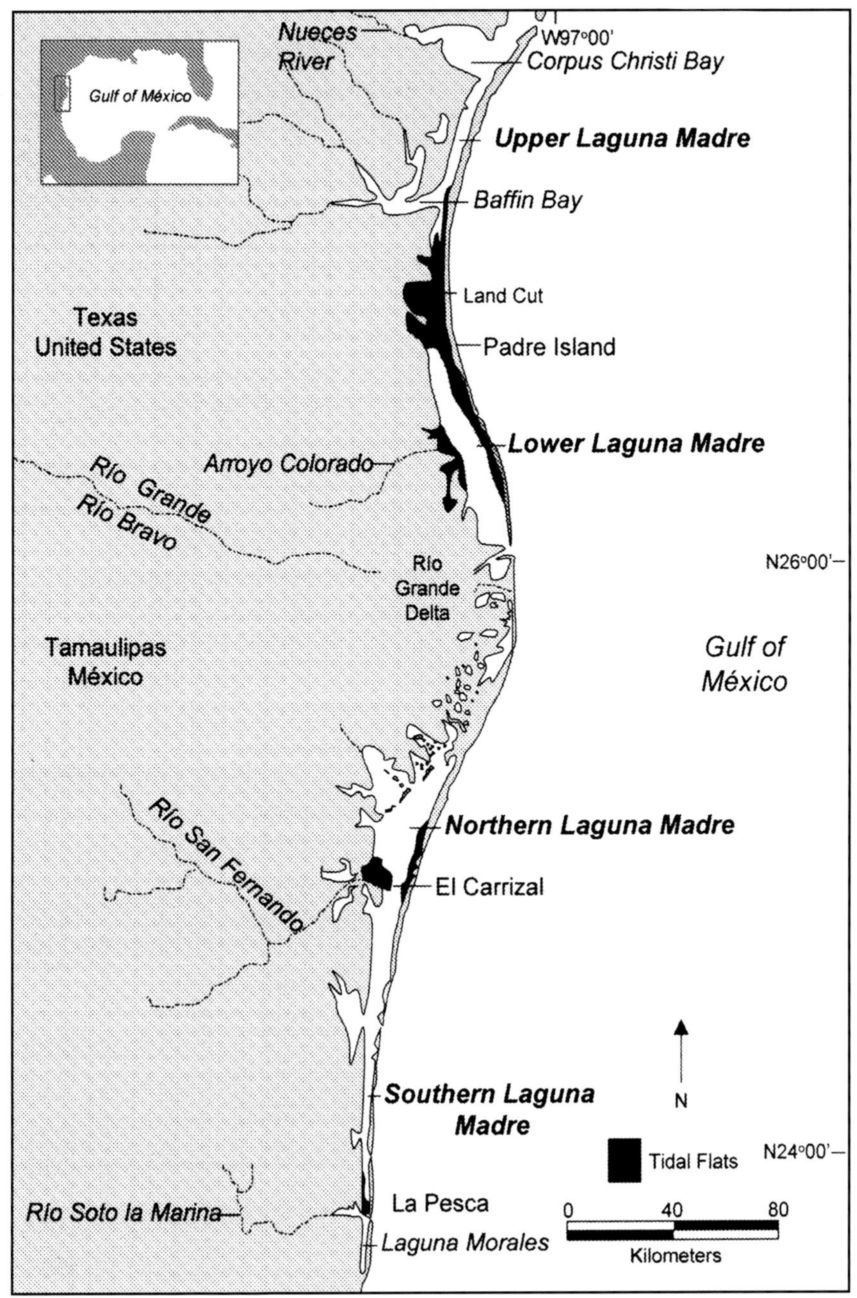

Fig. 1. Map of the Laguna Madre of Texas and Tamaulipas (modified from map in The Laguna Madre of Texas and Tamaulipas, *2002, by Tunnell and Judd, Texas A&M University Press).*

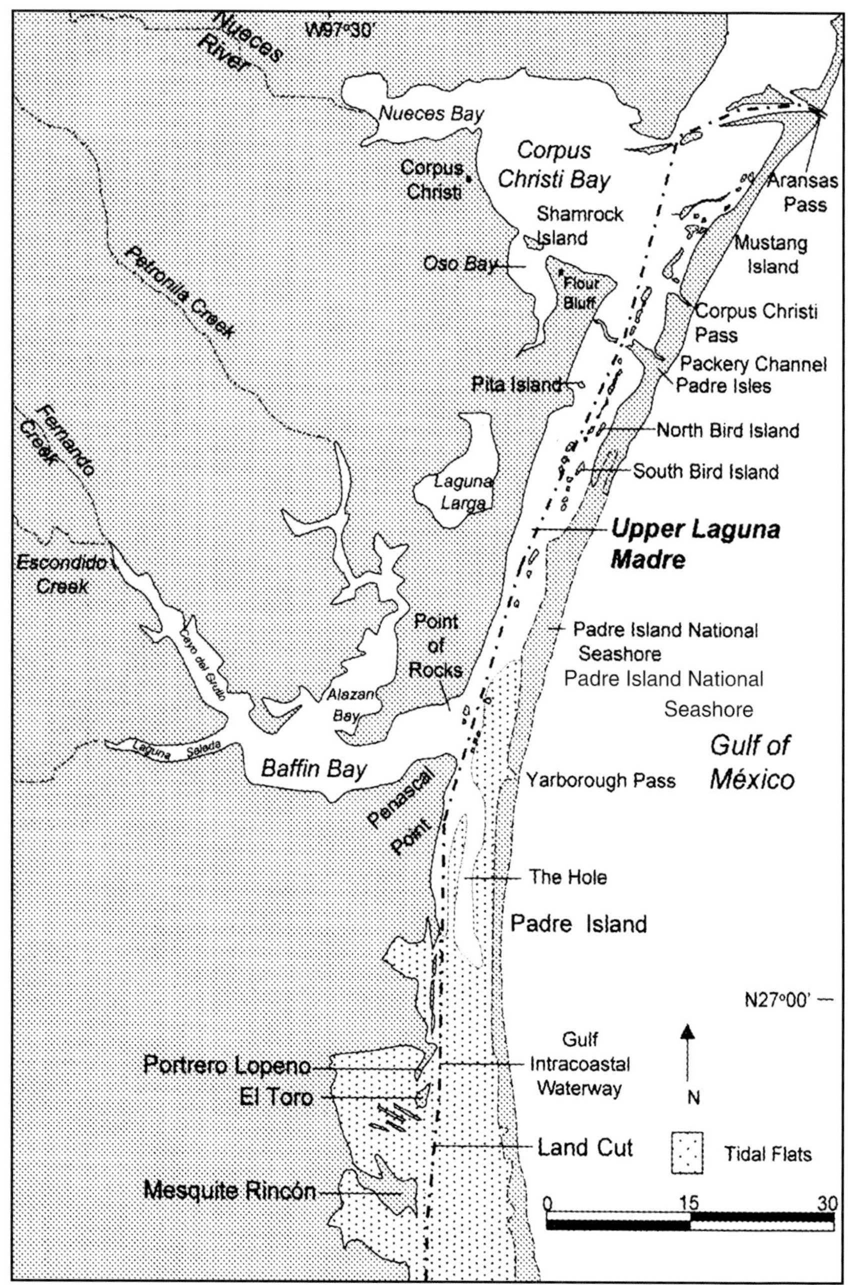

Fig. 2. Map of the upper Laguna Madre of Texas (modified from map in The Laguna Madre of Texas and Tamaulipas, *2002, by Tunnell and Judd, Texas A&M University Press).*

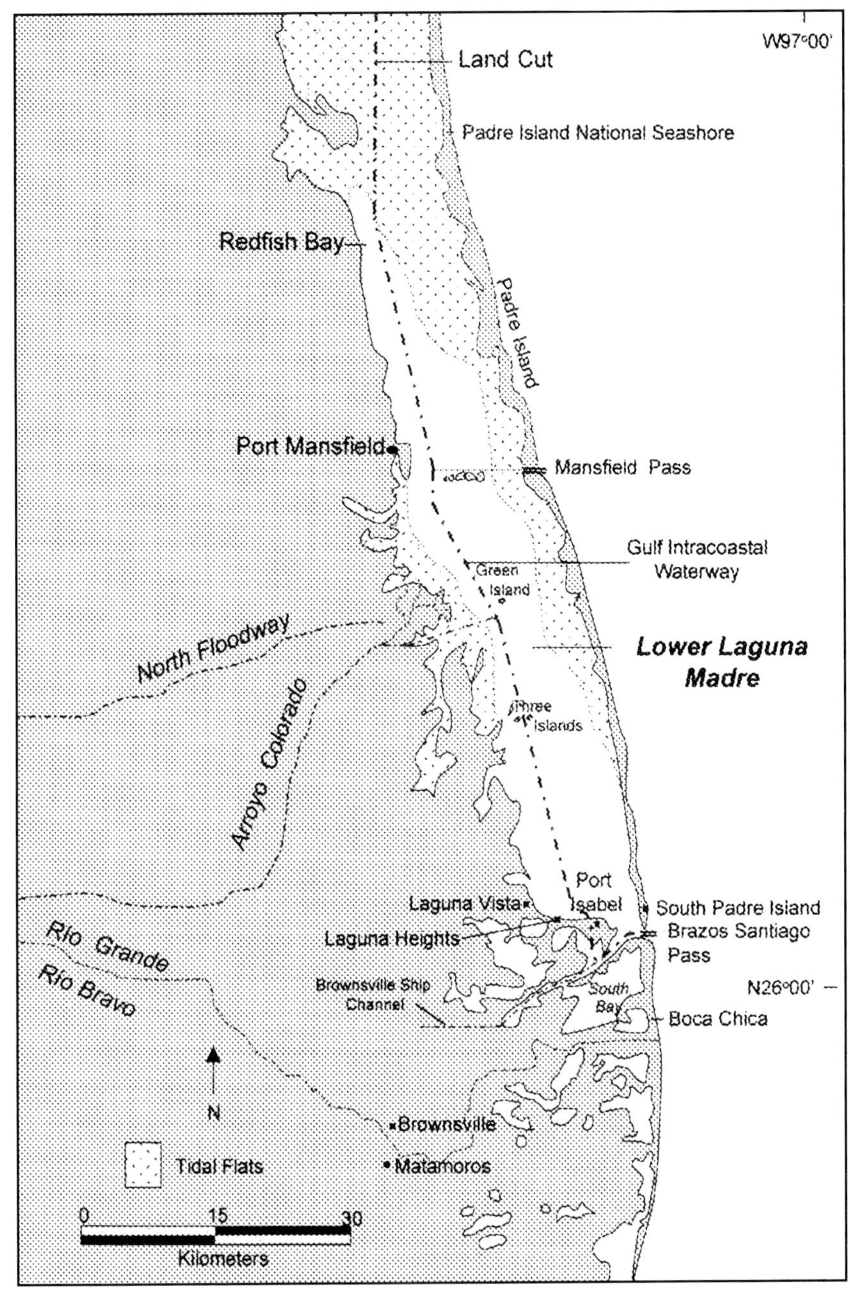

Fig. 3. Map of the lower Laguna Madre of Texas (modified from map in The Laguna Madre of Texas and Tamaulipas, *2002, by Tunnell and Judd, Texas A&M University Press).*

visitors to Baffin Bay must have had great respect for the area.

The surface area of the lower lagoon totals 150,000 acres and comprises three subdivisions (north to south): Redfish Bay (53,000 acres), extending south from the Land Cut to a point four miles south of Port Mansfield; the middle or lower lagoon (94,500 acres), extending south to the Brownsville Ship Channel; and South Bay (2,500 acres), terminating just south of Port Isabel.

The Texas Laguna Madre is bordered on the east by Padre Island, interrupted only by Port Mansfield Pass (East Cut). Most of the Laguna Madre is inaccessible to the public except by boat, making it largely secluded. The mainland shore to the west is protected by large ranches (King, Kenedy, Yturria), other smaller ranches, and the Laguna Atascosa National Wildlife Refuge. Both the private ranch land and large federal tracts have limited any significant commercial development to date. With the exception of South Padre Island, no commercial development exists on the barrier island. Other than the city of Corpus Christi at the northern end of the lagoon, the only other developments are on Baffin Bay (Riviera Beach and Loyola Beach) and the small township of Port Mansfield and several other small communities on the lower lagoon.

The shallow, clear Laguna Madre of Texas contains both natural and artificial (man-made) islands. In the upper lagoon only Crane, Pita, and North and South Bird Islands are naturally occurring. In the lower lagoon, only Green Island and Three Islands are natural (see Fig. 3). Natural islands are more common in the Laguna Madre de Tamaulipas than in the Texas Laguna Madre.

In both lagoons, islands form when strong winds push water up around low-lying wind-tidal flats. These are referred to locally as "lomas" (hill-like islands) or "potreros" (long islands lying parallel to shore). Numerous and widespread "spoil" islands exist throughout the Laguna Madre, created from bottom sediment dredged from the GIWW or from oil and gas exploration activities. Periodically the U.S. Army Corps of Engineers places new material (spoil) on the islands during scheduled maintenance dredging. New disposal sites are continuously being sought in both the bays and on the mainland. Open bay disposal is a highly controversial topic today. All natural islands and certain artificial spoil islands are designated as rookery islands for colonial bird species, including the piping plover (*Charadrius melodus*), snowy plover (*Charadrius alexandrinus*), and reddish egret (*Egretta rufescens*). The Laguna Madre is an important wintering area for the redhead duck (*Aythya americana*) and other migratory waterfowl. More than 80 percent of the North American breeding population winters in the western Gulf of Mexico, with the Texas and Mexican lagoons being home for more than 75 percent of that wintering population.

The Texas General Land Office (TGLO) issues permits and manages fishing cabins on the spoil islands. Of the 406 cabins on the Texas coast, nearly three-quarters are situated in the Laguna Madre, with 90 percent situated in the upper lagoon in the vicinity of Baffin Bay.

Drainage from the mainland into the Texas Laguna Madre is minimal. Several ephemeral creeks (San Fernando, Santa Gertrudis, Los Olmos, Petronilla, and several others) enter Baffin Bay and flow into the watershed following significant rainfall. Until recently, the upper lagoon had no direct connection to the gulf. In 2006, the redredging of Packery Channel was completed, allowing limited water exchange in the northernmost end. However, the lower lagoon has two inlets (passes) linking it with the gulf: Port Mansfield Pass and Brazos Santiago Pass. The distance between the Aransas Pass (at Port Aransas) and Port Mansfield Pass is ninety-three miles and the Brazos Santiago Pass is an additional thirty miles to the south. The only drainage into the lower lagoon is from the Arroyo Colorado and the North Floodway, which together drain more than one million acres of agricultural land in the Rio Grande Valley. The Rio Grande flows directly into the gulf and provides minimal benefit to the lower lagoon.

Hydrography

The Laguna Madre of Texas is classified as a negative estuary or hypersaline lagoon. Unlike typical bay and estuarine systems, which regularly receive freshwater inflow and exhibit both phytoplankton and salt marsh productivity, the Texas lagoon receives minimal and sporadic freshwater inflow. In the Texas lagoon, the water is typically clear, seagrass meadows predominate, and its shorelines are barren. The lagoon generally remains clear due to the composition of the bottom sediments (which are predominantly quartz sands) that do not easily resuspend, keeping turbidity to a minimum. Any resuspension of sediments quickly settles out when the winds subside.

In any hypersaline lagoon, evaporation exceeds precipitation, and this is certainly the case in the Laguna Madre. Evaporation from the water surface is high, often at twice the rate of precipitation. In the lower lagoon, the average annual rainfall is twenty-seven inches, with evaporation often totaling nearly sixty inches. Salinity values in a hypersaline estuary are usually between 40 and 80 parts per thousand (ppt) and the water is considered to be brine at salinities above 80 ppt, the level at which mass fish mortalities begin. The shallow nature of the Texas lagoon promotes evaporation due to a high surface-to-volume ratio. Salinity is high not only because of rapid evaporation but also because of low and variable rainfall, minimal freshwater inflow, limited inlets to the gulf, a small daily tidal range, and poor circulation. The shallowness of the lagoon, however, ensures that the water column is well mixed, meaning that both temperature and salinity are generally uniform from top to bottom with the exception of the deeper holes and channels. Average salinity between 1982 and 2000 in the upper lagoon was 38 ppt (with a range of 26 to 50) and 34 ppt (with values ranging from 31 to 37) in the lower Laguna Madre. The presence of the two passes in the lower lagoon, including the GIWW, moderates salinities and allows water exchange with the gulf, resulting in improved water quality. Before the GIWW was dredged in the mid-1940s, salinity levels in the upper Laguna Madre reached levels greater than 100 ppt. The redredging of Packery Channel (completed in late 2006) may slightly decrease salinity in the northern portion of the upper Laguna Madre (by some estimates perhaps as far south as Pita Island).

Meteorological tides (caused by wind and storms) are more important and much more pronounced than astronomical tides (caused by the gravitational pull of the sun and moon). Wind tides are the result of an increase in water height on the downwind side of a body of water caused by the friction of wind on the water's surface. This friction can result in an increase in water level of from one to four feet depending on wind velocity and fetch (distance). Strong southeast and north winds have been observed to inundate or cover as much as two hundred square miles of tidal flats in the lagoon in a short period of time and can push water to places where astronomical tides cannot. High water levels are normal in the Texas lagoon during late May and late October, with low water levels common in late February and late July. Water levels can fluctuate as much as twenty inches during these periods. Short-term (one to two weeks) water height fluxes are generally between four and eight inches. Daily astronomical tides usually account for only a one- to one-and-a-half-inch change in water level, with less vertical change seen as distance from the gulf passes increases.

Climate

The climate of the Texas Laguna Madre is semiarid to subtropical and characterized by high temperatures, deficiencies in moisture, and a combination of high humidity with occasional killing freezes. Long hot summers and short mild winters are also characteristic. The upper and lower lagoons experience similar average winter air temperatures (47°F). However, the upper lagoon average summer air temperature is somewhat cooler than that in the lower lagoon (92°F versus 97°F). Both lagoons experience from one to three frost days each year, and killing freezes occur on an average of once every seven years (between 1820 and 1997). (See the chapter on historical fish kills along the Texas coast.)

Average annual rainfall is highly variable in the Texas Laguna Madre (1917 saw only five and a half inches but more than fifty inches fell in 1992) and decreases slightly from Corpus Christi (twenty-eight inches) to Brownsville (twenty-seven inches). Rainfall occurs in two peaks: May/June and August/September. Generally the greatest rainfall is in September and is associated with tropical storm activity in the gulf. Overall, two-thirds of the annual rainfall occurs between May and October, the South Texas "rainy" season. Above average rainfall occurs during El Niño years. In general, winds averaging 12 mph predominate from the southeast for 270 days per year, from March through September, with "northers" interrupting that pattern during the winter (October through February). Humidity averages 88 percent annually with little seasonal variability (July = 90 percent, December = 85 percent).

Hurricanes and tropical storm activity regularly impact the Texas coast, with more than fifty storms striking or affecting the Texas coast since 1900. Twenty-four of these were categorized as "major" storms, and nine had some impact on the Laguna Madre. Beulah made landfall on the lower Texas coast in 1967, when high salinities were present in the Laguna Madre (upper lagoon salinities were between 55 and 63 ppt). The lagoon was first flooded with gulf waters following a six- to seven-foot storm surge and then by torrential rains following passage of the storm. Nearly twenty inches of rain fell in the watershed of the lagoon, dropping salinities to between 6 and 12 ppt. Hurricane Brett struck the Texas coast south of Baffin Bay in 1999 and created twelve shallow washover passes that connected the gulf and the lagoon for several weeks. Both hurricanes caused serious erosion on the gulf beaches.

Habitats

Habitats of the Laguna Madre of Texas include plant communities, beach rock, jettied inlets of the Port Mansfield and Brazos Santiago Passes, serpulid worm reefs, mangroves, oyster reefs, wind-tidal flats, and open bay.

PLANT COMMUNITIES

Four basic plant communities predominate in the Laguna Madre largely because of their great tolerances of environmental conditions. These plant communities include submerged seagrass meadows, phytoplankton, algal mats on the wind-tidal flats (mainly blue-green algae), and macro-algae (thirty species that grow best at salinities of less than 50 ppt).

Seagrasses provide oxygen and detritus and serve as both a refuge and an indirect source of food for larval and juvenile stages of numerous fishes and invertebrates. The seagrass meadows also contribute to the recycling of nutrients in this semi-enclosed lagoon system. Few marine herbivores eat seagrasses because they are difficult to digest. Any nutrient contribution from seagrasses in the Laguna Madre appears to be indirect and is made available only after the seagrasses are broken down by various microorganisms. Thus the top predators depend on seagrasses even though they directly eat fish, shrimp, and other invertebrates that rely on detritus as a food source.

Seagrasses are successful in the Laguna Madre because of its general shallowness and great water clarity, which provide a competitive advantage since these submerged plants require high light intensities for optimal growth. Seagrasses further reduce turbidity by holding the bottom sediments in place. Any turbidity is generally of short duration and is the result of plankton blooms, and along the Texas coast a brown tide (caused by *Aureoumbra lagunensis*) can be of long duration. The bloom following the 1989 freeze persisted from 1990 through 1995 and was still present to some degree in the Baffin Bay complex in 2007.

Extensive seagrass meadows are largely responsible for the high productivity of the Laguna Madre. Standing crops of seagrasses (meadows) compare in productivity to agricultural crops. Interestingly, one-half of all seagrass vegetative material is below the bottom of the lagoon. Seagrasses are firmly anchored in the bottom by a root-like system (rhizomes) and derive their nutrients through these rhizomes rather than obtaining nutrients suspended in the water. Due to generally poor water circulation in the lagoon, all nutrients are made available via recycling of dead plant and animal material. However, if better circulation and increased water exchange with the gulf were available it is likely that the necessary nutrients would be diluted and carried away from the lagoon. Because there is little freshwater inflow into the Laguna Madre, and thus little nutrient input from land, the availability of nutrients from the breakdown of seagrasses appears to be the primary reason for the vast and luxuriant coverage of seagrasses. The breakdown of the seagrasses has led to and supports a detritus-rich lagoon.

The Laguna Madre has 79 percent of the seagrasses present on the Texas coast even though the upper and lower lagoons occupy only 20 percent of the total surface area. In the upper Laguna Madre seagrasses cover 67,700 acres (67 percent of the total acreage), with shoal grass (*Halodule beaudettei*) dominating because of its ability to tolerate high salinity levels greater than 40 ppt. Other species include manatee grass (*Syringodium filiforme*), clover grass (*Halophila engelmannii*), and widgeon grass (*Ruppia maritima*). Seagrass coverage does not appear to be declining in either the upper or lower lagoon. However, the composition of species appears to be changing. In the upper lagoon, manatee grass appears to be increasing in coverage while shoal grass is declining, and there is some concern as to the quality of this new colonizer as suitable nursery habitat for larval organisms and what effects it may have on fisheries due to its greater above-ground shoot density. With a reported poor tolerance to higher salinities, widgeon grass is appearing in areas of the upper lagoon.

In the lower Laguna Madre, there is little expansion of manatee grass and turtle grass appears to be increasing. In the lower lagoon seagrasses cover 118,600 acres (79 percent of the total acreage), of which shoal grass comprises approximately 50 percent of the coverage, with manatee grass and turtle grass (*Thalassia testudinum*) making up most of the remainder. Both manatee grass and turtle grass are tolerant of salinities up to 40 ppt.

Overall, the Laguna Madre is considered to be a pioneer climax system, meaning that seagrasses invaded a previously barren environment and have become a stable community. The Laguna Madre has also been called a "thin-grass" system, causing recent concerns about propeller scarring and the decline of seagrass species throughout the Laguna Madre. The chapter on issues and concerns discusses these matters associated with seagrasses in greater detail.

Phytoplankton dominates the open bay areas of the Laguna Madre, and this community consists primarily of various species of diatoms and dinoflagellates. Phytoplankton densities have been found to be greatest between December and March and lowest during spring and summer. Phytoplankton density is dependent on temperature, salinity levels, and nutrient input from rainfall runoff. A survey in 1978 identified 135 species of phytoplankton in the upper Laguna Madre, with diatoms accounting for 86 percent of those species.

Blue-green algal mats are found on the wind-tidal flats along the shorelines of the Laguna Madre. These algal mats contribute to the recycling of nutrients and are an important food source for a variety of invertebrates, insects, and birds.

Numerous species of macro-algae ("seaweeds") are also found in the Laguna Madre. They thrive in this hypersaline environment, and because of the shallowness of the water they can easily photosynthesize throughout the water column. Dense macro-algal blooms may also be seen when there are increased levels of nutrients, such as nitrogen. Some species can be found drifting in the water or attached to hard substrates such as beach rock, jetty rocks, serpulid reefs, piers, and pilings. The most common species of drift algae are the red algae, while species attached to hard substrates are primarily green filamentous types.

Beach Rock

Beach rock or coquina rock (made up of clams, mussels, and other assorted molluscs) indicates the presence of a natural gulf shoreline at a previous high stand of sea level before the development of the lagoon system. This rock is present in the upper lagoon from Penascal Point to the Land Cut on the mainland (western) shore where it is part of the shallow "sill" that has formed across the mouth of Baffin Bay. These rocks are both exposed and submerged along the Kenedy Ranch shoreline and offer excellent places from which to fish. However, access to the shoreline is very limited, with few spots where one can anchor a boat and wade the shoreline. However, the water is fairly deep all the way to the shore and allows great drift fishing from a boat. In the lower Laguna Madre beach rock encloses the Laguna el Catán.

Jetties

Jetties line the edges of the channels along the two major gulf passes, Port Mansfield and Brazos Santiago. These aid in slowing down the siltation (sanding-in) process in the inlets. These constructed pink granite jetties provide abundant hard substrate for macro-algae and small invertebrates to live on, under, within, or behind. These three-dimensional structures attract an assortment of animals such as fish and sea turtles to the jettied passes to feed. They also serve as thoroughfares connecting the inner bays with the gulf and offer excellent places to fish throughout the year.

Serpulid Worm Reefs

Serpulid worm reefs occur only in Baffin Bay in the upper lagoon. These extensive (ten square miles of coverage) but extinct reefs are of two types: the reef fields in the westernmost reaches of the bay and patch reefs near the mouth and scattered throughout the remainder of the bay. Some of the best fishing in the upper lagoon is over and around these reefs that play a role in the bay similar to that of an oasis in the middle of a desert.

In the early attempts to stabilize the Aransas Pass at Port Aransas in the late 1800s, serpulid worm rocks from Baffin Bay were used because they were the only hard material available in the area. Hildebrand told of sailing craft making regular trips to Baffin Bay to take on load after load of these worm rocks to line the eroding and migrating pass. Those early efforts to stabilize the pass were unsuccessful. Refer to the chapter on the worm rocks of Baffin Bay for more information on this unique habitat.

Mangroves

Mangroves are present only in the lower Laguna Madre due to their poor ability to tolerate the winter weather farther to the north on the Texas coast. Although found in considerable abundance near the Aransas Pass (e.g., Harbor Island), the black mangrove (*Avicennia germinans*) is the only species of mangrove found in the Texas Laguna Madre (and is restricted to the southernmost portions of the lower lagoon). This mangrove species is much smaller (generally less than five feet tall) than those found in more tropical areas, where they can exceed thirty feet in height. The black mangrove is an intertidal plant that has its roots exposed to the air during low water and submerged during high-water conditions. Mangroves in the Texas Laguna Madre are fragile and experience mass mortality during extreme winter freezes like those in 1983 and 1989. It has been suggested that the Texas mangrove population may belong to a genetic group capable of surviving colder temperatures.

Oyster Reefs

Today oyster reefs occur only in South Bay in the lower lagoon due to the lower average salinities. Oysters are harvested commercially there, and the size of the harvests varies by area and with salinity levels. Because of the presence of oyster shells in the nearly 250 Karankawa habitation sites and middens mapped around Baffin Bay, it is supportive evidence that oyster reefs existed there in times past when salinity levels were undoubtedly lower and phytoplankton densities higher, most likely due to greater rainfall and freshwater inflow. However, the presence of old reef sites has to date not been documented in the upper lagoon.

Open Bays

The open bay habitat is unvegetated and interacts with the overlying water and adjacent habitats. It is supported primarily by the benthic (bottom) community, where organisms recycle nutrients in the sediment back into the water column. Most of the open bay habitat in the upper Laguna Madre is found in Baffin Bay where the water is deepest (averaging nine feet). Open bay bottom is estimated to cover 89 percent of Baffin Bay. As the extent of seagrass coverage increases in the upper Laguna Madre, open bay habitat has decreased and this has been attributed to the dredging of the GIWW. Open bay habitat has been increasing in the lower Laguna Madre since 1988 due to turbidity caused by maintenance dredging of the GIWW. Prior to 1988, seagrass habitat dominated in the lower lagoon.

Wind-Tidal Flats

Wind-tidal flats are harsh environments that are neither terrestrial nor marine. They are regularly flooded and exposed to the air due to meteorological tides (wind-caused) rather than by astronomical tides. The success of this habitat is dependent on nonliving factors rather than on the processes carried out by organisms living there. Wind-tidal flats are found only adjacent to hypersaline lagoons, and they replace salt marsh communities on the southern Texas coast due to the decrease in rainfall and in subsequent freshwater inflow. Extensive blue-green algal mats are commonly found on the wind-tidal flats where other vegetation is sparse or absent. Wind-tidal flats in the Laguna Madre are essential foraging habitat for wintering and migratory birds. Benthic invertebrate communities are present on tidal flats that are frequently flooded. These animals convert primary productivity into animal biomass that is used by higher consumers such as the resident and migratory shorebirds and wading birds when the flats are exposed.

Community Composition

All organisms in the Laguna Madre are not so much in competition with one another as they are in continuous competition with the harsh physical environment for their survival. None of the flora or fauna is completely adapted to the Laguna Madre. Rather, they simply tolerate a hypersaline environment that fluctuates between

30 and 70 ppt. The species are highly tolerant to a wide range of salinity levels. The hypersaline environment is a stress to all organisms and an even greater stress to those living in the Baffin Bay complex, where salinity levels are generally the highest. Hypersaline conditions cause stress for all organisms by affecting dissolved oxygen, pH, temperature, and osmoregulation (maintaining a preferred internal salt and water concentration). While the numbers of plant and animal species in the Laguna Madre are lower when compared to other marine environments, some species exist in great abundance. There are at least twenty-five species of animals that can withstand salinities between 75 and 80 ppt. These include many of the fishes, zooplankton (animal plankton), and various other invertebrates. Above 80 ppt few fishes are present except for two species, the inland silverside and sheepshead minnow, which tolerate salinities above 100 ppt for extended periods.

Recreational Fishing

Marine recreational fishing continues to be one of the most popular outdoor activities in the United States. It supports more than 350,000 jobs and contributes an estimated $30.5 billion to the national economy. Twenty-six of the thirty-one species of fish identified from the Gulf of Mexico estuaries by NOAA's Estuarine Living Marine Resources Program as having ecological, commercial, or recreational value have been reported from the Laguna Madre of Texas. In Texas, 1.7 million total fishing licenses and 823,000 saltwater licenses were sold in 2003. The most frequently caught species in the bays and passes of Texas (including the upper and lower Laguna Madre) were the spotted seatrout and red drum, respectively.

The Texas Laguna Madre is a popular area for many anglers. It produces 60 percent of the fishery landings for the entire coast while comprising only 20 percent of the total Texas bay area. The spring and fall periods are the best seasons to fish for spotted seatrout and red drum in the Laguna Madre. According to TPWD, the populations of spotted seatrout, black drum, and red drum in the upper Laguna Madre are at record levels in 2007. The population of spotted seatrout and the number of fish more than twenty-five inches in length in the upper Laguna Madre were at record highs. However, recent population declines for this species in the lower lagoon have been documented by TPWD, and a reduced bag limit (five per day) was scheduled to go into effect there in September 2007.

TPWD has been interviewing recreational anglers (including guides and tournament anglers) coastwide since 1974 and party boat anglers since 1983 at boat ramps to determine fishing pressure (effort in man-hours) and landings (number of total fish caught). For 2002–2003 (the most recent period for which data are available), the estimated annual fishing pressure was higher for the lower Laguna Madre (734,500 man-hours) than the upper Laguna Madre (498,100 man-hours). However, the total landings for the lower Laguna Madre were lower than for the upper Laguna Madre, 807,000 total fish versus 921,000 total fish, respectively. Up-to-date data on recreational landings and fishing pressure for all Texas bays may be obtained from the various Coastal Fisheries Field Offices of the TPWD.

Studies on the Laguna Madre

Previous studies on the Laguna Madre of Texas have focused on the unique physical and biological resources, but recently attention has centered on human impacts such as dredging of the GIWW and disposal of the resultant dredge material, water circulation changes due to the elevation of the John F. Kennedy (JFK) Causeway, the effects of Packery Channel, seismic and exploration activities, agriculture and other sources of nonpoint source runoff, boat propeller scarring of seagrasses, and vehicular impacts to the tidal flats on Padre Island National Seashore (PINS). In addition, natural perturbations, including fish kills from hypersalinity and freeze events and the nonlethal effects of brown tides, are well documented in the literature. The fish in Baffin Bay have been more thoroughly studied than those from the remainder of the Laguna Madre.

Hypersalinity has been a central focus of most studies involving the Laguna Madre. Low species diversity (numbers of species) and low productivity are commonly associated with hypersaline environments. However, numerous studies have shown the Laguna Madre to have very high productivity associated with the seagrasses, fisheries, and waterfowl. Although few species may be present in such "stressed" environments, the numbers of individuals in those species may be very high (great abundance). It has also been noted that in hypersaline environments the maximum size that a fish species attains tends to be larger. The "why" remains unknown, but it might be that despite the harsh environment, the conditions are more stable (there is less fluctuation), and for those species that can cope, it likely results in a longer growing season.

Because of the GIWW and the two gulf passes, Port Mansfield Pass and Brazos Santiago Pass, water circulation has improved and salinity fluctuations have been eliminated or reduced. Prior to completion of the GIWW in 1949, salinity in both lagoons was greatly elevated, especially in the upper Laguna Madre, where levels were two to three times that of the gulf and massive fish kills were common. Between 1946 and 1948, levels greater than 100 ppt were recorded in Baffin Bay and near 60 ppt in the lower lagoon. With the completion of the Port Mansfield Pass in 1962, salinities in the lower lagoon have rarely exceeded 40 ppt and those in the upper lagoon are rarely above 55 ppt.

The water of hypersaline lagoons has different chemical characteristics than normal sea water. At higher salinity levels the pH of the water decreases (becomes more acidic) during the early stages of evaporation and then decreases rapidly (becoming even more acidic) when calcium settles out of the water. These changes can have detrimental effects on organisms, including the fish. Salinities of 40 to 50 ppt have been found to be the optimal level for many species in the upper Laguna Madre. Studies have reported that larger or older individuals of a fish species are better able to tolerate higher salinity (and cold temperature) levels than are the smaller individuals. In the past, extreme hypersalinity levels (80 to 100 ppt) caused numerous fish kills. There has not been a significant fish kill caused by hypersalinity since the GIWW was completed (1949). However, small-scale kills occasionally occur in Baffin Bay during periods of extended drought. Refer to the chapter on historical fish kills for more information on this subject.

Construction of the JFK Causeway in 1949 prevented any appreciable improvements in water circulation and exchange in the upper lagoon from the inlets at Port Mansfield and Port Aransas. With the redredging of Packery Channel completed and the westernmost portion of the JFK Causeway now elevated, any significant changes in water quality over time in the upper lagoon remain to be seen. However, the opinion of many is that the effects will be minimal and restricted to the area north of Pita Island. Refer to the chapter on gulf passes and coastal processes for information on several passes and their histories of being open and flowing.

The remoteness and limited commercial development of the Texas Laguna Madre (as with the Mexican lagoon) have contributed to the protection and conservation of most marine resources and habitats. There also are many state and federal agencies that work together to monitor and limit impacts on the Texas Laguna Madre to protect the varied habitats and their living resources. Refer to the chapter on issues and concerns for more information.

Gulf Passes and Coastal Processes

Texas anglers have always wanted the gulf passes open and flowing into their beloved bays and lagoons, and currently there is much discussion and some activity concerning the reopening of some of the "old" ones. When considering such endeavors, it is necessary to examine the physical processes creating passes and their rates of success in remaining open. With this basic information, one has a better understanding of where re-openings would best be attempted to ensure minimum maintenance costs and maximum benefits.

Passes (or tidal inlets) generally exist as channels cut through the barrier islands linking the inner bay systems to the Gulf of Mexico. Passes are necessary as migration routes for fish and shellfish, for water exchange, and as navigational highways for humans. Concerning commercial shipping, the Gulf of Mexico is home to seven of the ten busiest U.S. ports. Natural passes are generally too shallow for deep-draft vessels to use and tend to sand-in over time. Thus there is a need to dredge and jetty natural passes and provide maintenance dredging to keep them open.

Passes are either natural or intentionally dredged and maintained. Natural passes are created (and maintained) in various ways, more commonly by storm tides "breaching" or washing over and/or through the barrier islands. In times past, most passes were also kept open by bays, swollen with river runoff, continuously flowing toward the gulf. Artificially dredged passes are lined with jetties and located at sites where natural passes once existed. Over the past 150 years, as many as thirteen passes have existed along the Texas coast, but only eight are open and flowing today.

By far the most ideal and least costly method of keeping passes open is self-maintenance by natural processes. This is accomplished by both tides and the prevailing winds moving water through the passes. Incoming or flood tides enter the bays through the passes; sediments (mainly sand) are deposited simultaneously (primarily at the mouth or seaward end).

If the ebbing or receding tide performs its job, the water flowing out of the pass should remove most of the sediment that was deposited on the incoming tide. For this process to work, there must be considerable velocity in the current flowing from the bay; if this "hydrostatic head" is sufficient, a balance is maintained. Those passes that periodically flow are usually opened by hurricane storm tides or surges. Rock jetties extending considerable distances into the gulf have been constructed at six of the eight passes currently open to slow down the sanding-in processes (only Cedar Bayou and Pass Cavallo are without jetties). Even so, all of them are redredged periodically to maintain depths sufficient for navigational traffic.

In bygone years, pass success was ensured because of a sufficient inflow of fresh water from the various river systems draining into the bays of Texas. This input of fresh water created a gulfward flow of water that not only aided in sand removal from the passes but also ensured the circulation and exchange of bay waters so vital to the continued health of the bays. However, most of the fresh water carried by rivers today is diverted and held in reservoirs behind dams for various uses, with the result being that much less water ever reaches the bays. Texas began constructing reservoirs during the 1940s and 1950s to retain fresh water for the growing number of users, and the "positive" flow of water from land to the sea is no longer sufficient to aid in the maintenance of passes. Today there are seventy-seven major Texas reservoirs and untold thousands of smaller ones retaining fresh water. If another drought similar to that of the 1947–57 period is experienced, even less fresh water will be available for the ever-increasing number of users.

An interesting aspect of natural passes (as noted by the late W. Armstrong Price) is the orientation and position of passes in the bay systems in which they occur. All natural passes were once oriented in a north-south direction; now most all have been dredged and jettied and extend in an east-west direction. However, Cedar Bayou, one of the most successful gulf passes, maintains its natural orientation largely because of prevailing winds, tidal exchanges, and storm surges. Another characteristic of natural passes (true for both jettied and maintained passes) is that all are positioned in the southeast portion of the bay system in which they occur. Examples include Cedar Bayou in the San Antonio Bay system, Pass Cavallo in the Matagorda Bay system, Aransas Pass in the Aransas Bay system, and the Brazos Santiago Pass serving the lower Laguna Madre. The orientation and position of passes in a bay are vital to both the success of the pass and the health of the associated bay system(s).

Prevailing southeast winds (averaging about 12 mph for 270 days each year along the Texas coast), together with the tides, push water through the passes and into the bays, allowing maximum circulation and mixing. During the remainder of the year the northerly winds push water in the opposite direction (out through the passes and into the gulf) and remove much of the sand that was deposited during the warmer months. In this way passes are "naturally" maintained. Jetties allow deep passes to be maintained more efficiently by greatly slowing the sanding-in process by redirecting the sediment carried in the longshore drift and depositing it at the mouth of the pass.

If we consider the upper Texas coast we see that the river systems are much more numerous because of the greater average annual rainfall (nearly twice the rainfall received on the lower coast). This disparity accounts for the greater number of passes on the upper coast. It also accounts for the lower salinities on the upper coast, due to greater freshwater inflow. The lower coast, with less rainfall, has at times experienced excessively high salinity levels, and, unfortunately, few passes exist to moderate these salty conditions with input from gulf waters. On the other hand, the lower Texas coast (from Matagorda Bay southward) has fewer rivers and less freshwater discharge, the level of evaporation exceeds precipitation, and "lagoon" type bay systems prevail.

After considering the physical aspects of passes, it is logical to look at several of the area gulf passes and their histories of remaining open. There is no better method of predicting the future redredging success of a pass than looking at its historical past. Yarborough Pass (comprising a two-mile-long complex with Boggy Slough) is a defunct pass south of Baffin Bay in the upper Laguna Madre. According to Spanish maps, it was apparently open between 1832 and 1882 and has generally been closed since. The first mention of reopening it was in 1925, and a major hurricane in 1933 accomplished just that (this storm also destroyed the Don Patricio Causeway linking Flour Bluff with Padre Island). There is no good record of how long Yarborough Pass was open, but it is known that the pass was dredged four times between 1941 and 1944, and each time it remained open only three to four months. The pass was opened again in 1945 (manually dug out by concerned fishermen) and in 1952 (using dynamite), only to close within months. Photographs of those efforts show a steam-powered dredge "landlocked" on Padre Island—the redredged pass filled in with sand faster than it could be removed ahead of the dredge! In the late 1940s, the Texas Game, Fish, and Oyster Commission (forerunner to TPWD) reported that the physical processes in play in that area of the gulf made it impossible to dredge and maintain this pass. Experts at the time stated that a pass dredged there, if kept open, would not be effective in exchanging enough water to moderate the high salinities persisting in the upper lagoon. In fact, a written report compared the pass to "a soda straw being used to drain a large water tank." When the pass was open to the gulf by storms, salinities in the upper lagoon were significantly reduced only within one mile of the pass.

In summary, all attempts to dredge and maintain a pass at Yarborough have failed. This failure is due primarily to the two converging currents in the gulf at 27° North latitude (the Little Shell–Big Shell area of Padre Island). Tremendous volumes of sand (not to mention plastic milk jugs, lightbulbs, hard hats, nylon rope, onion sacks, etc.) are deposited on the island as one of the currents turns shoreward. This natural process has prevented Yarborough Pass from remaining open. Today, active dune fields exist as far inland as Falfurrias because of gulf currents depositing sand in that area of Padre Island and the prevailing winds moving it inland. At best, this pass has never been more than a site of storm "washovers." With enough money and elaborate engineering and construction, the pass could be redredged and jettied, but maintenance costs would be prohibitive in trying to keep it open for any appreciable length of time.

Cedar Bayou has a much more successful history than Yarborough Pass in remaining open. This pass divides St. Joseph and Matagorda Islands and connects Mesquite Bay with the Gulf of Mexico. The pass was reported as being open from 1836 to 1927, closed between 1936 and 1938, and "mostly open" from 1938 to 1954. In 1955, Hurricane Janet closed Cedar Bayou, and after fishermen opened it in 1956 it closed almost immediately. In 1957, Hurricane Audrey opened Cedar Bayou, but it was closed by 1958. It was closed intentionally in 1979 in fear that oil from Mexico's IXTOC oil spill would enter the bays. In 1988, $5 million was spent to dredge the pass, but it was already showing signs of shoaling by 1989. Efforts to secure the funding and permits to redredge the pass continue today.

The long history of the opening and closing of Cedar Bayou has been blamed on decreased freshwater inflow and human activities. When the GIWW was dredged in the late 1940s, much of the bay water that would have helped maintain the pass was diverted. Reduced rainfall runoff in the Guadalupe River watershed and impoundment of the water has been an even greater factor contributing to the failure of this pass. Between 1950 and 1954, the annual freshwater discharge into the San Antonio Bay system was only one-third the amount entering the system during the 1939–50 period, an example of severe competition among a myriad of users for a decreasing natural resource.

Today this water exchange–only natural pass allows a limited but continual flow of water and fish/shellfish migrations through it. Its north-south orientation, position in the San Antonio Bay system, and periodic storm tides are largely responsible for its success in remaining open.

As of 2007, the redredging of Packery Channel was complete. This pass is actually part of a three-pass complex (including Newport and Corpus Christi Passes) that physically divides Mustang and Padre Islands.

Packery Channel, the natural pass for Corpus Christi Bay, was given its name because of the numerous meatpacking sheds that existed along much of its length in the 1870s. With direct access to the gulf, these businesses were established to process and ship oversupplies of cattle from area ranches. Sea turtles harvested from local bays were processed and shipped from there as well. History tells us the pass was open from 1835 to 1923, when all three passes closed. All three were redredged three times in 1928 and once each in 1938 and 1939, but in all cases each closed almost immediately. In 1939, and again in 1940, Corpus Christi Pass was even bulkheaded but to no avail. All three passes have been permanently closed since 1942 with few exceptions. Corpus Christi Pass was opened for six months after Hurricane Carla (1961), and following Hurricane Beulah (1967) it flowed for one year. Both Newport and Corpus Christi Passes (but not Packery) were breached by Hurricane Allen in 1980 and each flowed for about one year.

Price described Packery as "always long, narrow, and inefficient" despite its stable position in the southeast corner of Corpus Christi Bay, and he reported Corpus Christi Pass to be the most stable of the three. Price blamed the closing of all three passes on dredging activities in the Aransas Pass and Corpus Christi Ship Channels in 1923. These new and larger channels diverted much-needed water and were held responsible for reducing current velocities that had previously kept the Packery complex passes open. As a result, those passes sanded in and have remained closed since (with the exceptions stated above).

Yarborough Pass, if opened, would close quickly and while open would have only a limited effect on water quality in the upper Laguna Madre. A pass there would bisect Padre Island

National Seashore and few fishing enthusiasts or commercial vessels would use this pass; it is a great place for a pass but it was apparently not meant to be.

An open pass at Cedar Bayou is much needed to service both the San Antonio and Aransas Bay systems, and funds to reopen it are likely to be found and the pass redredged. However, natural passes can never be guaranteed to remain open and flowing. Thus, dredging to a greater depth, adding jetties, and securing funding for long-term maintenance dredging are necessary to ensure that a pass at Cedar Bayou remains open.

Anglers are already noticing improved water quality in Corpus Christi Bay in the vicinity of Packery Channel, and many enthusiasts are looking forward to running through it to the gulf for a day of fishing. Even with the Kennedy Causeway elevated, water quality improvement in the upper Laguna Madre will be limited to the northernmost area. However, recreationally and commercially important fish and invertebrate larvae spawned in the gulf will be carried through the pass and into the estuaries of Corpus Christi Bay and the upper Laguna Madre. The success of this pass will undoubtedly be dependent on sufficient maintenance dredging funds to keep it open.

It should be obvious that if we attempt to open old passes or construct new ones, we should follow the laws of Mother Nature—the best of all architects.

Historical Fish Kills on the Texas Coast

Most "seasoned" Texas pluggers well remember the freezes of 1983 and 1989 and the months prior, when all they could think about was the certainty of a new state record trout waiting to engulf their well-presented baits. When I initially drafted this section of text back in 1990, South Texas had just gone through its second fish-killing freeze in 1989 and Mike Blackwood was the reigning "Trout King" and state record holder (Baffin Bay, March 1975, 33.75 inches, 13 pounds, 9 ounces). Since then his record has fallen twice: first to James Wallace (Baffin Bay, in February 1996, 33.3 inches, 13 pounds, 11 ounces), after being held by Blackwood for twenty-one years, and then to Bud Rowland (lower Laguna Madre, May 2002, 37.3 inches, 15.6 pounds, sight-casted with a fly). It has become obvious that as the bar continues to be raised and the trout record broken, the Laguna Madre must be spared from the fish-killing Arctic fronts that periodically push through South Texas, often with catastrophic results.

However, fish kills are nothing new to the Laguna Madre or the rest of the Texas coast. Varying types and amounts of information are available on past fish kills, but the true extent of the early ones will never be known. Prior to the 1950s, marine biologists were few and far between along the Texas coast and getting to a fish kill to assess mortality (or even knowing a fish kill had occurred) could be difficult. Estimating losses was educated guesswork at best. Since the 1970s, the Coastal Fisheries Division of TPWD has been accurately assessing fish kills with a highly skilled coastwide staff utilizing extensive multiple-sampling techniques incorporating both shoreline counts and bottom trawls.

Red tides have taken their greatest toll on marine fish mainly in the Gulf of Mexico. The microscopic red tide organism, a dinoflagellate, kills by producing toxins that paralyze the gills of fish, rendering them incapable of extracting oxygen from the water and thus suffocating them. Red tide blooms are known to have caused fish kills in the Gulf of Mexico in 1935, 1948, 1986, 1996, and 1997. The 1935 kill was said to have extended 250 miles north of the Rio Grande, and mortality estimates ranged as high as 100 million pounds. While no figures are available for the 1948 event, more than 22 million total fish were lost to the red tide bloom in 1986. The red tide in 1986 killed one and a half times the total number of fish lost in the 1983 freeze. The 1996 red tide event was responsible for killing 3 million fish coastwide. This bloom reappeared in 1997, claiming an additional 21.8 million fish. Extensive and persistent red tides place great financial strain on coastal economies, especially the commercial oyster industry. As a result of the 1996 and 1997 blooms all Texas bays south of Galveston were closed to commercial oyster harvesting and some remained closed three months after the bloom dissipated.

High salinity or hypersalinity is unique to the upper Laguna Madre, and excessively high levels caused fish kills there in 1914, 1936, 1937, 1939, 1943, 1944, and 1945. The Laguna Madre was essentially one large lagoon before major hurricanes in 1900 and 1919 came ashore. These storms had dramatic effects on the entire Texas coast, and some speculate that they divided the Laguna Madre into the upper (north) and lower (south) lagoons by transporting a massive sheet of sand across from Padre Island and depositing it into the lagoon. Although slow natural processes are thought to have been filling in the upper lagoon, these storms are thought to have isolated the upper lagoon. Salinity levels rose quickly without a connection to the gulf in the lower lagoon to help moderate salinities. As a result, fish kills occurred regularly until the Gulf Intracoastal Waterway was completed in 1949. This engineering feat involved dredging a ditch 125 feet (wide) by 12 feet (deep) through the twenty-six-mile long sand flat known as the Land Cut. With the lagoons reconnected, no large scale salinity kills have since occurred in the upper lagoon. Salinity kills have generally been reported to occur at levels exceeding 80 ppt. Salinity in the Gulf of Mexico remains quite constant at 35 ppt, moderating hypersaline conditions with gulf waters entering through the Port Mansfield and Brazos Santiago (Port Isabel) Passes. Under hypersaline conditions even salinity-tolerant species such as red drum and black drum cannot replace their internal fluids and remove salts fast enough and they eventually “salt up” and die. Warm, salty water also holds less oxygen than cooler, fresher water, and short-term and small-scale summer and early fall fish die-offs from suffocation occur with some regularity each year.

The 1937 hypersalinity kill was reported to have killed 25 million pounds of fish. Today it is rare that salinities exceed 60 ppt in the upper lagoon, but there is always the threat of elevated salinity levels, especially during periods of extended drought. Prior to completion of the GIWW in 1949, salinities as high as 102 ppt were recorded at the mouth of Baffin Bay. In 1968 TPWD reported salinity levels in Alazan Bay to exceed 110 ppt, but no losses were reported. The Port Mansfield Pass, which is now greatly reduced in its water exchange capacity due to siltation, is responsible for not only moderating salinity levels but also ensuring good overall water quality in the upper lagoon. There is currently no plan (and thus no budget) for the Corps of Engineers to do any maintenance dredging of this very important pass.

Freeze kills along the Texas coast have a long and destructive history and are the only natural events that continue to claim large numbers of fish. These have been reported for the following years: 1527, 1820, 1845, 1846, 1856, 1868, 1882, 1886, 1889, 1890, 1899, 1909, 1917, 1924, 1930, 1940, 1941, 1942, 1945, 1947, 1948, 1949, 1951, 1962, and 1973. More recent freeze kills occurred in 1982, 1983, 1989 (February and December), and 1997.

Excerpts from newspaper articles appearing after some of the early freezes provide great insight into their severity:

> 1820—"The winter of 1820–21 was bitterly cold, so cold that Galveston Bay completely froze over."
>
> 1845–46—"General Zachary Taylor[,] bivouacked on the shore of Corpus Christi Bay during the winter of 1845–46[,] reportedly fed an army of 5,000 men with freeze-killed fish."
>
> 1889—"Nueces Bay completely froze from shore to shore. . . . Ice was so thick people rode horses across the bay." Corpus Christi Bay froze as well, encasing boats in the wharf area during that five-day freeze. "Local housewives had to buy their milk in chunks because it froze inside the delivery boys' cans." In Port Aransas (then called Tarpon), "the cove serving as the boat harbor was frozen over and the citizens spent Sunday morning walking on the ice among the boats and picking up fish that lined the shores."

The 1940, 1947, and 1951 freezes were fairly well documented and were considered to have been "catastrophic" in effect. The following is summarized from published reports: on January 18, 1940, the first freeze of the year arrived, dropping the air temperature from 65°F to 25°F in only four hours. Freezing conditions continued for ten consecutive days, with gale force winds persisting for the first four days. Copano Bay and the entire shallow Laguna Madre system were said to have been hit very hard. "Mush" ice formed on the shores of deeper bays, and some shallow bays froze out to nearly one-half mile from shore. This freeze was the benchmark by which later freezes would be measured and was considered to be the most severe freeze on record at that time. The only mortality estimate that could be found for this freeze was made by local commercial fishermen, who reported the losses at greater than a million pounds of fish. Considering the rapid onset and duration of the freeze and the low water temperatures attained, this mortality figure is most certainly on the conservative side.

In 1947, large trout to eight pounds were reported to be so thick on the surface of Baffin Bay that "they appeared like pepper on the white of an egg." Great numbers of snook were killed in the Brownsville Ship Channel. Nearly 16 million pounds of fish between San Antonio Bay and Mexico were said to have died in this freeze.

The cold front in 1951 came in slowly on January 28, and the air temperature remained between 19°F and 25°F for the following five days. Because two other freezes preceded this one, the losses were not considered to have been as great as in 1940, but the statewide losses of fish were estimated to be 60 million to 90 million pounds, with the Laguna Madre being the hardest hit. Brown pelicans and sea turtles also died. The catches then improved dramatically, and in March 1952 one gill net set by state biologists near the Land Cut yielded three "sow" trout weighing fifteen pounds each. The overall rapid increase in catches was attributed to fish migrating in from the gulf and/or from other bays. By 1954 the redfish and trout populations were considered to be at their normal levels.

The extent of mortality experienced during the more recent freeze-kills in 1983 (December) and 1989 (February and December) are difficult to compare with earlier ones for reasons previously mentioned. Also, early reports listed mortality as "pounds" of fish rather than "numbers" of fish, thus making comparisons virtually impossible. While bottom trawls work well to assess stunned and dead fish during and immediately following freezes, shoreline counts greatly underestimate mortality unless they are made one to two weeks following a freeze when water temperatures have begun warming and the fish have "gassed up" and started to float. After the 1997 freeze, TPWD noted that dead fish were not really seen until four to five days after the freeze and that fish were still floating to the surface eleven days after the freeze. TPWD determined that the two freezes in 1989 (February's being twice as destructive as the one in December) exceeded the 1983 kill on a statewide basis.

The December 1983 cold front broke record low temperatures in forty-five U.S. cities and was perhaps the coldest month since record keeping began in the 1870s. On December 26, Corpus Christi recorded a record low air temperature of 14°F with temperatures remaining below freezing for seventy-seven consecutive hours. Prior to this freeze, local bay water temperature had been in the mid-60s but within a few hours had dropped to 35°F. Nueces Bay was said to be frozen solid behind Gunderland Marine and gulf beach water was measured at 38°F. TPWD estimated that 14 million fish and 1 million invertebrates were killed coastwide (4.8 million of these were in the upper lagoon). This freeze was so far-reaching in latitude that it reportedly wiped out citrus crops as far south as Panama.

I toured the upper Laguna Madre south to the Land Cut on January 8, 1984, with the late Henry Hildebrand, who had written extensively about earlier Texas freeze-kills. This trip was eight or nine days after the freeze had ended and the water temperature had finally reached 60°F (it had remained near 40°F until January 4). Thus, most of the fish were already on the shores and few were seen floating. The intent of this trip was to visually observe the extent of the kill with no attempt to scientifically assess the damage. We carried only an Instamatic® box camera, thermometer, and measuring board. Weights were "guesstimates," but both observers were well-trained "guesstimators." Very few dead fish were seen until we reached Baffin Bay. A stop at my Twin Palms Island cabin yielded twenty to thirty dead fish beside the pier, among them seven trout between 7 and 9 pounds. In one two-hundred-yard stretch of shoreline near Rocky Slough, we counted twenty-four trout between 4.5 and 11 pounds, three reds from 7 to 17 pounds, and one black drum (25 pounds). Making two additional hundred-yard walks between Rocky Slough and the Land Cut we estimated that there were fifty reds and between five hundred and seven hundred trout (the last ranging from twenty to thirty-one inches). We made no attempt to estimate numbers of black drum and mullet anywhere we stopped as they were far too numerous to count. The "shell" spoil islands east of the Kenedy Ranch shoreline were littered mainly with trout, which were likely packing those deeper holes and seeking refuge from the cold conditions. We spent considerable time walking both shorelines in the north end of the Land Cut. Along with great numbers of red and black drum and mullet, large trout were stacked two to three deep in endless "windrows" on both shorelines as far south as we could see. We were "burning daylight" (a one-hour ride back to the boat ramp lay ahead of us) but idled at least another half mile south in my skiff; it all looked the same. There is no doubt that the entire twenty-six-mile-long "Cut" looked the same.

Aware of the reports of the large trout found dead after the 1951 freeze, I was very interested in seeing if others existed among the carcasses. I walked a quarter-mile stretch of beach, picking through the trout and looking for the largest ones. Due to the sheer numbers of fish, this survey took considerable time and I measured only the ones that were easy to grab. Surprisingly, I never found a trout longer than 33.5 inches in the short distance I walked, but there were literally hundreds between 28 and 31 inches. I'm sure there were larger ones to be found, but we ran out of time and had to head north. I would not even begin to venture a guess as to how many large trout we saw, or how many others that we didn't see, but there were more dead large trout in the north end of the Land Cut alone than either of us would have guessed would have been present in the entire Laguna Madre.

The February 1989 temperature drop was slower than in 1983 yet 11 million fish died coastwide (9.3 million in the upper lagoon). Included were twenty-six cold-stunned and dead green sea turtles stranded in the Corpus Christi area. Ice formed in all bays along the Texas coast and even in the lower Laguna Madre; the ice extended out from shore for fifty to two hundred yards.

TPWD estimated that 6 million fish were killed coastwide in the December 1989 freeze (703,000 in the upper lagoon). Although air temperatures during the December 1989 freeze were lower than those in 1983, they did not persist for as long. In West Matagorda Bay, twenty-nine Atlantic bottlenose dolphins (*Tursiops truncatus*) were found stranded and later died. Their deaths were attributed to the cold temperatures and the resultant catastrophic losses of an important food source, the striped mullet. Also of interest, 211 octopods were found dead on the gulf beach near Port Aransas where water temperature was measured at 34°F.

The January 1997 freeze affected mainly the lower Laguna Madre from the Land Cut to (and including) the Rio Grande. Water temperature fell to 37°F and remained below 50°F for more than five consecutive days. Reports reveal that 193,000 fish were killed in this freeze (48,000 of them in the Land Cut). Included were numerous snook in the lower lagoon. Twenty-five cold-stunned green sea turtles were found in South Bay. This freeze killed more trout in the lower Laguna Madre than did the two 1989 freezes and more black drum than either the 1983 or the 1989 freezes.

After reviewing water temperature data available from past freeze-kills, it is apparent that water temperatures approaching 48°F for greater than twenty-four hours will result in fish mortality. It is well documented that the extent of the fish-kill usually depends on the rapidity of the decrease in water temperature rather than the low temperature attained. The low temperatures recorded for some freeze-kills have been well above those of less destructive ones. Another factor influencing freeze-kills is whether or not a freeze was preceded by other cold weather events. The December 1983 freeze occurred after another near-freezing event that month, providing both an "acclimation" and a "forewarning," allowing fish to adjust and move to deeper and warmer bay waters and nearby gulf passes. When temperatures drop slowly fish can better acclimate and mass mortalities are generally avoided. However, severe cold fronts, in spite of acclimation considerations, will push temperatures so low that mass mortalities will result regardless.

Following the 1983 freeze, it took almost three years for catches in the upper lagoon to return to pre-freeze levels. Following the 1940 and 1947 freezes, commercial catches dropped by nearly 50 percent for the two years following those freezes compared to the three years prior. Shrimp catches were not seen to be affected. State biologists reported only four black drum captured in gill nets in October and November 1951 in the upper lagoon, but by February 1952 the catches were said to be one hundred pounds per night. By mid-1953 the fish were so abundant that it was nearly impossible to haul in the nets, and by mid-1954 both redfish and trout populations had returned to their pre-freeze levels.

One fortunate aspect of freeze-kills is that younger individuals of a species are generally less susceptible to cold-death than are the adults. The younger individuals usually survive the freezes and show up in the catches rather quickly afterward, thus allowing rapid rebounds to occur in a fishery. To my knowledge, no data exist to support recruitment via migration from the gulf or other bays following freeze-kills, but the rapid appearance of large fish in the fishery certainly hints strongly at this phenomenon.

It is widely known that fish concentrate in the Land Cut prior to advancing cold fronts. Most of the dead fish observed after the 1983 freeze had their mouths and gill cavities chock-full of bottom sediment, and it has been speculated that this fish-kill may have been exacerbated by barge traffic during and after that freeze. Prop-wash from barges is substantial and could not only have destratified the water column but also pushed cold-numbed fish into the mud and buried them. Major barge carriers with the Gulf Intracoastal Canal Association have had several discussions with TPWD, the Coastal Conservation Association (CCA), and Texas A&M University–Corpus Christi to consider temporarily ceasing barge activity during and following cold fronts when lethally low water temperatures are anticipated. CCA and TPWD have funded temperature sensors that are placed in the Land Cut to monitor and forecast conditions during the winter months.

Various kinds of natural disasters have long been responsible for great losses of our living marine resources. Freezes are the greatest constant threat and will no doubt continue to claim large numbers of Texas fish in the future. We are continually reminded that Mother Nature taketh away as quickly as she giveth.

Considering the trout population, we know that some huge individuals have been landed in the past and continue to show up in angler catches and in TPWD sampling in the Laguna Madre. If we all fish responsibly, keep only a modest amount to eat and release the remainder, and if Mother Nature spares the Texas coast from frequent freeze-kills, it is almost a given that South Texas will eventually claim the spotted seatrout world record now held by a fish taken near Fort Pierce, Florida (May 1995 39.5 inches, 17 pounds, 7 ounces). Jim Wallace's record fish was estimated to be six years of age, and I would estimate that the more than three-foot monster female released by Bud Rowland in May 2002 was seven or eight years old. Assuming good water quality conditions that allow maximum growth, it seems reasonable to expect that we will need at least ten years between killer freezes (remember that they recur and average of every seven years) to produce a fish surpassing the one landed in Florida. I'm keeping my fingers crossed and doing the "anti-freeze" dance.

The Worm Rocks of Baffin Bay

Novices and longtime "lagunatics" alike are well familiar with the "worm rocks" in Baffin Bay. They can make one's day by producing fish and then quickly spoil the day by bending a prop shaft or even cracking a hull or transom. What anglers probably don't know is the interesting geological history of these "fish holders" and the conditions under which the worm reefs were formed and the rate at which certain reefs are being flattened.

First of all, these rocks should not be confused with the beach rock extending from Penascal Point south to the Land Cut along the Kenedy Ranch shoreline. The beach rocks are the remains of an old gulf shoreline (at least five thousand years old) and are formed primarily of sand, clay, and the shells of a variety of molluscs. Worm rocks (referred to as "reefs" when found in concentrations) are quite rare and known only from Baffin Bay, parts of Florida, and near Veracruz, Mexico. The rocks are actually layer upon layer of the calcified tubes of a group of marine worms called serpulids (specifically, *Hydroides dianthus*) that feed by filtering tiny planktonic organisms from the water. The individual rocks are "about the size of a man's head" (to use an old description) and were formed as the planktonic larval worms settled from the water onto hard substrate, often on caliche rocks. The reefs in Baffin Bay are of two distinctly different types: reef fields (extending only three to twelve inches above the bottom) occurring in the upper reaches of Baffin Bay (mainly in Cayo del Grullo, Laguna Salada, and Center Reef across the mouth of Alazan Bay) and patch reefs (generally circular in shape and rising several feet above the bottom). Good examples of this type are found in the Bad Lands, Point of Rocks, East Kleberg Point to Starvation Point, and Penascal Point. If all vegetation is removed, one can closely examine the formations and see that the small tubes exhibit two different types of growth forms: "oriented" growth, where individual tubes are parallel to one another, and "random" growth, where the tubes have grown in all different directions. Oriented growth has been attributed to favorable or stable environmental conditions and random growth to harsh or fluctuating conditions. All in all, the worm rocks are estimated to cover ten square miles in the Baffin Bay complex. Old records tell us that sailing craft would travel from Port Aransas to Baffin Bay and back in the late 1800s and return with this rock, which would be used to line the unstable gulf pass. In South Texas, naturally occurring hard material is certainly in short supply, and this abundant worm rock was the only option. This effort to stabilize the pass obviously was a futile attempt, and not until the 1940s was this pass truly stabilized with the pink granite rock present today.

Of great interest are the results from radiocarbon dating studies of the worm rocks, revealing that they began forming approximately three thousand years ago and that the worms continued building reefs until a few hundred years ago. No more than a few living worms in their translucent tubes can be found today in Baffin Bay, so the reefs are considered to be fossils with no more of this great three-dimensional structure being formed. The question is, why aren't the reefs building now as they once did?

Investigation reveals that conditions in the Laguna Madre are markedly different today from what they were in the past. Ancient middens or garbage dumps near Karankawa habitation sites around the rim of Baffin Bay have yielded oyster shells in considerable abundance. These shells were undoubtedly collected nearby. The bay is far too salty today for this mollusc to survive. In fact, the upper lagoon is considered a negative estuary because evaporation exceeds precipitation and freshwater inflow (by a ratio of 2:1). Oysters, like serpulid worms, are filter feeders and occur where salinities are midrange due to moderate rainfall, thus allowing nutrients to be carried into the bays to support their food supply (microplankton). Today's generally dry creeks such as Los Olmos, San Fernando, Jarachinal, and Petronilla flowed continuously in wetter times, creating a fresher and more turbid environment because of the increased sediment load. Evidence of this can be observed today by digging around the reef fields in Laguna Salada: the reefs rise only slightly above the bottom because sediments carried into the bay during wetter periods filled in around them. The worm rocks extend far below the surface of the sediments, showing that sediments nearly covered them up. Conditions were so different during those earlier times that there was likely little seagrass due to murky water and lower salinity. There were probably fewer spotted seatrout but an abundance of black drum (determined from fish ear stones found in the middens). Today's salty, clear-water, nutrient-poor conditions resulting from decreased rainfall over the last several hundred years have created an unfavorable environment for both the serpulids and oysters. Current conditions favor abundant seagrasses, spotted seatrout, and both red and black drum.

The conditions that allowed these reef-building worms to flourish were the result of a natural cyclic event of the past. Under current conditions no more of that prime real estate that put Baffin Bay on the map as the premier coastal big-trout hotspot is being created. Another negative element is that certain reefs are being destroyed due to human activities (lower units, hulls, and anchors tearing them apart and waders stomping them down). The two reefs that parallel the King Ranch shoreline at Point of Rocks/Compuerta Pass have been reduced from a nearly continuous four-hundred-yard-long patch reef that once was two feet off the bottom to not much more than a long mound of rubble in only fifteen years. When I started fishing Baffin Bay in the 1970s, one could not run a boat across the main reef without hitting it, even on high water. Today most people do not know the reef even exists because it has literally been flattened. A wader stepping on individual rocks often creates a chalky cloud in the water as the calcium carbonate crumbles into a fine powder. The only "good" example of a patch reef still present today is on the south shore of Baffin Bay. This reef is basically a single rock at least eight feet in diameter that rises nearly to the surface in six to seven feet of water, surely the result of hundreds or even thousands of years of growth. What a beautiful example of how Baffin Bay must have once looked. Thus far, this rock has remained intact, but a large drill site within several hundred yards of it was under review in 2005. Fortunately, potential environmental impacts prevented drilling at that site. Currently, fifty-five drill sites are proposed for the area between the JFK Causeway and Baffin Bay.

Aside from reef destruction, a big concern for wade-fishing enthusiasts is safety. Debris such as leaders hooks, lures, monofilament, rope, anchors, and even pieces of old houseboats abound on and around the reefs. Waders generally like to walk near the reefs, casting around and over them, but this is nearly impossible as the reefs appear to "grow up" around you. Two steps into a rock pile often means eight to ten steps to get back out. A fishing buddy of mine nearly drowned on one of the large reefs on the north shore twenty years ago when he stepped into a mid-thigh-deep hole in a reef and fell over backward. The only reason he is alive today is because he was able to get his popping rod behind his head and repeatedly push his face above the water so he could breathe. He continued doing this until he was able to push himself up into a sitting position. He came very close to drowning with only six inches of water covering his face.

Over the years, all attempts to permanently mark the reefs have failed. Locals have felt that the newcomers should learn their way around Baffin Bay via the hit-and-miss method of navigation. While it would be impossible to mark all the reefs, the major areas should be marked or they will continue to be flattened. Boats should always anchor away from the reefs and waders shouldn't walk into them. These worm rocks are largely responsible for the tremendous big-trout fishing success in Baffin Bay. Unfortunately, those little worms aren't cranking out that rock anymore. Like all aspects of today's marine environment, we need to save what we've got while we've still got something to save.

The Summer House

Veteran upper lagoon anglers regularly refer to the Summer House as a landmark and great fishing area along the Kenedy Ranch shoreline, but few know the history of this structure. The ranch hands actually called it the Tide Gauge Cabin because of the government-built tide gauge pier put there in the 1940s to monitor water levels. Most anglers are familiar only with the other tide gauge pier that still stands behind the northern end of the Tide Gauge Bar in Baffin Bay.

All that stands today of this one-time favorite retreat of Sarita K. East are the crumbling remains that can still be seen above the tree line on the western shore just before one enters the north end of the Land Cut. Cabin construction began in 1950 under the supervision of Fred Yaklin Sr. and Louis Turcotte, both longtime Kenedy Ranch employees. It was built primarily as a getaway for East, but it was also used by the "coast rider" cowboys during cattle roundups and sweeps and by ranch security and game wardens when they were working the eastern part of the 200,000-acre ranch. The structure rested on a massive twelve- to fifteen-inch-thick slab of concrete and consisted of a kitchen, adjoining central living quarters, a wide screen porch, and even a carport. Butane lights, refrigerator, and cooking stove were in place along with a wood-burning stove. Drinking water was hauled in by trailer in a five-hundred-gallon cypress tank. The encampment was planted with various types of native vegetation and was enclosed with a barbed-wire fence in an attempt to keep deer, feral hogs, and javelinas from consuming East's yard plants and produce from the garden. The six-foot knoll on which the Summer House was built provides a magnificent panoramic view of the surrounding tidal flats, Laguna Madre, and the ranch.

The cabin was frequently occupied because it was only a half-day drive from the ranch headquarters and county seat in Sarita (her namesake). It was the only place for anyone to stay on the eastern section of the ranch. A sand/clay/caliche road was actually constructed across the mudflats so that vehicles could reach the island where the cabin sat.

Sarita East would stay there for weeks on end, and she loved to fish from the tide gauge pier. She would even wade the worm reef flats in front of her beloved Summer House to catch redfish, speckled trout, and drum. She used the cabin until her death in 1961. Thereafter it was used less and less, and by the mid-1970s it was beyond repair. The thatched roof can still be seen just above the tree line as one enters the Land Cut. A word of caution: this area is private property, so do not trespass—the "coast riders" might intercept you!

The worm reefs that dot the flats in front of the cabin all the way to the Intracoastal Canal are very good fish-holders. The unique beach rock reminiscent of an old Gulf of Mexico shoreline beginning at Penascal Point continues along the shoreline in front of the cabin. From an angler standpoint, the Summer House area is unique not only because of the reefs but also because all fish moving south on that shoreline stack up there before entering the Land Cut and all fish leaving the Cut fan out on the shoreline as they head north. I have made many productive wades and drifts in front of this structure of simple elegance.

No photographs of the Summer House in its heyday were available when I first wrote this piece in 1995. Instead of seeing how the place looked in contemporary photos, I "saw" it through the descriptions of Louis Turcotte (now deceased), who also provided the history of the famous structure.

But I also have my own memories of Sarita and the area around the Summer House. My grandfather Sam Hunt was sheriff of San Patricio County for thirty years, and his brother Louis Hunt was sheriff of Kenedy County. We would occasionally visit Uncle Louis and his wife Hattie (the postmaster) in Sarita. In the 1950s we would drive to the flats in the area of the Summer House, where my Uncle Louis stepped from the car, removed his boots, rolled his pants to his knees, and took off in search of redfish with his single-action .45 Colt. Somewhere the family has a picture of that tall, long-legged cowboy and lawman grinning and holding up a redfish he got with his pistol on that wade. I do remember the sound of gunshots in the distance that day and I swear I can almost remember eating redfish that night.

Issues and Concerns

Corpus Christi is the only center of population in the northern end of the upper Laguna Madre, but the 25-mile trip to Baffin Bay is only a short boat ride with the high tech hulls and outboard engines available today. South Padre Island is the most populated center in the lower lagoon, and the summer tourist season pushes its population much higher. Port Mansfield has become a shallow-water fishing destination for many anglers, and despite its remoteness, this small fishing village swells with anglers during the summer. Until the 1940s, the Texas Laguna Madre was unknown to all but local commercial fishermen, but slowly and surely it has been discovered. It is not uncommon for Corpus Christi fishing guides to make a daily run with their customers to Port Mansfield (150 miles round trip) when the fishing is slow in the upper lagoon. Loyola Beach and Riviera Beach on Baffin Bay have been discovered as well. Over the last several years guides from as far away as Houston and Galveston have located there, primarily during the winter for the prime trophy trout fishing. In 2002, a large "floating hotel" capable of accommodating forty anglers and ten guides was towed into Baffin Bay. TPWD ultimately determined that it was not a legally permitted floating cabin and the owners were ordered to remove it. It was returned to its home port in Chandeleur Islands, Louisiana.

Overall, boating and angling activity has increased dramatically since 1990 along the Texas coast, and this is especially true for the Laguna Madre, which had long been overlooked or bypassed by fishing enthusiasts. The word is out about the phenomenal fishing it has to offer and the masses are coming. The popular and much-refined tunnel hull boat floats in only five to eight inches of water and gets onto plane easily in water just a little deeper. Once on plane, these boats will easily run in water only four to five inches deep. The characteristics of the tunnel hull boat coupled with a high horsepower outboard engine with shallow-water intakes and jet drive engines have allowed a lot of folks to access shallow water that twenty years ago could be reached only by anchoring in waist-deep water and wading to it. Such boats are top sellers at marine dealerships and popular throughout both lagoons. Many consider the ultimate shallow-water engine to be the Yamaha TRP (twin rotating propellers), and nearly three-quarters of them are sold to boat owners operating in the Texas Laguna Madre.

Wetland losses on the Texas coast between 1955 and 1992 are estimated at 210,600 acres or about 5,700 acres per year. Although these losses have decreased dramatically, more and more people are using the water. Slow but continuous destruction of the worm reefs in Baffin Bay has been occurring since the 1980s due to damage by outboard lower units. Marking of the major reefs must be done to preserve this unique environment and the essential habitat and great fishing opportunities they provide.

Boater education is essential in preventing more damage by outboard motors and to ensure safety on the water and improved traffic flow at the increasingly crowded boat ramps. All first-time boat buyers should be required to successfully complete short courses in basic navigation and boat operation. Learning the rules of the water, as the driver of a wheeled vehicle must learn the rules of the road, should be required of boat operators as a matter of course.

Another problem shared by both lagoons is determining where to dispose of the spoil from maintenance dredging of the GIWW by the Army Corps of Engineers and from new channels needed for oil and gas activities. Many spoil island sites are occupied by fishing cabins, with 90 percent of the total number of coastal cabins situated in the upper lagoon between the JFK Causeway and the Land Cut. Some islands without cabins are designated exclusively as bird rookery islands and are unavailable for spoil disposal. Thus, other sites must be identified for spoil disposal. Neither Padre Island National Seashore (PINS) nor the King or Kenedy Ranches have agreed to accept spoil. Open bay disposal is a controversial topic that will encounter many permitting problems, as few are in favor of taking away bay bottom to create islands from dredge material. As of 2007 more than fifty drilling permits were in various stages of approval for oil and gas exploration in the upper lagoon between Corpus Christi and Baffin Bay. All drilling projects will ultimately result in spoil that must be disposed of. Additional sites have been approved for drilling on PINS.

By-catch from gulf and bay shrimp boats along the Texas coast continues to be a very controversial topic. The southern flounder has recently been identified by TPWD as a species of great concern in the by-catch issue. Their data reveal that more than 80 percent of flounder mortality is caused by shrimp boats. The smaller males that cannot avoid the nets are the bulk of the mortality in the bays, while gulf shrimpers catch the larger females in their trawls. Many experts also blame the bay shrimpers and their by-catch for a reduction in the number of older and larger Atlantic croaker along the Texas coast. Rarely are individuals older than three years seen today, whereas in the not too distant past considerably older (and much larger) individuals were very common.

Among natural events, the red and brown tides appear to be occurring more frequently and are now termed "harmful algal blooms." Red tides produce toxins causing primarily fish to die from suffocation as their gills become paralyzed and unable to remove oxygen from the water. The toxins can be harmful to humans who consume infected shellfish (e.g., oysters) or breathe the toxins, which can cause respiratory complications. The red tide occurring in the Texas Laguna Madre is caused by a planktonic dinoflagellate (*Karenia brevis*). Another dinoflagellate (*Alexandrium monilatum*) is responsible for red tide blooms in the northern and eastern gulf. Red tides tend to be more associated with the nearshore gulf, and thus far only the lower lagoon has been affected to any extent.

The Texas brown tide is caused by very small planktonic algae, *Aureoumbra lagunensis,* that can persist for long periods of time, having the ability to reduce the number of types of plankton present and affect the seagrasses by reducing light. Brown tide organisms are ever-present in the upper reaches of Baffin Bay (Laguna Salada and Cayo del Grullo) but not at the high densities seen between 1990 and 1997. Although "brown water" periodically covers large areas of the upper lagoon, researchers have not determined that it is caused by the brown tide organism.

Killing freezes that have occurred on the average of once every seven years since 1820 will no doubt continue to take a heavy toll on fish populations in the future. Fortunately, history has shown us that the effects on certain species of fish, by even the most devastating freezes (e.g., 1983 and 1989), are generally short-lived, with fish populations generally returning to their pre-freeze levels within four to five years. Hypersalinity and the resultant kills appear to be catastrophic events of the past. Additional information on these topics is included in the chapter on historical fish kills in Texas.

With the opening of Packery Channel, salinities are slightly reduced in the northernmost end of the upper lagoon. However, little attention has been focused on the silting-in of the Port Mansfield Pass and the overall importance of this pass to both Texas lagoons. This pass must be maintained to ensure water circulation in both lagoons and as a "highway" for fish and other organisms that spend portions of their lives in both the gulf and the lagoons. The efficiency of this pass is greatly reduced, and unless it is redredged, not only the water in the lagoons but also the organisms living there will eventually diminish in quality and quantity.

Propeller scarring is a problem common on the lower Texas coast (from Aransas Bay southward), especially in the shallow upper and lower lagoons. Increasing boat traffic in shallow water results in increased propeller scars in shallow seagrass beds. This damage is a major concern because seagrass is an essential habitat for many larval and juvenile stages of organisms living temporarily or permanently in the Laguna Madre. The seagrass beds are also the main source of primary production (photosynthesis) in the Texas lagoon, and any significant decline will ultimately affect the well-being of most organisms living in the Laguna Madre ecosystem. Recently, such groups as the Nature Conservancy and Coastal Conservation Association (CCA) have begun joining forces to mark existing channels and shallow areas in the upper lagoon to limit seagrass destruction by outboards. Boaters who have been observed doing any damage to seagrass meadows (e.g., causing propeller scars) may now be subject to fines in the Redfish Bay State Scientific Area (to the north) and within the boundary of PINS in the upper lagoon.

As the numbers of commercial guides and recreational anglers continue to increase on the Texas coast, boat traffic and fishing pressure (angler hours spent fishing) will increase as well. The population of Texas in 2006 stood at 21 million, with 6 million (28 percent) of those making their homes along the gulf coast. The latest data available from TPWD (2002–2003) reveal that nearly 600,000 saltwater fishing licenses are issued annually. Estimates are that in thirty years, the Texas population will be 34 million and 1.2 million saltwater anglers will be fishing along the Texas coast. This translates to a doubling in the number of people fishing in saltwater in the next three decades. Currently, fishing pressure in the lower lagoon is nearly twice that of the upper lagoon. However, this estimate is based only on day trips (less than twelve hours in duration) with trips of longer duration not included. Since most cabins are situated in the upper lagoon and many of the trips are overnight ones (longer than twelve hours), the two lagoons essentially become more similar in terms of fishing pressure. It should also be noted that of the eight Texas bay systems, the upper lagoon receives the least amount of fishing pressure. In fact, together, the upper and lower lagoons account for only 20 percent of the coastwide fishing pressure in Texas. It follows that with increasing numbers of boats on the water (and many of them owned by new anglers), many will search out those areas like the upper lagoon where the fishing is exceptional and boat traffic is minimal. I think the Texas Laguna Madre (along with the San Antonio Bay system) is the last frontier on the Texas coast and that it will experience some of the fastest growth in angling and boating coastwide. Boat dealerships in Corpus Christi fully realize this, and the two largest ones are greatly expanding their operations to capitalize on this growth. To quote one dealer, "Our future is in fishing boats, especially the first-time buyers."

One of the most popular and fastest growing segments of tournament angling is the saltwater market. Several of the large national tournament organizations and their television sponsors are interested in holding annual events in the Laguna Madre, knowing that it is an untapped, shallow-water mecca. The money awarded in bay tournaments is nearly equal to that paid to winners of bass fishing tournaments. TPWD has noted a decrease in the sale of freshwater fishing licenses for some time (along with a decrease in hunting license sales), while saltwater license sales have continued to increase.

In spite of these activities, the Laguna Madre remains largely secluded, and commercial development on PINS and the large mainland ranches is expected to be minimal in the foreseeable future. However, with time, development is inevitable. In the 1980s, the Kenedy Ranch took advantage of its tremendous hunting and fishing opportunities and opened a lodge offering world-class guided fishing and hunting services in the upper lagoon. Although this venture lasted only a few years, it was quite successful. In the early 1990s, a Japanese tour-company representative visited the Corpus Christi area with the intent of developing a tourism business offering Hovercraft trips throughout the upper lagoon, concentrating its tours in Baffin Bay. This never came about, but many are of the opinion that these early endeavors were simply ahead of their time and that similar ones will be successful in the future because the unspoiled Texas lagoons have so much to offer. Different types of activities and business ventures will undoubtedly be investigated and some will surely be executed in the not-so-distant future. The fastest growth in the Corpus Christi region is on Padre

Island, and most of the homeowners there are also boat owners. Not all of these boats are fishing boats; some are "pleasure boats" that are used for rides and sightseeing. With Packery Channel open and flowing, many boaters new to the upper lagoon are sure to investigate this inviting body of water from one end to the other, in addition to the gulf.

Padre Island National Seashore is in the process of developing a ten-year management plan, and among the items under consideration is the creation of additional camping and recreational areas similar to Bird Island Basin, with the goal of increasing public access to the upper lagoon. A plan to initiate a ferry system from Port Mansfield to the Port Mansfield Pass jetties was introduced in 2003, but thus far it has failed to gather much support. Any such activity would certainly increase pedestrian and boat traffic on both the barrier island and in the lower lagoon. PINS is intent on making more of the lagoon available to its park visitors, and it is likely that additional camping, kayaking, sailboarding, and boat ramp facilities will be developed in the near future.

Although the Texas General Land Office (TGLO) is issuing no new permits, all spoil island and floating cabins are now required to dispose of all sewage, garbage, and general refuse in an approved manner. This agency is interested in making more of the Laguna Madre accessible to the general public and has suggested the concept of developing rest areas and camp sites at specific locations in the lagoon and in the Land Cut. On-the-water vendors could provide ice, bait, and beverages to boaters and anglers as well. The latter is not a new idea because in the 1950s and 1960s at least one bait barge operated in the upper lagoon offering these items to anglers.

The Texas Laguna Madre has slowly changed and will continue to change as the fishing and boating public continue to discover the serenity and magic of this shallow-water paradise. The large private ranches and federal landholdings are ultimately in control of the fate of the Texas Laguna Madre. It is hoped that sustaining the health of the "Mother Lagoon" will be of paramount importance to these stewards making decisions about commercial development along its shorelines. It is crucial that all users respect the lagoon and what she has to offer and that they leave her as good as they found her.

An Introduction to the Fishes

The fishes are the most numerous and diverse of the vertebrate group of animals (which includes the amphibians, reptiles, birds, and mammals). They dominate the waters of the world and have a great variety of morphological, biological, physiological, and behavioral adaptations. Their great diversity is clearly reflected in the large number of living species. A recent compilation lists 23,250 living species of fishes but estimates the number to be closer to 25,000, with 200 new species being described each year. The total may eventually reach 30,000 species.

For the book by Tunnell and Judd on the Laguna Madre of Texas and Mexico, Kim Withers compiled a list of the fish families and species present on the Texas coast, Corpus Christi Bay, both the upper and lower lagoons, and the Mexican lagoon. For the Texas coast, she reports a total of 548 species, with 86 for the upper lagoon, 94 for the lower lagoon, and 115 for Corpus Christi Bay (adjacent to the upper lagoon). The Mexican lagoon is reported to have 142 fish species. These numbers clearly show the reduction in species in the two Texas lagoons when compared to the Texas coast and to Corpus Christi Bay. Elevated salinity is certainly a partial explanation for the reduction in fish species in the Texas lagoons. The increased number of species reported for the Mexican lagoon can be explained not only by the greater number of shark and ray species but also because of certain physical and climatic differences between the Texas and Mexican lagoons. The Mexican lagoon has more gulf passes than the Texas lagoons, and the Mexican lagoon experiences a greater frequency of hurricanes and tropical storms striking the coast and opening the passes. This storm activity allows a great improvement in water quality and increased recruitment of fish from the gulf into those waters. After a storm makes landfall, fishery productivity is very high in the Mexican lagoon and remains high for five to six years before the passes silt in. Slowly, salinity levels increase and fishery production declines as water quality continues to decline. This pattern amounts to a "boom and bust" cycle long noted by Hildebrand.

Worldwide, fishes occupy an extraordinary variety of habitats. They can be found thriving in seasonal ponds, intermittent streams, cold mountain streams, tiny desert springs, hypersaline lagoons, deep ocean trenches, and countless other aquatic environments. Physiologically, this diversity of habitats means that fish may be found living at temperatures from 28°F to nearly 104°F and in water with pH values ranging from 4 to above 10. Fish also occupy waters with dissolved oxygen values near zero and at salinities from fresh to well above 100 ppt (dissolved solids expressed as parts per thousand). Some live as much as three miles above sea level and others at nearly seven miles below the surface of the ocean.

One would expect to find the greatest number of fish species in the oceans because salt water covers nearly three-quarters of the earth's surface. By volume, salt water is 97 percent of all water. Fresh water amounts to less than 1 percent of all the available surface water. Interestingly, only 60 percent of all fish alive today are marine and 40 percent are freshwater inhabitants. This is because fresh water consists largely of thousands of distinct and isolated "islands" in a "sea of land" (the continents) and thus freshwater bodies comprise an amazing diversity of different habitats to which fish have had to adapt over time. This has led to a great diversity in the number of freshwater fish species. In contrast, most marine habitats consist of open ocean that is relatively stable in temperature and salinity, has sunlight penetrating only the surface waters, and is thus largely unproductive. Additionally, few nutrients are available in the open ocean, further limiting productivity. Furthermore, only about 15 percent of all fish species are inhabitants of the open ocean environment. Nearly 80 percent of marine fishes live in coastal embayments (bays) and in a narrow band of shallow water along the margins of the continental land masses. As a result, most fish species live in close proximity to both land and humans. Also, most fishes are found in warm environments where annual temperature fluctuations are minimal.

Despite the diversity of aquatic habitats, the range of environmental conditions encountered, and the physiological adaptations necessary to cope with them, most fish are easily recognized as fish. This is because the physical and chemical characteristics of water impose a great number of constraints on the functional design of fish. Most of the fish-like characteristics are adaptations allowing the most efficient use of the water by these mobile vertebrates. The properties of water that exert the greatest influence on fish design are its density, low compressibility, solvency, and transparency.

Water is eight hundred times more dense than air. This greatly reduces the effects of gravity and enables fish to remain suspended in the water column with little effort when compared to the great amount of energy required for birds to stay airborne. Most fish are neutrally buoyant and as a result, most all muscle is devoted to swimming, with little wasted on fighting the effects of gravity. Also, more thrust can be exerted against water than against air. On the negative side, the greater density of water means that there is more resistance, or drag, experienced when fish attempt to swim through it. This friction is largely offset by a streamlined body shape that lowers resistance and by the fact that most of their muscle mass is devoted to forward motion. Together these factors provide an efficient means of pushing the body and tail against the water to propel the fish forward.

The resistance of water to organisms moving through it occurs because water is not very compressible. Movement through air is much easier because it compresses against an animal's body, flowing smoothly alongside, thus not needing to be completely displaced. In contrast, water literally must be pushed out of the way by an organism moving through it. This creates turbulence along the sides of the body and in the wake of the organism, further increasing drag. This creates problems for fish, but they have adapted to take advantage of the situation. Fish have a lateral line system, which is a very acute sensory mechanism capable of detecting minute amounts of water turbulence and displacement produced by its own movements and by other organisms or objects. This system enables them to acutely detect nearby stationary objects, school mates, and predator and prey organisms. The slight compressibility of water allows sounds to be easily transmitted through it, especially those of low frequency. Sound is carried farther and nearly four times faster in water than in air because of its greater density. This has allowed most fish to have keen senses of hearing and to produce sound. External ears are not necessary because fish are of nearly the same density as water and are said to be "transparent" to sound waves, allowing sound to easily pass through their muscles. However, sound waves are interrupted internally by structures in the fish that are either more dense (otoliths or ear stones in the skull) or less dense (air bladders). The statement proclaiming the oceans to be a "silent world" is truly a myth. Many fish produce sounds and most can hear.

Perhaps the most important aspect of water that enables it to support life is its unique property of being the nearly universal solvent. Natural waters contain a complex mixture of dissolved gases, salts, and various compounds, many of which are essential to fish to sustain life. These are absorbed directly by the gills and skin or indirectly through food intake. The most important gas is oxygen, which is present in very small amounts compared with oxygen levels in the air (1 to 8 parts per million in water compared to about 210 parts per million in air). Fortunately for fish, their gills are very efficient at extracting oxygen at such low concentrations, although their activity is greatly reduced under low oxygen conditions. Assisting in oxygen transfer to the blood, the surface area of the gills is quite large and allows a high percentage of the blood to be brought into contact with the water to assist in gas exchange. However, the great surface area of the gills causes fish to be very sensitive to changes in salinity, making it difficult for most fish to move between fresh water and salt water. Certain waste products and carbon dioxide in the blood are eliminated at the gills as well. The gills also readily absorb harmful contaminants present in the water.

Another key characteristic of water is the poor penetration of light through it compared to air. Even in the clearest ocean water, light does not penetrate deeper than about six hundred feet, with most absorbed in the first three hundred feet. This becomes important when considering that the average depth of the world's oceans is nearly thirteen thousand feet (two and a half miles). The majority of fish rely on sight to capture prey and avoid predators, but many have sensory structures such as barbels (chin and snout whiskers) and electric organs that allow them to navigate and find food under low light or even completely dark conditions. Below the lighted zone, some fish communities produce their own light to communicate with one another, attract prey, and confuse predators.

The hypersaline aspect of the Laguna Madre places various physiological stresses on fish. In addition, tidal currents are weak, water circulation is poor, and the residence time of water in the lagoon is long (especially in the upper lagoon). Especially during extended droughts, fish in the Laguna Madre must tolerate these harsh conditions or move to where conditions are more favorable. The most important physiological adaptation to the high salinity environment that all living plants and animals must make is controlling their salt and water balance. All marine organisms (plants and animals alike) tend to lose water and gain salts, and this rate increases as salinity increases. As salinity levels increase, fish rapidly dehydrate and increasingly accumulate salt in their blood and tissues. To maintain suitable salt levels, fish excrete salt via specialized cells on the gills (chloride cells). To replace water lost to their environment by dehydration, marine fish drink salt water and produce dry, salty feces to help conserve water and further expel the buildup of salts.

Temperature plays an important role in the chemical composition of water and the conditions to which the fish must adapt. Oxygen availability is reduced as temperature increases and is another problem faced by all organisms living in hypersaline environments. The solubility of oxygen also decreases as salinity increases. Warm, salty water holds less oxygen than cooler, fresher water.

In times past, heavy commercial fishing pressure, along with the harsh environment of the Laguna Madre, has had negative effects on the abundance of certain fish species. In order to monitor fish populations in the Laguna Madre, extensive data are collected throughout the year by the TPWD Coastal Fisheries monitoring program to determine abundance, recruitment, and harvest/mortality of selected fish species. Additionally, the Stock Enhancement Program stocks red drum and spotted seatrout into all Texas bays when necessary to ensure good angling success. Southern flounder are also being stocked on a limited basis. Bag and size limit regulations for the recreational fishery are established and enforced by TPWD in the Laguna Madre, all other Texas bays, and in the gulf to 9 nautical miles (10.4 statute miles). Current information regarding recreational angling regulations (bag and size limits) can be found on the TPWD's Web site: http://www.tpwd.state.tx.us/publications/annual/fish/.

External Characteristics of Fishes

Sharks

Fig. 4a. Shark characteristics. [Illustration by Janice D. Fechhelm from Saltwater fishes of Texas: a dichotomous key, *1995, by E. O. Murdy, Texas A&M University Sea Grant College Program]*

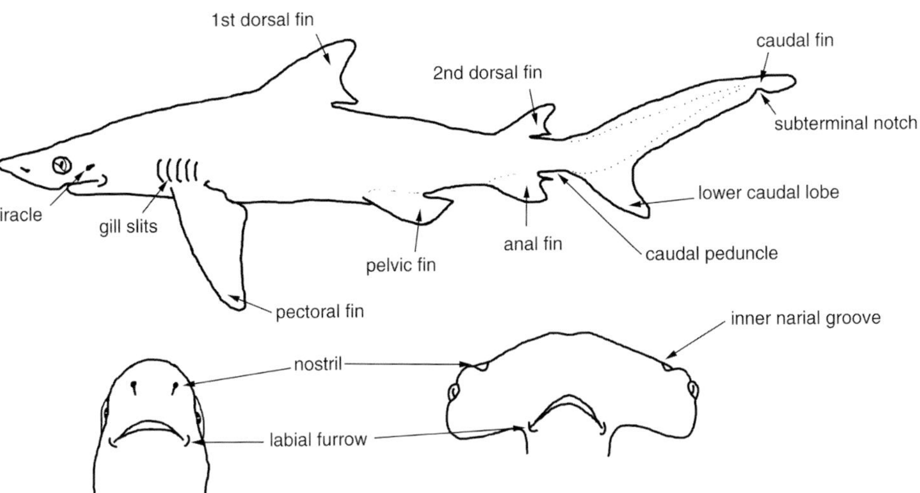

Skates and Rays

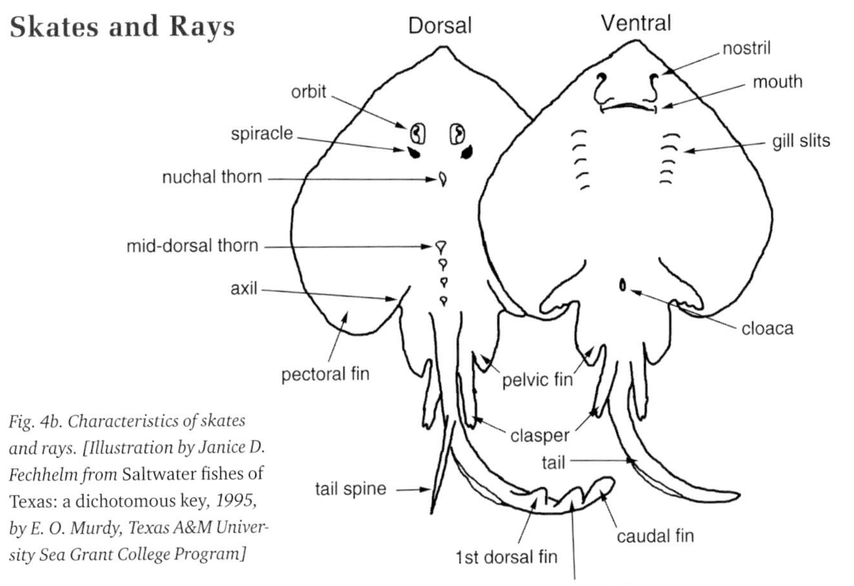

Fig. 4b. Characteristics of skates and rays. [Illustration by Janice D. Fechhelm from Saltwater fishes of Texas: a dichotomous key, *1995, by E. O. Murdy, Texas A&M University Sea Grant College Program]*

Bony Fishes

Fig. 5a. Characteristics of bony fishes. [Illustration by Janice D. Fechhelm from Saltwater fishes of Texas: a dichotomous key, *1995, by E. O. Murdy, Texas A&M University Sea Grant College Program]*

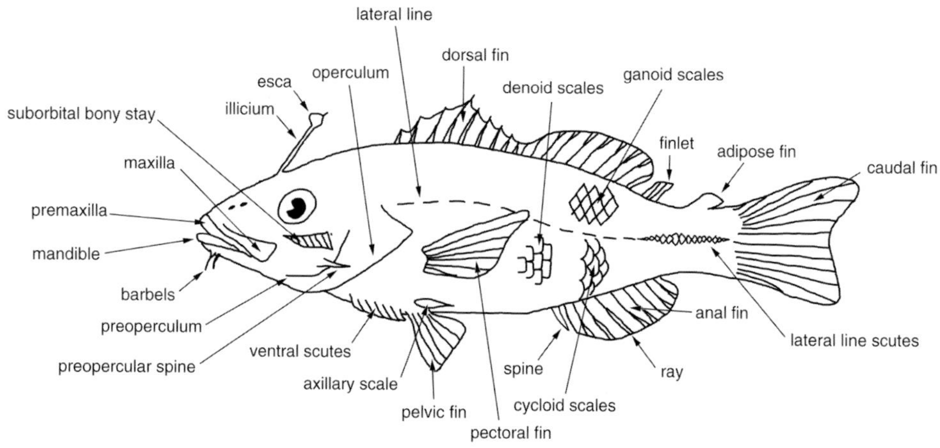

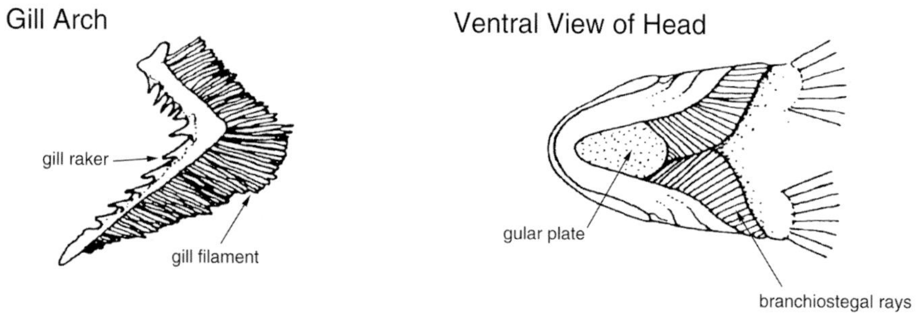

Fig. 5b. Gill arch and ventral view of head. [Illustration by Janice D. Fechhelm from Saltwater fishes of Texas: a dichotomous key, *1995, by E. O. Murdy, Texas A&M University Sea Grant College Program]*

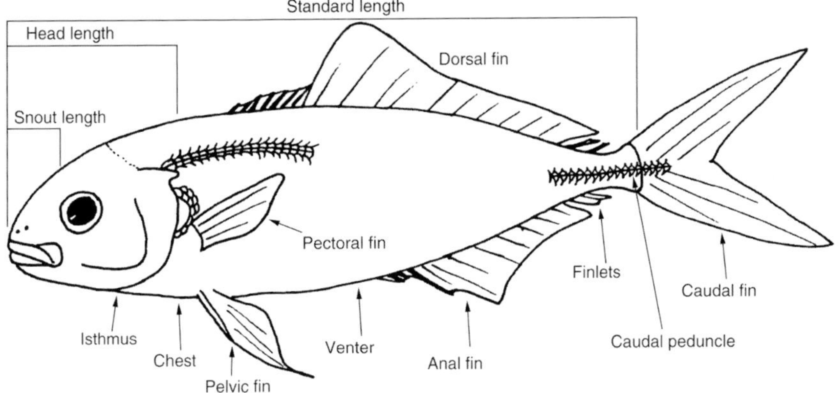

Fig. 6. Important parts and measurements of a hypothetical fish [Illustration from Fishes of the Northern Gulf of Mexico, *1975, by Jerry G. Walls, © T.F.H. Publications, Inc.]*

Fishes of the Texas Laguna Madre

Kingdom—Animalia
Phylum—Chordata
Subphylum—Vertebrata (with backbones)
Super Class—Agnatha (jawless fishes)
Super Class—Gnathostomata (jawed fishes)

Cartilaginous Fishes—Class Chondrichthyes

This class includes sharks, skates, rays, and chimaeras. Although not the oldest group of the fishes (that distinction belongs to the ancestors of lampreys and hagfishes), members of this class have changed little since they first appeared in the fossil record more than 400 million years ago. They appeared in marine deposits, indicating at least a good portion of their evolution occurred in salt water. They are an easier group to define mainly because there are only about 850 species total. Also, except for their teeth, they have not been preserved well and it is assumed that the early forms are quite similar to the species alive today.

The cartilaginous fishes are characterized by having skeletons of cartilage; the body covered in small sandpaper-like placoid scales (or dermal denticles); teeth that are not fused to the jaws and are replaced in rows; single, ventral nostrils on each side of the head; a spiral valve intestine; and claspers (reproductive organs) on the pelvic fins of the males. The sharks and rays possess five to seven pairs of gill slits that open externally and separately and are not covered by an operculum (gill cover) as in the bony fishes. The chimaeras have four pairs of gill slits with a single opening on each side protected by a soft gill cover. There are approximately 375 species of sharks, 450 species of skates and rays, and only 30 species of the bizarre, deepwater chimaeras (sometimes called rattails).

The various reproductive methods practiced by this group are some of their most interesting traits. All species of cartilaginous fishes undergo internal fertilization. Most species are either viviparous (placental development and live birth) or ovoviviparous (eggs hatch inside the female and are born alive), giving birth to only a small number of young. A few species are oviparous (egg layers) and deposit eggs in capsules that can survive extreme environmental conditions before hatching. Regardless of the mode of reproduction, all enter the world as well-developed juveniles.

Most all of the cartilaginous fishes are marine, although a few species, such as the bull shark (*Carcharhinus leucas*), implicated in many shark attacks on humans, can live permanently in fresh water. There are true freshwater species in two families of tropical stingrays. Rays range in width from 4 inches to a wingspan of more than 20 feet in large manta rays. Skates are generally smaller, but there are considerably more species of them.

Sharks are generally large animals, with many species averaging nearly 6 feet in length. The whale shark (*Rhincodon typus*) is the largest of all fish, with adults reaching more than 40 feet in length. There are generally five gill slits present, although a few species have six or seven. The spiracles, remnants of forward gill slits, occur behind each eye on some sharks and on all rays. The upper lobe of the caudal fin is longer than the lower one and is reinforced by the vertebral column.

The skin of certain shark species has long been valued as a tough and wear-resistant leather and is sometimes made into a product called shagreen, which is used as an abrasive, like sandpaper. Many species are the targets of the world's ocean fishing industries, not only for the harvest of their flesh and fins but also for their jaws and teeth, sold as souvenirs. Sharks and rays are often considered to be distinctly different, but some species such as the angel sharks clearly show the characteristics of both.

Because of their relatively large sizes and reputations as man-eaters, sharks have always attracted great public interest. Shark attacks are not common anywhere and have been rare in the Gulf of Mexico. While some have occurred along the gulf coast, most attacks have been on Florida's east coast in the Atlantic Ocean. In 1987, there were three attacks at Port Aransas, Texas, with two in a single day in the surf zone. These occurred the year following a red tide event that killed large numbers of fish in the gulf. Single attacks in South Texas were reported the summer after devastating freezes in 1962, 1983, and 1989. All involved aggressive attacks and small but serious wounds. The only fatality was in 1962. A tooth recovered from one of the Port Aransas attacks was identified as being from a blacktip shark (*Carcharhinus limbatus*); other evidence suggests that small sharks were involved. Another attack in 1977, a year of great shark abundance along the Texas coast, was the result of a shark escaping from a seine in a local bay. Since 1990, a small number of unconfirmed attacks have occurred along the coast.

In general, sharks are much more common in the gulf than in the bays. However, since 2006 sport anglers wading in Matagorda Bay have reported that they are continually approached by aggressive sharks attracted to fish on their stringers. Many new and novel fish-holding baskets have been constructed in an attempt to mask their catches from the roving schools of sharks. Because of high salinities in the upper lagoon, sharks are seldom encountered. They are somewhat more common in the lower lagoon.

GROUND OR WHALER SHARKS—ORDER CARCHARHINIFORMES

This order is a large assemblage comprising eight families and nearly 270 species, and it contains many of the more familiar species of sharks, including the requiem sharks (Carcharhinidae) and hammerhead sharks (Sphyrnidae). General characteristics of this order include two dorsal (back or upper surface) fins, an anal fin, and five gill slits with the last one to three slits situated above the base of the pectoral fins. Gill rakers are lacking, and the eyes are equipped with a nictitating fold or membrane (movable lower eyelid). Spiracles are usually present, and the intestinal valve is of the spiral or scroll type. Embryo development is highly variable; it may be oviparous, ovoviviparous, or viviparous. The members of this order are found in virtually every marine habitat. Many species occur in coastal areas and the open ocean in temperate to tropical zones of the Atlantic, Pacific, and Indian Oceans and the Gulf of Mexico, while some inhabit estuarine areas and a few even make use of freshwater habitats.

Requiem Sharks—Family Carcharhinidae

The requiem sharks comprise one of the largest shark families and are the most abundant of sharks, being named for the tendency of some species to occur in large "masses" near the surface. There are about sixty species in this worldwide group, with fifteen to seventeen species occurring in the Gulf of Mexico. While most species occur in temperate and tropical marine waters, the bull shark (*Carcharhinus leucas*) is known to enter freshwater systems, including the Mississippi River, where it has reportedly made attacks on humans.

The requiem sharks are generally medium to large (3 to 10 feet long) in size, and they have a moderately slender to rather stout body. The long, arched mouth is equipped with blade-like teeth that are often different in the upper and lower jaws. Characteristically, the upper teeth are broadly triangular with serrated edges, while the lower teeth are narrow and smooth-edged. No barbels or nasal grooves are present, and spiracles are usually absent. The first dorsal fin is moderate to large in size and is situated between the pelvic fin base and the pectoral fin base.

This family contains several well-known species inhabiting tropical and temperate waters. The ridgeback sharks (those with a pronounced ridge between the dorsal fins) are common pelagic species, whereas most other species live near the bottom. However, this is a loose distinction. Some sharks in this group are "ram-ventilators," meaning they must swim constantly to oxygenate their gills, while others can lie on the bottom for extended periods. Many are more active at night or dawn and dusk than during the day. Some are solitary or socialize in small groups, while other species are schoolers. A few give specialized threat or defensive displays and may also become aggressive when encountered by humans. The requiem sharks are major predators, generally consuming a wide variety of prey. Their diet generally consists of bivalves (clams, mussels), cuttlefishes, squids, octopods, crustaceans, fish, sea turtles, sea birds, marine mammals, and even other sharks. Most species are viviparous while a few are ovoviviparous. This is the most economically important shark family, as many species are utilized for food, oil, leather, shagreen, fish meal, and various other products. Some cause great losses to the longline fisheries by their predation on hooked fish and to trawl fisheries by causing damage to their nets. A few species are also dangerous to humans. Most cannot tolerate fresh water, and apparently few can tolerate the high salinity characteristic of the Texas Laguna Madre.

BLACKTIP SHARK—*Carcharhinus limbatus*

Other names: spotfin, ground shark, tiburón

The blacktip shark is more abundant than any other species in anglers' catches from piers and the surf zone in the Gulf of Mexico during the summer months. The blacktip shark is found worldwide in temperate and tropical waters from the western Atlantic throughout the gulf and Caribbean to Brazil. This species has been reported from all of the saltier Texas bays, including the upper and lower Laguna Madre. It has been recorded as plentiful in the upper Laguna Madre during less saline periods. The snout is slender and pointed, and both the upper and lower teeth are

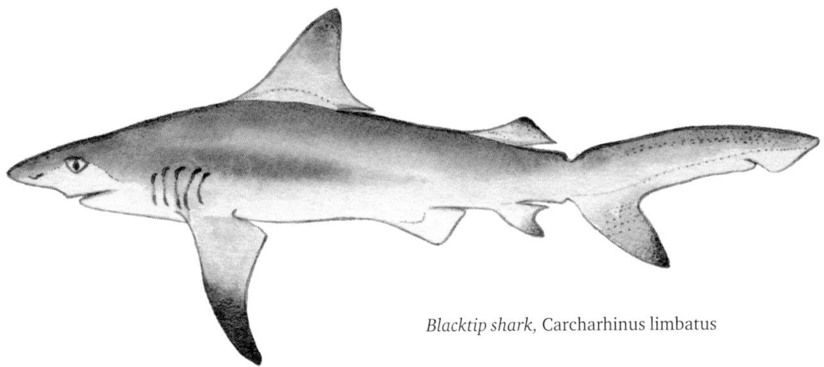

Blacktip shark, Carcharhinus limbatus

slender and symmetrical. The body is dark gray, bluish gray, or dusky bronze dorsally and white to yellowish in color on the belly. In adults, the dorsal, pectoral, and caudal fins are tipped with black and the anal fin is white, but the black-tipped fins become less distinct with age. The blacktip is a very active, strong swimming and schooling species and is especially abundant in areas of swift water. Thus, in passes, channels, and the surf zone, congregations are often encountered.

This species can be a spectacular leaper, like the spinner shark (*C. brevipinna*), and is frequently observed in a nose-up twirl leaving the water. It may display this behavior at the end of a feeding run on small schooling fishes. Even within sight of land, especially in early summer, one can watch this breathtaking exhibition. Blacktips are often segregated by age and sex. Females migrate seasonally to cooler waters during the warmer months and return to give birth near the beach or in inshore nursery grounds after a ten- to twelve-month gestation period in alternate years. During this time, females may occur in larger aggregations. Litter sizes range from one to ten "pups" (usually four to seven). Young are 15 to 28 inches in length at birth, and the young of the year are sometimes caught in the surf by anglers. Adults can reach 8 feet in length. This species is good sport and table fare. The Texas record is 190.0 pounds and 8.1 feet long (Gulf of Mexico, 2003).

Atlantic Sharpnose Shark—*Rhizoprionodon terranovae*

Other names: sand shark

The Atlantic sharpnose shark is extremely common in coastal waters during the summer months and is one of the more abundant shark species in Texas waters. It ranges from the Bay of Fundy, along the northeastern coast of the United States, south to

Atlantic sharpnose shark, Rhizoprionodon terranovae

the Yucatan. It has also been found in the Pascagoula River in Mississippi. This species is a year-round resident off South Carolina, the Florida Keys, and in the gulf. The Atlantic sharpnose is replaced in the Caribbean by a very similar, closely related species, the Caribbean sharpnose shark (*Rhizoprionodon porosus*). This shark is recognized by its long snout (longer than the width of the mouth) and by the presence of long labial furrows or grooves along the corners of the mouth. The teeth are triangular, strongly notched on their outer margins, smooth edged, and similar in both jaws. The body color is brownish, olive-gray, or bluish gray with metallic hues shading to white below. Adults usually have white spots on the upper body. Juveniles have black-edged dorsal and caudal fins, and the second dorsal fin is set slightly behind the anal fin.

The Atlantic sharpnose is common in the surf zone and enclosed bays. It forms large schools of individuals of similar size and sex. Sexes generally are segregated during most of the year, and loose aggregates of males or females often roam coastal waters. Off South Carolina it is found at depths of 40 feet or less in the summer, moving to deeper waters (90 feet) during the winter months. Food items include shrimp, molluscs, and small fishes. Development is viviparous and sexual maturity is reached at about 33 inches. The gestation period is about one year, and shortly after giving birth in late spring the females mate again. The pups (usually four to seven per litter) are born during early June in estuarine or shallow coastal waters and are 9 to 14 inches in length at birth. Pups are common in the surf and bays during the summer. The Atlantic sharpnose shark is often considered a nuisance to sport anglers because it takes bait intended for more desirable game fish. Along with the blacktip shark (*C. limbatus*), it is commonly caught by surf and coastal pier anglers. The adults grow to about 4 feet in length, but the average size is 3 feet and 4 to 6 pounds. The state record is 17.1 pounds, 43.5 inches long (Gulf of Mexico, 2000).

SPINNER SHARK—*Carcharhinus brevipinna*

The spinner shark is a fast-moving species with an almost circumtropical distribution, having been reported from the Atlantic, Indian, and western Pacific Oceans and the Mediterranean Sea. In North American waters, it ranges from North Carolina to Florida and the Gulf of Mexico, being common throughout its range during the warmer months. Spinner sharks roam offshore waters, although this species appears to be more common in inshore waters. It is characterized by a snout as long as, or longer than, the width of the mouth and by the first dorsal fin originating over or posterior to the free tips of the pectoral fins. The teeth have narrow, triangular, broad bases. The upper teeth have finely serrated edges while the lower teeth are smooth. Juveniles may have smooth-edged upper teeth. The body color is gray or bronze with a band of gray extending downward over the white belly from the level of the pectoral fins to the pelvic fins. Those less than 28 inches long have unmarked fins. Adults have black tips on the second dorsal, anal, and pectoral fins and on the lower lobe of the caudal fin. The spinner is often confused with its smaller cousin, the blacktip shark (*C. limbatus*), which has similarly marked fins (except for the white-tipped anal fin), but the eyes of the blacktip are somewhat larger.

This species is often seen in schools, leaping from the water while spinning, hence its common name. The reasons for spinning are not known, but the spinning is often attributed to the feeding behavior when pursuing schools of prey from

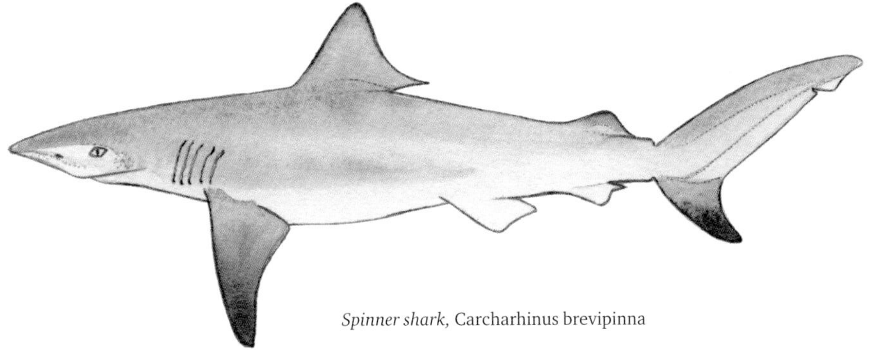

Spinner shark, Carcharhinus brevipinna

beneath the school and then spiraling upward, engulfing them. The spinning behavior has also been attributed to a mating ritual. The spinner shark's food consists of small schooling fishes, squid, and small sharks and rays, but it will eat almost anything it can catch. Development is viviparous and males mature at about 67 inches, with females becoming sexually mature at about 71 inches. The pups measure 24 to 30 inches at birth and litters usually consist of six to twelve pups, born in early summer. The spinner shark appears to migrate to offshore waters in winter. It has been reported to be a rather aggressive shark and has been blamed for attacks on divers and swimmers. The average size is 6 feet and 120 pounds. The state record is 212.6 pounds, 89.8 inches long (Gulf of Mexico, 2000).

Hammerhead Sharks—Family Sphyrnidae

The hammerhead sharks are among the more common sharks found in tropical and warm temperate waters, and their distribution is circumtropical. They inhabit open ocean waters and continental shelves from the surface to at least 900 feet and are sometimes found in large schools. There are eight species in this family, and at least three species occur in the Gulf of Mexico. Family members possess a tall first dorsal fin. These medium to large sharks are characterized by flat, lateral expansions of the head, so when viewed from above or below the outline is that of the letter T. The eyes and nostrils are borne on the outer edge of the head. Several hypotheses have been advanced to explain the function of the expanded head. The wide snout is thought to be an aid in locating prey by smell, but it may also help to dislodge food on the bottom. It may also aid these swift animals in making very tight turns, thus increasing their maneuverability. The shape of the head can be used to distinguish most species at a glance. They are reported to have hearty appetites and to feed on a variety of prey, including other hammerheads, stingrays, squid, octopus, crustaceans, and an array of bony fishes. These sharks are viviparous and produce living young. The hammerhead sharks were once sought for their vitamin-rich liver oil. The fins are very valuable, and commercial fisheries and their by-catch fisheries have depleted populations of these sharks in many areas. Hammerheads die quickly when hooked or entangled, so live release is usually not successful.

BONNETNOSE—*Sphyrna tiburo*
Other names: bonnethead, shovel-head shark, cornuda, cabeza de pala
The bonnetnose was once one of the most abundant sharks in South Texas bays and has only been reported from

Bonnetnose, Sphyrna tiburo

the Laguna Madre near Port Isabel. At one time anglers commonly landed the bonnetnose along gulf beaches during the warm months of the year. The bonnetnose occurs in the eastern Pacific and western Atlantic from Massachusetts and through the Caribbean to Brazil. It inhabits the shallower areas of the continental shelves and bays. The bonnetnose can be easily distinguished from other family members by the notchless, rounded, and shovel-shaped head. There are often dark spots on the body, and the teeth are smooth and without serrations. Both the upper and lower jaws are equipped with twelve to fourteen rows of similarly shaped teeth. This species is gray to greenish gray on the sides with a light-colored belly.

The bonnetnose is a migratory and social species, often found in groups of three to fifteen individuals and rarely found alone. Their behavior is well studied and complex. The bonnetnose usually remains near shore, but there is some evidence based on shrimp trawl catches that it moves offshore during the winter. On the Texas coast, adults feed mostly on crabs but may consume bivalves (clams, mussels), octopus, and small bony fishes. Pregnant females are more common in shallow water and produce litter sizes ranging from four to sixteen pups. The young are born during late summer and are 13 to 16 inches in length. In Mexico, this small shark is an important food fish. Adults attain 4 feet in length. The Texas record is 24.3 pounds and 50.1 inches (Gulf of Mexico, 2004).

Skates and Rays—Order Rajiformes and Order Myliobatiformes

Members of these orders have the head, body, and pectoral fins combined into a flat disc (wings) with a slender tail bearing very small dorsal and caudal fins. All skates and rays are characterized by having ventral (belly or lower surface) gill openings, no anal fin, and eyes and spiracles (respiratory openings) on top of the head. Most familiar are the skates (Rajidae), a nearly cosmopolitan marine group found from shallow estuaries to great depths in the world's oceans in both warm and cold waters. Some species are more than 6 feet wide, but most do not grow to more than 2.5 feet. Unlike the rays (livebearers), the skates are oviparous (egg layers). Their eggs are enclosed in leathery cases called "mermaid purses." The barb or stinger on the tail is a spine modified from a scale and the poison is produced by glands in the grooves on the spine. The spines will regenerate if lost or broken. Stingrays may have several of these serrated spines and can inflict painful wounds that can become infected. The toxin is heat labile (easily broken down with heat), and anyone receiving a puncture should treat the wound with hot compresses or with hot water. Chemical heat packs are widely available today. Common practice is for these exceedingly painful wounds to be treated with a tetanus shot and antibiotics to prevent infection. At least one fatality is known from Texas waters. Some of the larger species are fished commercially in Europe. The thickest parts of the wings provide white, mild flesh that is very good to eat.

Stingrays—Family Dasyatidae

This family comprises 118 species worldwide, with 7 species occurring in the Gulf of Mexico. Most stingrays are warm-water, bottom-occurring animals, burying themselves in the sediment with only their eyes and spiracles exposed. They are usually found near the shore in shallow waters, generally along tropical and subtropical coasts, but they often enter rivers. They feed on a wide variety of benthic organisms, including shellfish and fish, some of which they "mine" hydraulically by jetting water into the sediment to dislodge them. Some stingray species damage commercial clam and oyster beds by preying upon them for food. Stingrays are generally shy and avoid humans if left alone. While stingrays are plentiful in the bays and surf, swimmers and waders generally make sufficient noise to scare away those that might be in their path. Stingrays may be safely handled by carefully and firmly picking them up by the tip of the tail or by grasping them from the front with the thumb and forefinger inserted into the spiracles, the safest being to combine both methods. A stingray will readily take a baited hook, and because of its flat body it can put up a determined resistance. They are

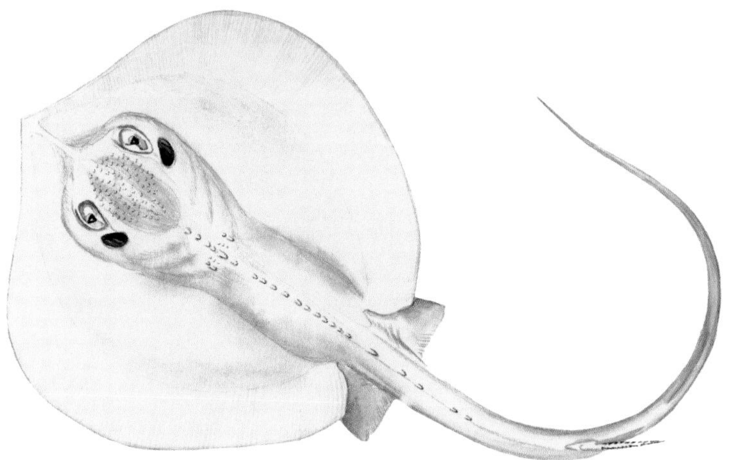

Atlantic stingray, Dasyatis sabina

not great fighters but are very strong and burrow into or onto the bottom like a suction cup, which can test an angler's stamina and patience. They can also be the shallow-water angler's friend as they create trails of silt in their wake when feeding and often attract red drum.

Atlantic Stingray—*Dasyatis sabina*
Other names: stingaree
This is the smallest and most common stingray and likely the most dangerous, since it is very abundant in shallow bays where anglers and swimmers regularly encounter them. It ranges from Chesapeake Bay to south Florida and throughout the Gulf of Mexico. The disc has very rounded outer corners and rear edges, with the length of the disc equal to its width. The snout is triangularly pointed and projecting, and a mid-dorsal row of spines is present on the body, with a few on the tail beyond the pelvic fins. It has a very slender tail with brown folds of skin both dorsally and ventrally. The body color is tan to brown above and white on the underside. The Atlantic stingray is common in shallow coastal waters to depths of about 70 feet. It often enters fresh water but prefers sandy estuarine areas and depressions in shallow lagoons. It leaves bays and migrates to the gulf during the colder months but remains on the inshore shelf.

The "wings" are edible and are similar in texture and taste to that of scallops. Litters of a half dozen off-spring are born live in the spring and

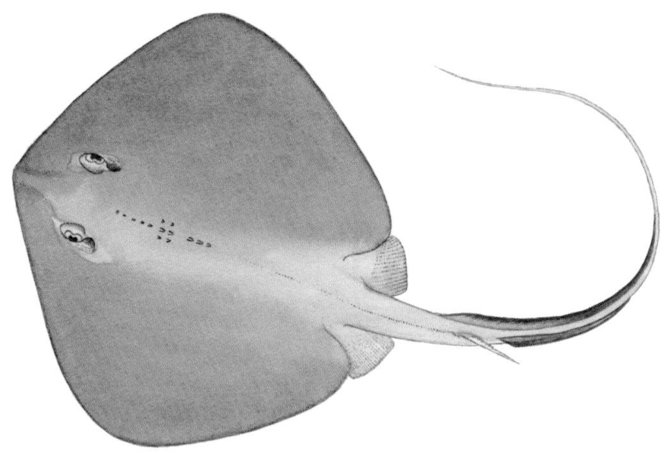

Bluntnose stingray, Dasyatis say

summer, with the young being fully developed and ready to face the challenges of their environment. This species has been reported to give birth to young in Corpus Christi Bay during June and July. The state record is 10.8 pounds, 41.5 inches long (Galveston Bay, 1994).

This is the ray that will most often be encountered by anyone wade fishing in the bays and on the gulf beach. If anglers pay attention to the area in their path, these rays will often be seen swimming up in front of or directly beneath the feet. It amazes me how many we encounter and how seldom we come in contact with their poisonous spines. Shuffling the feet when wading is advice well taken, especially for those of us who have come in contact with them.

Bluntnose Stingray—*Dasyatis say*

This species is found from the New Jersey coast and throughout the gulf to Argentina; it is widespread in the coastal waters of the West Indies. The body is dark, often nearly black. Well-developed black to dusky-colored dorsal and ventral finfolds are present on the slender tail. The disc is smooth and broadly rounded at the corners with about ten mid-dorsal spines and sometimes a few small spines on the wings. The snout is short, relatively blunt, and not projecting. The bluntnose stingray is primarily an inshore species with large individuals present there during the summer when bearing their young. They do not commonly enter bays. Individuals may grow to 3 feet wide. The Texas state record is 36.7 pounds (Galveston Bay, 2003).

Southern Stingray—*Dasyatis americana*
Other names: raya
This is one of the largest stingrays along the southeastern and gulf shores, ranging from the New Jersey coast south to Brazil. An inshore ray over much of its range, it occurs in the northern gulf in the saltier bays and estuaries to the edges of offshore reefs. It has been reported from the Laguna Madre but apparently does not regularly enter hypersaline waters. The disc is almost a perfect rhombus (diamond shape) with pointed corners, and it is usually a uniform dark brown color on the upper surface (grayish in the young). The ventral finfold on the slender tail is long and pronounced. The dorsal finfold is absent or reduced in prominence, and both finfolds are black in color. A mid-dorsal row of low spines is present on the body along with a few short rows of spines near the shoulders. It can exceed 6 feet in width and 7 feet in length. The state and world record is 246.0 pounds, 8.0 feet (Galveston Bay, 1998).

In 1982, I was wading alone in an area well north of Rocky Slough (between Baffin Bay and the Land Cut), where I had recently caught two common snook. I was "hit" by a 4-foot-wide southern stingray lying in one of the few large sandspots on that shoreline and would have drowned from the immediate incapacitation and pain from that one and only encounter had I been in water more than waist deep. I nearly died several times before the pain subsided. All entering the coastal waters should be aware that heat or hot water applied

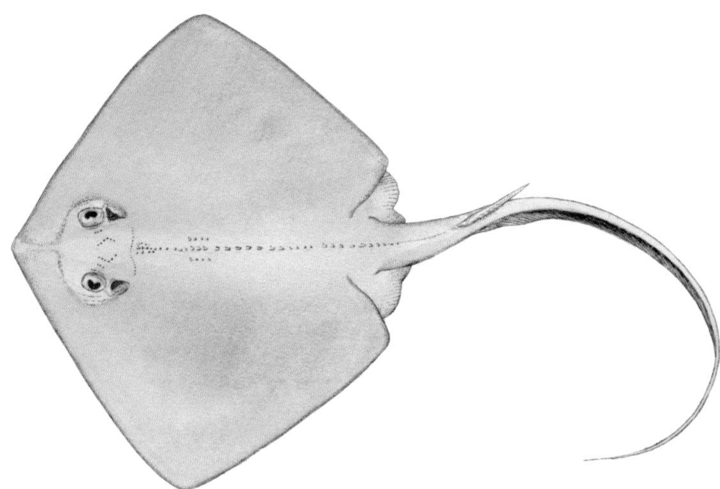

Southern stingray, Dasyatis americana

to the entry wound will relieve the pain immediately. It is highly recommended that one visit a physician as soon as possible because these puncture wounds are very "dirty" and antibiotics will likely be prescribed.

Eagle Rays, Manta Rays, and Cownose Ray—Family Myliobatidae and Family Rhinopteridae

There are nearly thirty species in this group, and most occur in tropical and warm temperate latitudes. At least five species occur in the Gulf of Mexico. All bear live young, and most species are found offshore. Eagle rays are large, free-swimming rays with wide, pointed wings and a blunt snout. Schools of eagle rays are said to "fly" through the water, flapping their powerful pectoral fins. They will gather in schools of hundreds or even thousands, with some undertaking long seasonal migrations. Most reach a large size, up to 4 feet in width, and have a strong, serrated spine with venomous tissue near the base of the tail, yet they are inoffensive and present little danger to swimmers since they do not lie on the bottom and thus cannot be stepped on. However, they can be dangerous if speared; native fishermen have been wounded by the spines, sometimes fatally (due to the wound itself or subsequent infection). Manta rays are giant, free-swimming rays that also move through the water by "flying" movements of the wing-like fins with the long, whip-like tail held straight behind them.

The feeding habits vary greatly among the different species in this family. The eagle rays and cownose ray feed while cruising along the bottom in search of food such as oysters, clams, and crabs, which they grind and crush between their large plate-like teeth. They often dislodge prey from the bottom with the hydraulic action of powerful movements of their large wings. The manta rays unroll their large, flexible "horns" or cephalic fins to direct and channel large plankton and schools of small fishes and crustaceans into the very broad and wide mouth. These rays are preferred food for some large shark species; eagle and manta rays are often seen with bite-sized chunks missing from a wing.

Both eagle and manta rays are apt to show up in the bays, especially in areas near the gulf passes. As a teenager I frequently saw both from the gulf piers in the summer. A vivid memory is of a 15- to 20-foot wide manta ray that stayed near Horace Caldwell Pier (Port Aransas) in the 1960s. One day it finally tired of having many anglers purposefully foul hook it, and it then headed south, taking all their fishing line with it. In the 1980s on a student field trip aboard the R/V *Katy* into Corpus Christi Bay near Ingleside, we watched a small manta ray (conservatively 8 feet wide) do countless aerial crashing leaps before tiring and swimming away.

Cownose Ray—*Rhinoptera bonasus*
Other names: cowfish
The cownose ray is a coastal resident that is most abundant in the shallow gulf but regularly enters estuaries. This species ranges from the New England coast to Florida and throughout the gulf to Trinidad, Venezuela, and Brazil. The disc is brown to olive colored above and lacks any spots or markings. The wings are long and pointed with concave rear edges. The snout projects forward with an indentation at the center, and a deep groove is visible from the side. There are usually seven rows of teeth (crushing plates), and the eyes are situated on the sides of the head. A cownose ray will occasionally leap free of the water, landing with a loud crash, likely a territorial display. Populations in the gulf are reported to migrate clockwise, with schools of up to ten thousand rays making a mass exodus at the onset of cold weather, leaving the west coast of Florida for the Yucatan Peninsula. Large schools are found in saltier bays and on the inshore shelf during the summer. During spring and summer, the cownose ray is commonly seen in the Laguna Madre and can be very common in Baffin Bay.

Anyone fishing the lagoon regularly will see schools of cownose rays,

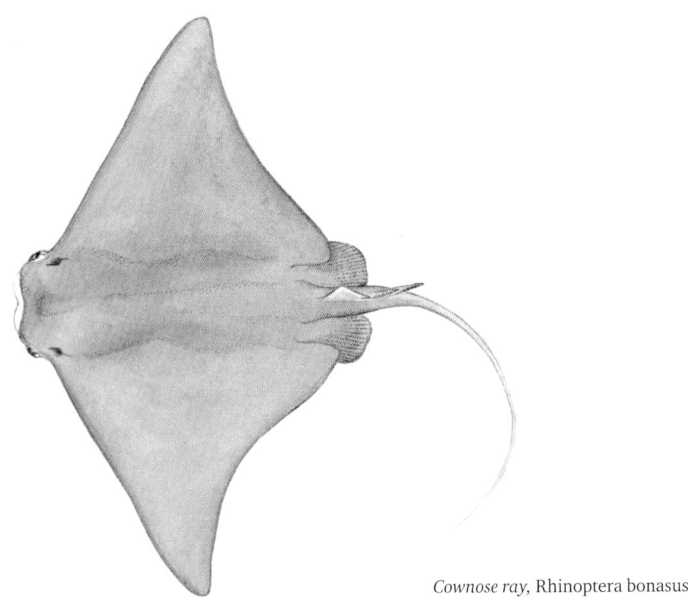

Cownose ray, Rhinoptera bonasus

especially in the summer months. They travel in schools of up to thirty or forty individuals and alternate between swimming near the bottom virtually unnoticed and at the surface. Generally a few wingtips and "nervous water" are all that will be seen. They will take soft plastics on occasion but are often foul-hooked. The cownose ray has been captured at salinities as high as 60 ppt. They average 2 feet in width, but may reach 7 feet wide and 100 pounds. The state record is 50.5 pounds and 52.0 inches in length (Gulf of Mexico, 1986).

Bony Fishes—Superclass Osteichthyes, Class Actinopterygii

This class includes most of the living fish-like vertebrates, with bony fishes representing nearly 40 percent of all known vertebrate species. This is a large and diverse group with a fairly rich fossil record. As a result, this is a difficult group to clearly define. The most distinctive characteristics for all bony fishes include the presence of an entirely or partially bony skeleton (rather than cartilage), bony scales, and soft rays in the fins. Some (e.g., lungfishes) even have modified air bladders that function exactly like lungs. There are currently between 23,500 and 25,000 named species with as many as 55,000 species when subspecies are considered. As many as 200 new species are described each year, especially from freshwater systems in South America and from deep ocean basins. The two main groups of the bony fishes are the lobe-finned or fleshy-finned fishes (the coelacanth and lungfishes) and the ray-finned fishes, consisting of four types: (1) bichirs and reedfishes (fringe-finned ganoids), (2) sturgeons and paddlefishes (cartilaginous ganoids), (3) bowfin and gars (bony ganoids), and (4) the teleosts ("true" bony fishes, the largest group by far, comprising nearly 23,000 total species). About 60 percent of the bony fishes are confined to marine waters, with the remainder found in a wide variety of freshwater habitats. A very small number of bony fishes alternate between fresh water and salt water (diadromous). The bony fishes are found from deep abysses to above the high tide line in the oceans and bays, from oxygen-poor boggy swamps to the rushing torrents of high-altitude mountain rivers, and from extremely hot springs to marine waters so cold that a natural antifreeze is required in the blood to keep the fish from freezing. They swim using various methods and walk and wriggle into and out of water; they leap, glide, and even fly. They range in size from tiny quarter-inch gobies to giant tunas, marlins, and swordfishes, all reaching lengths of 10 feet or more.

Their colors rival those of the butterflies and birds, their shapes and postures are simply fascinating, and their modes of life and certain of their anatomical and behavioral adaptations for feeding and breeding are almost unbelievable.

TARPON AND LADYFISH—ORDER ELOPIFORMES

This order includes two families and eight species. The tarpon is commonly found in nearshore gulf waters, and although it has been caught with some regularity in the Texas lagoon, especially around Port Isabel, it is not included here because it is not common in the Laguna Madre. All members share the leptocephalus larval stage with the eel-like fishes. Although having teeth, the nonfeeding larvae are nearly colorless and ribbon-like, often having the shape of a willow leaf. Larvae in this order differ from those of eels in that they have forked caudal fins. In addition to the general features of a primitive bony fish, all members have a gular plate, which is a bony structure between the branches of the lower jaw. These fishes show some relationship to the herring-like fishes and were once included in that order (Clupeiformes).

All are streamlined and predatory with silvery scales (very large in the tarpon) and deeply forked caudal fins. They are shallow-water, tropical to subtropical marine species that often enter fresh or brackish water. Although poorly regarded as table fare except in Mexico and Central America, the tarpon and ladyfish are popular sport fishes because of the spectacular leaps and aerial displays they perform when hooked.

Tarpon and Ladyfish—Family Elopidae

LADYFISH—*Elops saurus*
Other names: skipjack, ten pounder, banana, chiro, machete, matajuelo real, lisa Francesca
The ladyfish is familiar to most coastal anglers because of its determined runs and repeated jumps from the water. Its alternate common

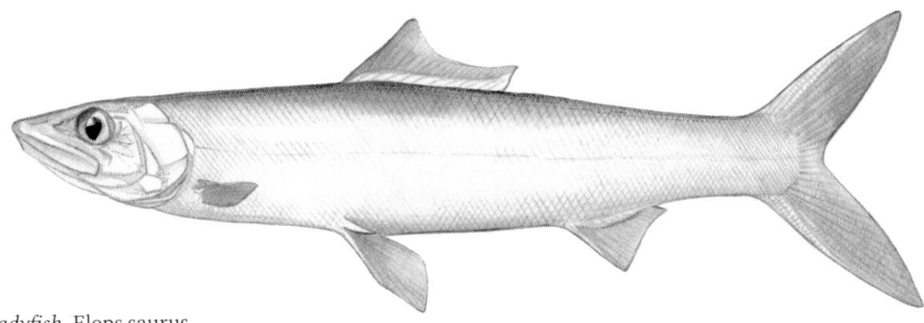

Ladyfish, Elops saurus

name "ten pounder" comes from the fact that it fights as if it weighed that much or more. However, unlike the tarpon, it has little appeal as a game fish because of its small size. The ladyfish is elongate, with a green back and brilliant silvery sides and tiny scales that are easily knocked off. The caudal fin is deeply forked, and the mouth is large and very bony. It is an aggressive, swift, and voracious predator that strikes and slashes reflexively at almost anything in its path.

This species ranges from the Atlantic states south to Venezuela. It is common in the surf, around passes, and in the bays, with apparently no preference for a particular habitat. Instead, ladyfish tend to follow whatever baitfishes are available, feeding on small schooling species such as anchovies and silversides. Rarely do they break the surface of the water when "frenzy" feeding. Rather they swirl in great schools just below the surface, producing a "boil" as they dash back and forth until the last of their prey is consumed. Although the spawning sites are not fully known, ladyfish are reported to be offshore spawners. The larvae have been collected from January to April in Oso Bay (Cayo del Oso). Adults are common in the hypersaline Laguna Madre in the summer. When the temperature drops in the fall, they leave the coast and may migrate southward.

The ladyfish is a savage striker and a strong, showy fighter, though not highly esteemed by Texas sport anglers. It is also an aerial acrobat, jumping frantically and continually from the water in an attempt to dislodge the hook from its bony mouth (which it generally does). An old saying was that only one of ten tarpon or ladyfish hooked would actually be landed. They are often seen at night beneath pier lights where they wait to ambush unsuspecting prey. They can be caught on a wide variety of natural and artificial bait; however, the soft flesh is of poor quality, being both oily and bony. Whether fact or fiction, the ladyfish has long been considered a favored prey of large female spotted seatrout in the lagoon. The average adult size is 1 to 3 pounds, with the largest always found in the gulf. Although they are known to reach 6 to 7 pounds, the current Texas record is 5.0 pounds and 28.5 inches long (Aransas Bay, 2005).

TRUE EELS—ORDER ANGUILLIFORMES

This is a large order of marine and catadromous (able to migrate from fresh water to salt water) species comprising about twenty families. These are the "true" eels and are thought to have their origin in a bonefish-like ancestor. The obvious link between the tarpon/ladyfish and the eels is the leptocephalus larval stage, seen in both groups. The eels are greatly elongate, with the dorsal and anal fins continuous with the caudal fin. Scales are absent in many families, and the gill openings are usually small and placed behind the edge of the concealed gill cover, which is hidden by a fleshy flap of skin. Modern eels all lack pelvic fins and many are also without pectoral fins.

The large diversity of the different types of eels that exist is poorly known. Worldwide, there are approximately 730 species belonging to 15 families in this order. Their public image has been formed largely by the culinary and sporting qualities of freshwater eels and by lurid descriptions of fierce moray eels attacking divers on coral reefs. However, all species are quite secretive in the varied types of habitats they occupy. Representatives inhabit lakes, streams, coral reefs, and even the deep sea, but most live in shallow tropical or subtropical marine habitats. Many temperate adult eel species make extensive migrations to lay their eggs in areas where oceanic currents favor the growth, survival, and return "home" of their larvae to the freshwater environment in which they themselves matured.

Snake and Worm Eels—Family Ophichthidae

This family is the largest in the order, with nearly 250 known species. Approximately 28 species in 15 genera are reported from the Gulf of Mexico. The snake and worm eels are common in various habitats where they burrow tail first into the sediment. The snake eels have a hard, pointed, finless tail; the worm eels possess a caudal fin. The spike-like tail of the snake eels allows them to quickly penetrate sand and mud bottoms. Several tropical species lack pectoral fins. Most are found in shallow water and are brightly colored but rarely seen. These eels are difficult to collect because they burrow into soft bottoms during the day but are nocturnal and most active at night. Snake and worm eels do not have permanent burrows; they use them by day and abandon them at night. When in their burrows, they leave only their heads with two pairs of nostrils exposed at the surface. Oceanic species are commonly eaten by groupers, snappers, and other benthic fishes. Some have been known to burrow through the wall of a predator's stomach, die in the fish's abdominal cavity, and become mummified.

Speckled Worm Eel—*Myrophis punctatus*

This is one of the most common eels found on muddy bottoms of the inshore gulf, lagoons, and bays of Texas, and it is known to occasionally enter fresh water as well. It can be especially abundant in grass flats in the upper Laguna Madre, but it does

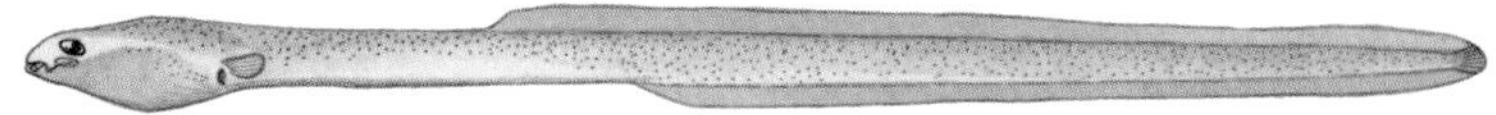

Speckled worm eel, Myrophis punctatus

occur in all Texas bays. The upper body surface is profusely speckled with obvious, pepper-like black spots, and the snout is pointed when viewed from above. The speckled worm eel ranges from the coast of North Carolina to Bermuda and throughout the gulf to Brazil. It is commonly found from mangrove swamps to offshore reefs. On the Texas coast, the adults migrate to the gulf to spawn. Generally, only the juveniles are found inshore, with the strange leptocephalus larvae probably drifting in from offshore spawning areas and appearing along the coast between December and May. Adults may reach up to 2 feet in length.

SHRIMP EEL—*Ophichthus gomesii*
This eel is a common inshore species usually found in muddy habitats in the shallow gulf and in high salinity bays. The sides are dark brown fading to dark gray above, sometimes with a bluish or reddish cast. The belly is generally pale in color. The dorsal and anal fins are dusky in appearance. This eel ranges throughout the Gulf of Mexico south to Brazil. This is the common eel caught by anglers fishing in the saltier bays of Texas. It has been reported to be somewhat common in the Intracoastal Canal near Flour Bluff, Texas. Individuals to 30 inches have been reported. The current Texas state record is 11.1 pounds and 24.5 inches (Gulf of Mexico, 1990).

PALESPOTTED EEL—*Ophichthus puncticeps*
This is an uncommon species sometimes taken by anglers from hard bottom areas. It is highly variable in its color pattern and maximum adult size. This is a large, very heavy-bodied eel and is commonly confused with the shrimp eel. It can be distinguished by the series of large pale spots generally found along the dark tan to gray sides. The upper jaw projects forward and is equipped with one row of palatine teeth. It occurs from North

Shrimp eel, Ophichthus gomesii

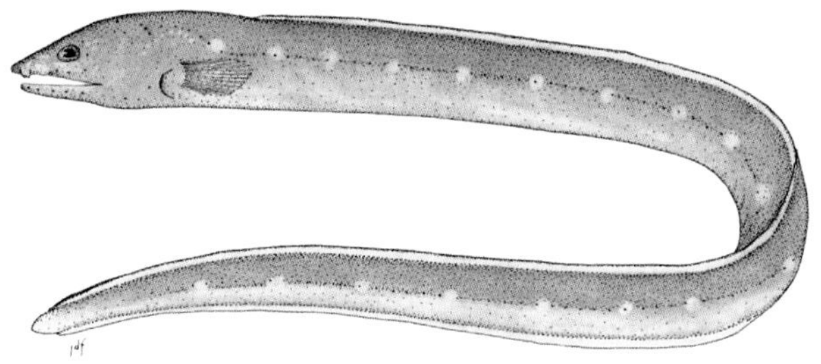

Palespotted eel, Ophichthus puncticeps. *Illustration by Janice D. Fechhelm*

Carolina throughout the northeastern gulf, and adults may attain lengths of more than 6 feet.

Herrings, Shads, Menhaden, and Anchovies—Order Clupeiformes

The herrings and anchovies are thought to be related to the tarpon and ladyfish but lack some of the latter group's primitive characteristics. This order usually has silvery deciduous (easily lost) scales; many have compressed, keel-like bellies, often with specialized, posteriorly directed scales (scutes) on the ventral midline. This group lacks a lateral line (sensory pores along the sides of many fish species). All are adapted for living in the well-lighted surface waters of both salt water and fresh water. Most species are filter feeders and form massive schools that feed on plankton. Their most conspicuous adaptations for this lifestyle are reflective silvery scales, a compressed body, a flexible mouth, and fine gill rakers on the gills to filter plankton from the water. The scales, which scatter light from above, and the compressed body shape, which obscures their profile when viewed from below, greatly reduce their visibility to aquatic predators.

Herrings, Shads, and Menhaden—Family Clupeidae

There are about 181 species in more than 50 genera in this group, with 16 species occurring in the Gulf of Mexico. Most of the herrings, shads, and menhaden have an elongate or thread-like last ray of the dorsal fin. The profile of the belly is moderately to deeply curved. Herrings and their kin are spindle shaped to moderately deep bodied and slightly to strongly compressed, with a terminal mouth and a deeply forked caudal fin. Clupeids have a sense of hearing that is among the most acute in all fishes. The teeth, when present, are small. The eyes are large and situated in the anterior half of the head and gener-

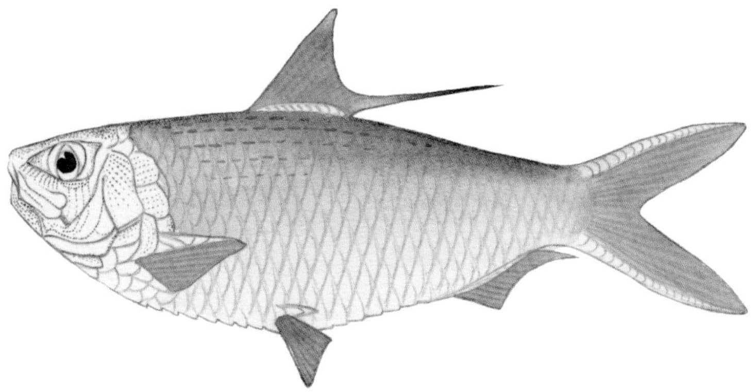

Atlantic thread herring, Opisthonema oglinum

ally covered by an adipose eyelid. The pectoral fins are set low on the body, the dorsal fin is short, the pelvic fins are positioned below the base of the dorsal fin, and the anal fin is small. Most species have a complete series of scutes along the belly.

This group occurs worldwide from tropical to polar latitudes. They are generally present in coastal marine waters, but a number are anadromous and some live exclusively in fresh water. Most are schooling fishes that feed on plankton. Embryonic development is oviparous. Most species in this family are popular live bait or cut bait.

Atlantic Thread Herring—*Opisthonema oglinum*

Other names: greenie, shiner, hairyback, machuelo

The Atlantic thread herring is a popular baitfish in some areas and has been reported as a latent fishery for the Texas coast. The body usually has five to seven dark lengthwise streaks and a dark spot above the gill cover followed by one or more spots.

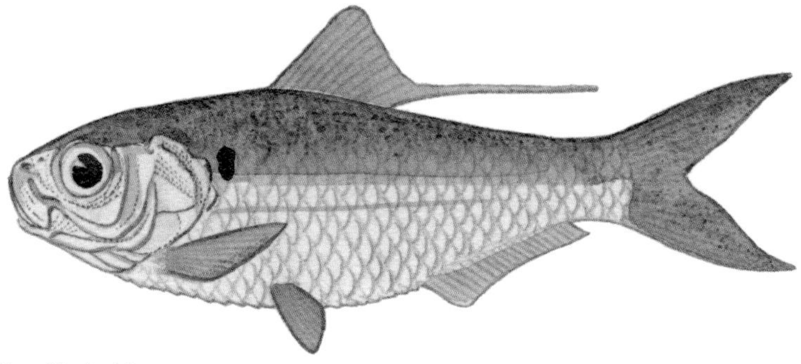

Threadfin shad, Dorosoma petenense

Common in saltier waters, its range is from Cape Cod throughout the gulf to Brazil. This species is commonly 4 to 6 inches long but may attain a length of up to 12 inches.

THREADFIN SHAD—*Dorosoma petenense*

This is a freshwater species that enters coastal embayments. All ages and sizes have a black shoulder spot and six to eight dark stripes on the upper sides of the body. It is apparently absent from the Laguna Madre during high salinity years, but during low salinity periods it has been reported in great abundance in Baffin Bay. The Texas record is 7.6 inches and 0.13 pounds (Richland Chambers Reservoir, Corsicana, 1998).

GIZZARD SHAD—*Dorosoma cepedianum*

This is another freshwater species that regularly enters bays and is found in the Laguna Madre during times of low salinity. Both juveniles and young adults have a dark shoulder spot. They have a thick-walled, muscular stomach that is gizzard-like in function. Once they enter the bays, especially during times of floods, many never return to the rivers. They live and grow in the bay and they may even survive hypersaline conditions. This species reaches a length of 14 to 20 inches. The Texas record is 2.7 pounds, 18.0 inches (Town Lake, Austin, 1997).

SCALED SARDINE—*Harengula jaguana*

Other names: white bait

The scaled sardine is one of several similar species of sardines and it may be the most common inshore member of the family. One to several shoulder spots may be present, and the dorsal fin lacks an elongate filament. This species ranges from Florida to Brazil and is widely distributed on the inner

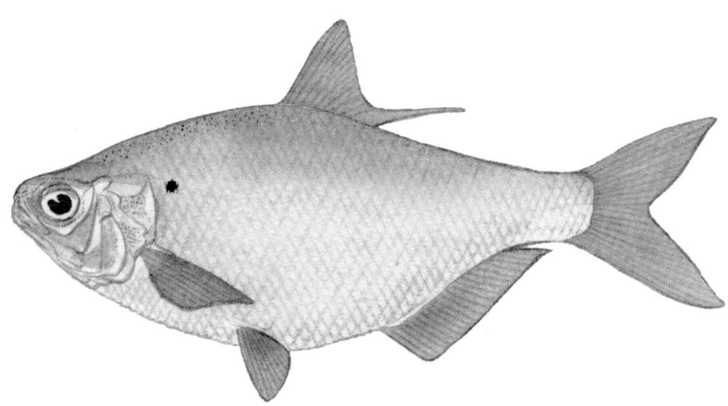

Gizzard shad, Dorosoma cepedianum

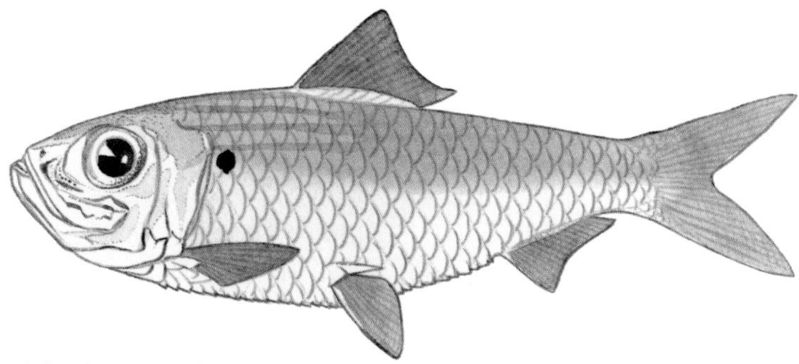

Scaled sardine, Harengula jaguana

continental shelf. In the fall, this species may be found in the more saline bays far from any pass. It is often captured with wire hoops for use as baitfish in some areas. The Texas record is 11.8 inches (Gulf of Mexico, 1995), but most adults are 5 to 7 inches in length.

Finescale Menhaden—*Brevoortia gunteri*

This species is of some importance to commercial fisheries in some parts of the gulf, and it is used primarily for the manufacture of fish meal and oil. It is more common off southern Texas. This menhaden is very silvery in color, it never has more than one spot on the sides, and the fins are dusky to yellow in color. Small individuals of this species are difficult to separate from the gulf menhaden. It will enter brackish waters along the Texas coast and ranges from the Chandeleur Islands west and south to the Yucatan Peninsula. There is little information on the relative abundance of this species in the Laguna Madre, though it is common during some years. The finescale menhaden is a spring spawner while the gulf menhaden is primarily a fall and winter spawner. It grows to 10 inches in length.

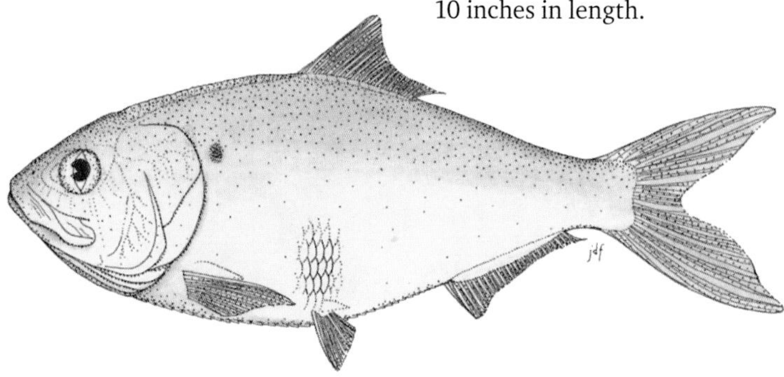

Finescale menhaden, Brevoortia gunteri. *Illustration by Janice D. Fechhelm*

GULF MENHADEN—*Brevoortia patronus*
Other names: pogy, mossbunker, alewife, fatback
The gulf menhaden is an important commercial species and most abundant in western Louisiana. Adults are found in most Texas bays and especially in the gulf waters close to shore. It ranges from Florida to Yucatan, Mexico. This species is distinguished from similar species by having a dark shoulder spot followed by a series of smaller ones. The pogy catch is the largest poundage of marine product landed in the Gulf of Mexico, and during times past it was reported to be the most important single fish species in the United States. In some years, more than 1.1 billion pounds are processed into fish meal, used for its oil, or turned into pet food and fertilizer. Nearly all these fish are commercially harvested between Galveston and Mobile, Alabama. In 2000, the gulf menhaden fishery was the greatest by volume (1.3 billion pounds) in the Gulf of Mexico and the second largest based on value ($80.7 million). Tagging returns indicate that fish between Nueces Bay and the Arroyo Colorado migrate eastward to Louisiana. This fish is an estuarine-dependent species, meaning the early life stages require estuarine habitat. In some low salinity years, it occurs in great abundance in Nueces and Baffin Bays. During high salinity years, it is virtually absent from Baffin Bay. The current state record is 13.6 inches (Sabine Lake, 2005).

Anchovies—Family Engraulidae

The anchovies are the most abundant of the schooling fishes in tropical and subtropical coastal waters and estuaries around the world. They are translucent fish that inhabit inshore areas where plankton densities are high, although a few species inhabit fresh water. There are 15 to 20 genera and about 140 species of anchovies,

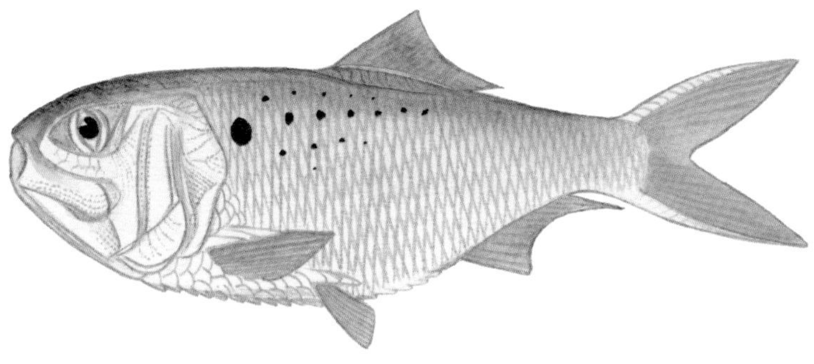

Gulf menhaden, Brevoortia patronus

with a dozen or so found along the Atlantic coast and throughout the Gulf of Mexico. Four species have been confirmed from the northwestern gulf, but other tropical species should be expected offshore during the summer. Although individuals of different species are occasionally found together, large schools usually consist of a single species.

Anchovies are distinguished by their overhanging snouts and long upper jaws, which extend behind the eye almost to the edge of the gill opening; these characteristics produce the classic "anchovy look." Due to their jaw structure, anchovies can open their mouths to an incredible extent, producing round openings that are efficient for filter feeding on plankton with their fine, close-set gill rakers. Most are usually less than 5 inches long, and local species are too small to be of commercial value. However, they serve as an important food source for many larger predatory fishes. Some herrings are the focus of major commercial fisheries as well. One of the greatest of these is the anchovetta fishery off Peru. They are fished commercially in areas where labor costs are low, and populations may fluctuate dramatically in response to changing oceanographic conditions and collapse rather quickly when overfished. Larger species are sometimes sold fresh; others are canned whole or used as a paste and are widely used as bait. Despite their importance, most species remain poorly known. Although anchovies are quite small, they can be present in enormous schools that occupy large areas of the surf zone and bays.

Whether coincidence or not, the arrival of anchovies in the Texas surf in the spring and fall usually means the tarpon are not far behind. On the Atlantic coast of Florida, the experienced tarpon anglers know that the arrival of the white mullet (*Mugil curema*) signals that the tarpon (*Megalops atlanticus*) will not be far behind.

BAY ANCHOVY—*Anchoa mitchilli*

Other names: glass minnow

The bay anchovy is the most abundant fish species in all Texas bays but is common in the Laguna Madre only during hypersaline years. They have been reported to occur in greater numbers than any other species. The bay anchovy is found everywhere and is a crucial link in the estuarine food web between the zooplankton and fish such as trout, flounder, and red drum. The bay anchovy ranges from the cold water estuaries of Maine southward throughout the Gulf of Mexico to Yucatan. These fish are olivaceous in color with a silver stripe that runs almost the entire length of the body and is slightly narrower than the diameter of the eye. The stripe is variable, it may be

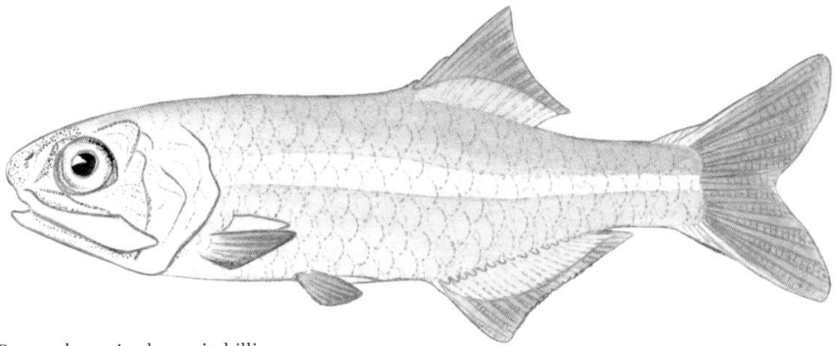

Bay anchovy, Anchoa mitchilli

absent anteriorly, and it is narrower than the eye in southern populations and as wide as the eye in northern populations. They are filter feeders and spend their entire lives in or near estuaries. The abundance of this species has been considered to be an ideal indicator of the overall health of estuaries. Anchovies are responsible for roughened patches on the water's surface as they feed. Beneath the surface, the school attracts many species of fish and above the surface, terns and gulls. They are also used as a baitfish in some areas. The average size is 2 to 4 inches.

Dusky Anchovy—*Anchoa lyolepis*
Other names: "red ball" minnow
The dusky anchovy ranges from the northern Gulf of Mexico and southeast Florida to Venezuela. It is found primarily in the gulf, but there are several reports from the upper Laguna Madre. This poorly known anchovy appears along the Padre Island surf in great schools in the late spring a few days prior to the arrival of tarpon. It can concentrate again in late fall causing another showing of tarpon schools. The body is elongate and the dorsal fin begins at a point well in front of the anal fin. The silver stripe on the body is about equal to

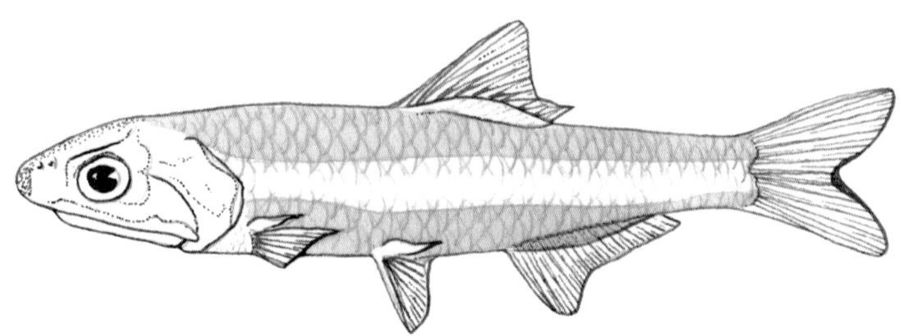

Dusky anchovy, Anchoa lyolepis

the eye diameter and is generally bordered above by a narrow dark stripe. The body color is dusky and iridescent above, and there is a golden spot on the top of the head. It may reach a length of 3.5 inches.

STRIPED ANCHOVY—*Anchoa hepsetus*
The striped anchovy is primarily a resident of the open gulf, and when found in the bays it occurs in clearer and saltier waters than does the bay anchovy. The striped anchovy ranges from Chesapeake Bay through the northern Gulf of Mexico to Uruguay. The back is usually greenish with some yellow present on the head. The dorsal fin begins at a point well forward of the anal fin, and the silver stripe on the body is about three-fourths of the eye diameter. Over the years this species has been collected in small numbers in the upper Laguna Madre. Millions of striped anchovies have been observed in the first two cuts along the beach of Mustang and Padre Islands. This event has always occurred in the fall when there is little surf action and the water is clear and calm alongshore. Massive schools of these fish have been observed to stretch for ten continuous miles and scattered all the way to the Rio Grande. They may grow up to 6 inches.

CATFISHES—ORDER SILURIFORMES

The catfishes are one of the most distinctive groups of fish. They have no true scales, and the skin is either naked or covered with bony plates (dermal denticles). The pectoral and dorsal fins usually have prominent spines at the leading edges. These spines are provided with a locking mechanism that holds them erect when the fish is alarmed. Many species have venom glands associated with the spines, and the wounds from some species can be extremely painful or even fatal. All catfishes have barbels around the mouth, and a fleshy adipose fin is usually present

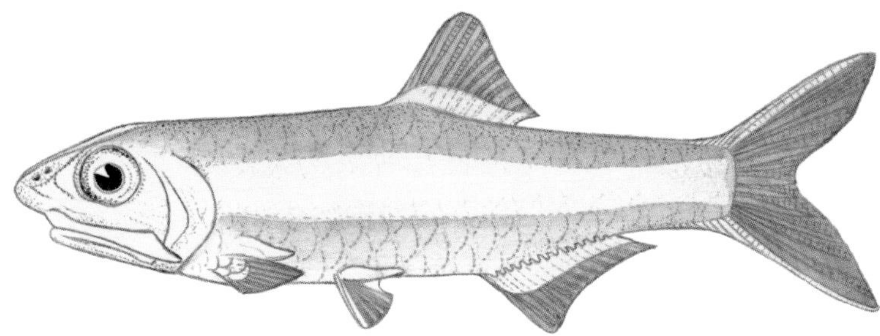

Striped anchovy, Anchoa hepsetus

far back on the tail stock. The heads are usually flattened with small eyes, and the mouth contains numerous sandpaper-like teeth.

This is a very large order containing approximately thirty-one families and twenty-six hundred species of catfish, with more than half occurring in South America. They are known from every continent except Antarctica, although fossils have been found there. Some catfish families are strictly freshwater occurring and are rarely found in water of more than 2 ppt salinity. Members of the Ariidae family are widespread in warmer latitudes. Most catfish species are nocturnal predators that consume large amounts of food and grow very rapidly. However, others are scavengers, omnivores, or even herbivores. Some are very important as sport fish, and the aquaculture industry has long relied on certain freshwater species due to their fast growth and mild flavor. No captures of freshwater catfish have been reported in the Laguna Madre, even during extended periods of low salinity.

Marine Catfishes—Family Ariidae

The marine or sea catfishes have two representatives in the northwestern Gulf of Mexico. Both species resemble typical catfish in appearance, lacking scales and having prominent, serrated spines on the leading edges of the dorsal and pectoral fins. Treatment of minor punctures from these spines usually provides little relief of pain. Although the pain can be intense, it is usually of short duration. Catfish may be safely handled by firmly grasping the body from the front with the whole hand so that the fingers push against the rear of the pectoral spines while holding the dorsal spine flat against the back. However, most people prefer to use pliers when removing fish hooks. Catfish often produce a loud clicking noise that comes from the pectoral spines moving in their bony joints as the inflated air bladder vibrates.

Sea catfish are bottom scavengers, feeding on a variety of benthic invertebrates and relying largely on their sensory-laden barbels to detect them. The great abundance of marine catfish may lead one to think that they congregate in great schools or aggregations when in fact they are generally solitary animals. Both species of sea catfish exhibit oral incubation in which males carry the fertilized eggs in their mouths. They are common in tropical and temperate coastal waters, especially in bays, muddy areas near the mouths of rivers, and in the surf zone. The skulls of sea catfishes are commonly found on beaches. Viewed from below, the bone structure suggests a crucifix, and for this reason, some refer to them as "crucifix fish." They are considered nuisances by anglers and shrimpers.

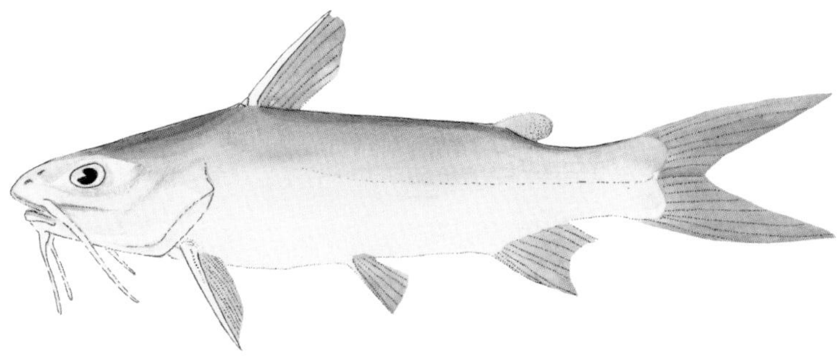

Sea catfish, Ariopsis felis

Sea Catfish—*Ariopsis felis*
Other names: hardhead, seacat, tourist trout, TR, bagre de mar
This famous "whiskered" bait thief has the distinction of being at the top of the heap in terms of being a "trash fish." It is probably the fish most frequently caught by saltwater anglers and yet it has no commercial or sport value. However, it has allowed many youngsters to catch fish on an otherwise fishless day. Like its cousin the gafftopsail catfish or gafftop, it occurs from Cape Cod through the Gulf of Mexico and as far south as Panama. Surprisingly, both of these marine cats are absent from much of the Caribbean. It is widely distributed throughout all Texas bays (except the Laguna Madre during periods of high salinity) and the nearshore waters of the gulf. The far more common hardhead has four chin barbels and two on the snout, each "whisker" being round in cross section. There are probably more injuries in marine waters due to punctures from the spines of this fish than from any other injury. Hardheads, especially the smaller ones, are extremely active and wiggly when being removed from a hook. Deep punctures sometimes result in broken spines having to be surgically removed when barefoot beach strollers accidentally step on the dried carcasses. Generally, the largest individuals are taken from the gulf. Spawning occurs in June and July, and this species leaves the shallows during the colder months, with many moving offshore during the winter. The current state record is 4.0 pounds and 23.0 inches (Corpus Christi Bay, 2003).

Gafftopsail Catfish—*Bagre marinus*
Other names: gafftop, bandera
The "gafftop" is far less numerous than the hardhead, but it reaches a much greater size and has much greater appeal to anglers, although it

is poorly utilized. It is distinguished by its larger, flatter head, the presence of only four flat ribbon-like barbels on the head, and long fleshy filaments extending from both the dorsal and pectoral fins. The gafftop tends to frequent deeper and muddier areas of bays and channels during the warmer months of the year. It apparently prefers waters of intermediate salinity, and it is not found in as low or as high salinities as is the more tolerant hardhead. Both are scavengers, although the gafftop is said to be a bit more predatory in its feeding behavior. Although armed with stout spines at the leading edges of both the dorsal and pectoral fins like the hardhead, far fewer punctures from this catfish occur. This is because the spines are less pointed and are covered with a thick tissue. This species is also far less active when landed and much easier to subdue while being handled.

Spawning takes place between April and August with an apparent peak in April and May. All sea catfish males are mouth brooders and as many as sixty-five eggs (to 1 inch in diameter) can be carried in the oral cavities of large individuals. Incubation can last for sixty-five days, during which time the males do not feed. I always check both species for the presence of the large eggs and occasionally find a male with a mouthful. The best fishing period for gafftop is during the months of March through July when they are moving into the bays from the gulf.

Gafftopsail catfish, Bagre marinus

Many anglers consider the gafftop to be the "slime king" of the bays. Anyone who has handled one is thoroughly familiar with the mucous that quickly coats the leader, hands, and anything else that comes in contact with the fish. Larger gafftops may be sold commercially and their flesh is considered to be excellent, although there is no basis for it being of better quality than that of the hardhead. Pieces of cut fish and whole squid fished on the bottom of deep channels near gulf passes have long produced good numbers of larger individuals. In the Aransas Pass at Port Aransas as recently as the 1970s one could routinely catch gafftop that were in the 8- to 10-pound range. Like many species today, the numbers and average sizes are greatly reduced from times past. The state record is 13.3 pounds and 34.0 inches (Gulf of Mexico, 1981), but adults larger than 6 pounds are uncommon today.

Lizardfishes—Order Aulopiformes

This order contains twelve to thirteen families and is a mixed bag of odd fishes, all of which are related by the unique structure of the gill arches. Most inhabit the water column far from shore but also occur at great depths. The exception to the rule is members of the Synodontidae family, one of which inhabits coastal bays.

Lizardfishes—Family Synodontidae

There are approximately fifty-five species in this family and nine species occur in the Gulf of Mexico, but only one is found in the Laguna Madre. The lizardfishes (known as cigarfishes in some areas) are members of a family of mostly small- to medium-sized bottom-dwelling and carnivorous fishes. They are commonly found in shallow bays and along the shores of warm waters. All are elongate, possess a fleshy adipose fin, and lack scales. Many species have a strong, pungent, and somewhat musky odor coupled with a lizard-like appearance due to their slender cigar-shaped body, flattened bony heads, large mouths, and pointed snouts. The jaws are sinister looking and armed with numerous small sharp teeth. The behavior of tropical forms is said to be lizard-like in movement, in that they will scurry along the bottom in search of prey. Lizardfishes are voracious predatory fishes, and most of the deep-sea forms have highly distendable stomachs, enabling them to consume large prey items. They are non-schooling loners and conceal themselves to ambush prey by resting quietly on their pelvic fins or by hiding in the sandy or muddy bottom sediments. Early juvenile stages differ considerably from the adults. They are occasionally caught on hook and line and show up regularly in shrimp trawl by-catch, but they are of no commercial value. They are the bane of gulf shrimpers because they are of the right size and shape to "gill" themselves in the mesh of the nets. In areas of the southern United States, lizardfish bites are mistakenly considered to be poisonous. A large lizardfish might inflict a painful bite, but none are known to possess any toxin or venom.

Inshore Lizardfish—*Synodus foetens*
Other names: snakefish, sandpike, galiwasp, chile
This species ranges from the Massachusetts coast, throughout the Gulf of Mexico to Brazil. Adults are brown with a greenish tint on the dorsal surface and at least eight diamond-shaped marks along the sides, giving them a camouflage advantage. Younger individuals have six large black spots along the belly anterior to the anal fin and numerous small black spots along the base of the anal fin. The inshore lizardfish will enter brackish water, and the largest individuals occur offshore in waters hundreds of feet deep. The scientific name *foetens* refers to the fetid, putrid odor the fish rapidly develops when dead and left in the sun. However, even when alive they have a distinct, nauseating odor. Postlarvae, juveniles, and adults have all been collected in bays and lagoons, but adults are not common in the Laguna Madre. They are sometimes caught by anglers on rod and reel (often on spoons and highly reflective lures) but are considered a nuisance. Marine biologists often receive calls about this reptilian-looking fish. Many anglers are shocked when they first encounter this fish because they think they have caught an evil and long-extinct species. In the Laguna Madre they may reach 16 inches in length. The Texas record for this fish is 1.9 pounds, 20.0 inches (Gulf of Mexico, 1991).

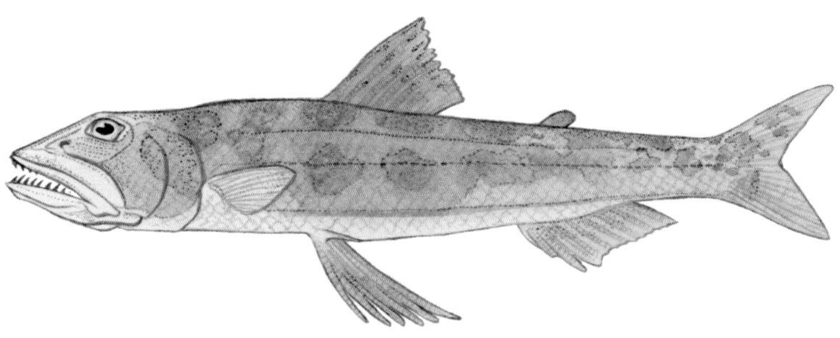

Inshore lizardfish, Synodus foetens

"Cod" Fishes, Grenadiers, Hakes, and Burbots—Order Gadiformes

This order contains the cods and their allies, and with few exceptions all species are found in marine waters. Their characteristics are considered to be both primitive and advanced in terms of their placement in the taxonomy of the bony fishes (teleosts). They are generally elongate with long dorsal and anal fins. There are no spines in the fins, and the mouths are near the end of the head, often with barbels. Although many have long tapering tails, a distinct caudal fin is present in about two-thirds of the species.

This group contains twelve families and more than 480 bottom-oriented marine fishes, some of which play major ecological roles, especially in deepwater benthic communities.

Cods and Their Allies—Family Gadidae

By far, this is the most important family in the order Gadiformes from an economic standpoint, and it contains about fifty-five species of cod, haddock, pollock, lings, and whitings. All have great commercial value as food fish or as a source of high-quality fish meal. The true cods are distinguished from other cod-like fish by having separate caudal and dorsal fins, the latter being divided into two or three sections. Most are somberly colored, without bold patterns on the body. Most swim about on or near the bottom, feeding on crabs, fish, and molluscs. Some species make extensive seasonal migrations between spawning and feeding grounds. Many have the gas bladder in connection with the inner ear, which is thought to increase their acuteness of hearing. Members of this family are found in temperate, cold, and arctic waters of both hemispheres and occur mainly in continental shelf and slope waters, retreating to deeper water during the winter.

Southern Hake—*Urophycis floridana*
The southern hake ranges from the Atlantic off North Carolina throughout the Gulf of Mexico, residing primarily in coastal waters and entering bays following cold spells during the winter. It has been reported from the Laguna Madre but is not a regular inhabitant. The sides are reddish brown above and whitish or silvery below. A series of dark spots are present on the cheeks, and sometimes these spots fuse into "facial bars." Two spots are often present on the gill covers. The lateral line is alternately black and white and is darker overall than the rest of the body. Each pelvic fin has two long, filamentous rays that extend to or slightly beyond the origin of the anus. Unlike closely related species, there is no elongate ray in the dorsal fin. Individuals grow to 12 inches in length.

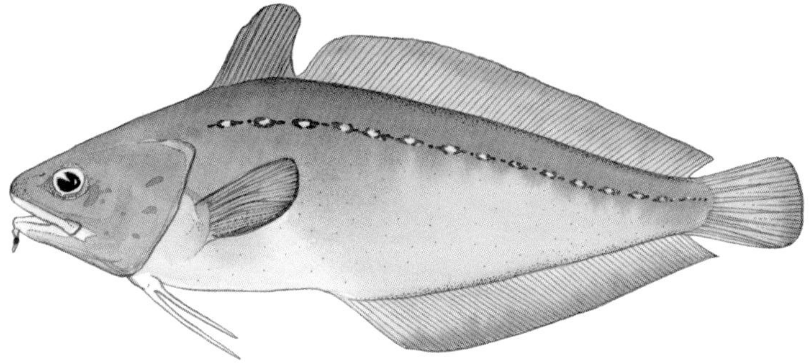

Southern hake, Urophycis floridana

Cusk-Eels and Brotulas—Order Ophidiiformes

This order contains a variety of species, many with elongate tapering bodies and long dorsal and anal fins continuous with the caudal fin. The pelvic fins are supported by small spines in some species and resemble elongate barbels. These are mostly marine benthic organisms living on or near the bottom, with few freshwater representatives. As many as four hundred species have been reported, some of which live at great depths. The cusk-eels and brotulas residing at great depths generally show extreme adaptations for living there, including poorly developed eyes. In fact, some of the deepest living of all fishes are brotulas. Curiously, some species of brotulas have adapted to underwater caves in both brackish and freshwater environments.

Cusk-Eels and Brotulas—Family Ophidiidae

The cusk-eels and the closely related egg-laying brotulas are grouped into this family. There are about fifty genera and 210 species worldwide, and 35 of these occur in the Gulf of Mexico. Most species in this group are small and not particularly common. All are bottom-dwelling, ranging from the shallows to great depths in mainly temperate and tropical shelf waters of most seas. Most species are dull in color (tan to dark brown), but some have a conspicuous pattern on the sides and all are elongate fishes possessing filamentous fins. Most are strongly nocturnal, remaining hidden in crevices or in burrows during the daylight hours.

Crested Cusk-Eel—*Ophidion welshi*
This species ranges from Georgia's Atlantic waters south and west

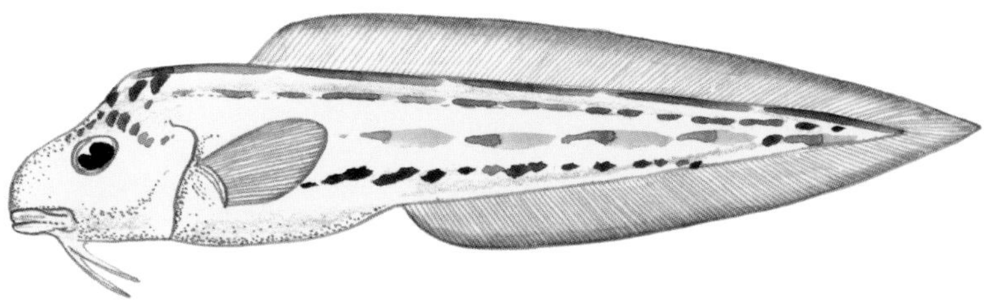

Crested cusk-eel, Ophidion welshi

throughout the Gulf of Mexico. The body has three rows of dark spots, with the upper row usually fused into a solid stripe and the middle row of spots often partly fused. This cusk-eel inhabits bays and nearshore waters to 180 feet deep and is the second most abundant cusk-eel from the Texas gulf shrimp grounds. Large males (more than 6 inches in length) are generally distinguished by having a swollen nape or crest behind the head. The pelvic fins consist of two moderately flattened rays. Adults may reach 10 inches in length.

BEARDED BROTULA—*Brotula barbata*
This species is primarily an offshore species and occurs from Florida throughout the gulf to South America. Small individuals are found over muddy bottoms in the shallow gulf (mostly from sixty feet deep to the upper continental slope) and are regularly taken by shrimp trawlers. Larger individuals are taken near jetties and passes, where their identity commonly perplexes anglers. Near rocky bottoms this is a somewhat common species, though it is not often caught on a hook and line. At

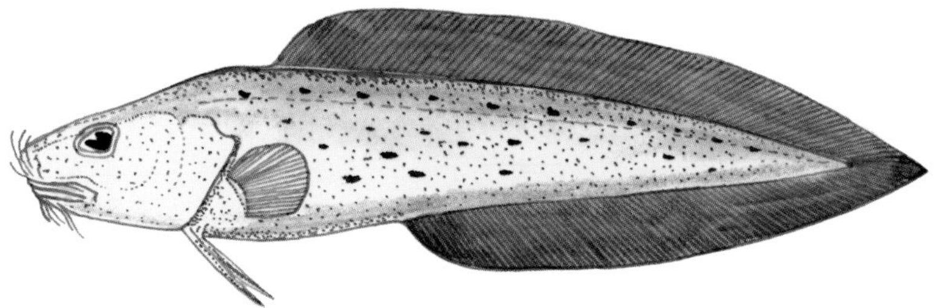

Bearded brotula, Brotula barbata

least one individual has been reported from the Intracoastal Canal near the JFK Causeway. They are spotted as juveniles but lose their spots to become a rich, maroon to olive-brown color as adults. Distinctive stripes are found on the cheeks of young but are lost with age. Bearded brotulas are likely nocturnal feeders, relying on their numerous highly developed snout and chin barbels to locate food. They grow to 3 feet in length.

Toadfishes and Midshipmen—Order Batrachoidiformes

This order contains nearly seventy species of toadfishes and midshipmen, generally broad-headed, bigmouthed bottom fishes of tropical and temperate seas. The body is squat, usually without scales, ribs are lacking, and only one jaw contains teeth. They are commonly encountered in shallow marine waters, especially off North America, and are closely related to the anglerfishes and sargassumfishes. Venom is produced in glands at the bases of the dorsal spines in some species and injected through the hollow spines. Many species can produce a variety of sounds with muscles that vibrate the air bladder. These sounds have been described as resembling snorts and grunts, with some species producing sounds during the spawning period that resemble boat whistle blasts.

Toadfishes and Midshipmen—Family Batrachoididae

This family comprises sixty-nine species in nineteen genera, and four species occur in the Gulf of Mexico. Fishes in this group are primarily small to medium-sized benthic fishes living in bays, lagoons, and coastal waters of tropical and temperate regions, spending most of their time on or buried in the bottom sediment. There are three spines in the first dorsal fin, and most have barbels and skin flaps around the mouth. The head is large and distinctly flattened, and they have multiple lateral lines that are well developed. All lack light-producing organs, or photophores, except for the Atlantic midshipman. Some members of the family are highly venomous; however, of the local species, only the Atlantic midshipman produces venom, although not sufficient to affect humans. They attach their eggs to hard substrates, even inside cans and pipes. The eggs are guarded by the male, and the larval stages are not capable of swimming. Toadfishes and midshipmen feed on other fishes and crustaceans.

Gulf Toadfish—*Opsanus beta*
Other names: oyster dog, mudfish, dogfish

This species is restricted to the Gulf of Mexico and its bays and the West Indies and ranges from Florida through the gulf to Campeche,

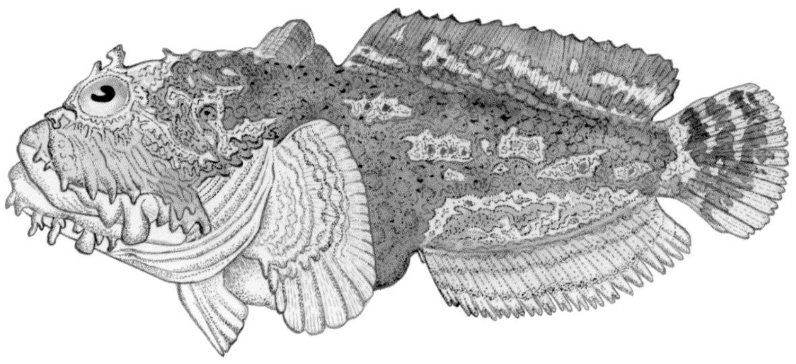

Gulf toadfish, Opsanus beta

Mexico. It is common in seagrass beds and in coastal bays and lagoons. The toadfish is primarily a bay species found on oyster reefs and around jetties, pilings, and even in old tires. Small individuals sometimes take refuge in sunken cans or jars and feed on other animals seeking shelter there. They often grow to fill them and become trapped. Toadfish are sedentary and rely on camouflage for ambushing fish and shellfish, but they sometimes feed as scavengers. The head and body are dark tan and white with irregular light blotches or crossbars. They are variously mottled and marbled, with the darkest and most solidly colored portions above and toward the head. The pale areas often form "rosettes" toward the rear of the body, and the fins have dark brown bars. The large, flat head, spiny dorsal fin, and gill covers give the toadfish a sinister appearance.

While they are weak swimmers, gulf toadfish can engulf prey in a single gulp thanks to their large, highly expandable gills and mouth. Contrary to the belief of many anglers, the toadfish, though capable of delivering a painful bite and punctures with its sharp spines, is not venomous. Toadfish prefer quiet, low-oxygen areas that are often unsuitable for other fish. Their massive gill capacity allows them to thrive under these harsh conditions where other species cannot. In the Laguna Madre, the species is much more abundant at moderate salinities than in hypersaline conditions. The state record is 3.0 pounds and 15.9 inches (Gulf of Mexico, 1989).

Atlantic Midshipman—*Porichthys plectrodon*

The common name of the Atlantic midshipman refers to the rows of light-producing organs (photophores) on the sides that were thought to resemble the buttons on a nineteenth-century naval midshipman's uniform. This species ranges from the coast of Virginia and the Gulf of Mexico to South America. It has a broad distribution ranging from the bays to the brown shrimp grounds in the gulf. The sides are silvery to golden with irregular dark brown (often bluish) spots above that sometimes fuse to form U-shaped marks. The sides and ventral surface of the body are covered with regularly arranged rows of photophores, and the fins may have rows of dusky marks. A large luminous area below each eye is set off by an area of black pigment below. The gill covers end in a sharp spine through which the fish may inject venom.

Members of the genus *Porichthys* are the only North American shore fishes that possess light-producing organs and, in fact, are among the few shallow-water fishes anywhere that produce light. They make loud noises when courting, much to the annoyance of people who live in boats anchored near a spawning area, because boat hulls can amplify the loud buzzing sound. They are also nocturnal and rarely seen by anglers. Individuals are generally 4 to 6 inches long but may attain a length of 9 inches.

Clingfishes or Skilletfishes—Order Gobiesociformes

All 120 species of clingfish are adapted for adhering to rocks in the pounding surf of the intertidal zone (between the high and low tides) or clinging to swaying vegetation. They are mostly small, tadpole-like fish, with a ventral sucking disk used to attach themselves to rocky bottoms in the surf zone or to plants. This disk comprises the modified pelvic fins and part of the pectoral fins and has patches of short fleshy knobs that may be useful for identifying the various species. They lack scales, spines, and an air bladder. They range from tropical to cold temperate

Atlantic midshipman, Porichthys plectrodon

seas throughout the world with the greatest diversity of species found in colder waters. The greatest diversity found in North America is in the tropics, and four Mexican and Central American species are restricted to fresh water.

Clingfishes—Family Gobiesocidae

This family comprises 120 species worldwide, with only 10 occurring in North American waters. Members of this family are a group of small, bottom-dwelling fishes sometimes called "skilletfishes" because of their large, flat heads and slender, tapering bodies. These scaleless fishes with soft-rayed fins (without spines) are found off tropical and temperate shores, although some do enter fresh water. Only one species is common inshore and has been reported from South Texas. Other species are known to occur on offshore gulf reefs and hard bottoms. Individuals can exert enough suction that they are often difficult to dislodge from a smooth surface.

SKILLETFISH—*Gobiesox strumosus*

The skilletfish is truly one of the strangest fish one will ever see. It is usually a dark olive-brown with a mottled, net-like pattern, often with reddish or green pigmentation. A dark band may be present at the base of the caudal fin, and the lower lip has conspicuous fleshy bumps. The skilletfish ranges from Bermuda and the northern gulf to Brazil but is absent from the Bahamas. It is the only clingfish on the U.S. coast north of southern Florida in the Atlantic Ocean. This fish occupies grassy and rocky shallows and is common around pilings, oyster reefs, and other protected habitats, frequently laying its eggs in oyster shells. It appears to occur over a wide range of salinities but is generally not found in hypersaline waters. Waders may be startled to see one of these fish dart from cover to latch onto the underside of their foot. It does not draw blood, sting, or bite, so one should not be alarmed; gently remove it by hand and let it go.

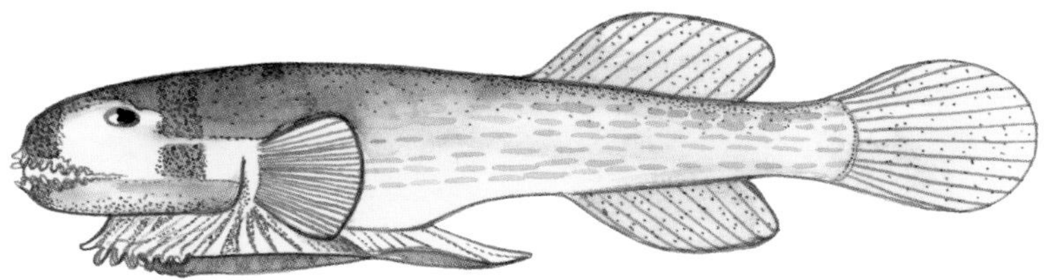

Skilletfish, Gobiesox strumosus

They make interesting aquarium fish because they regularly attach themselves to the glass walls of the tanks. They attain about 3 inches in length.

FLYINGFISHES, HALFBEAKS, AND NEEDLEFISHES—ORDER BELONIFORMES

This order includes the marine flyingfishes, halfbeaks, and needlefishes that share several characteristics related to their life near the surface of the water (epipelagic zone). Members are characterized by the single dorsal and anal fins that are approximately equal in size and situated far back on the tail stock. The lateral line is well developed and set low on the sides of the long and narrow body, while the pectoral fins are situated high on the sides. These are active marine fishes, mostly inhabitants of warm and temperate seas, but about one-third of the halfbeak and needlefish species live in fresh water. Worldwide, there are nearly forty genera and 180 living species in this order.

The flyingfishes are best characterized by their elongate pectoral fins, which enable them to leave the water and glide for considerable distances. The halfbeaks frequently jump from the water or skip over the surface, and although they cannot "fly," some halfbeaks do possess relatively long pectoral fins. These fins aid them in their extended leaps and indicate a close relationship with the flyingfishes. An elongated, flattened lower jaw on the halfbeaks is highly characteristic. Though these features are usually characteristic of this group, there are flyingfishes with short pectorals and halfbeaks lacking the elongate lower jaw. Careful observation of a flyingfish on takeoff or in the process of gaining additional gliding time when near the crest of a wave will reveal the lower part of the caudal fin in an extremely rapid sculling (side to side) motion, with that portion of the caudal fin being the only part of the fish in contact with the water. "Flight" distances of 165 feet and speeds to 55 miles per hour have been reported for some species.

More than fifty species of flyingfishes are known, and they inhabit tropical coastal and bay waters and the open sea, and at least one species lives in fresh water. Most of those found in U.S. waters live near the surface. Ecologically, there are two groups: those that are basically offshore species inhabiting waters more than two hundred miles from land and inshore species living less than two hundred miles from land that often enter the bays. However, this division is not absolute because several offshore species occasionally venture into inshore waters.

While feeding, the elongate lower jaw of most halfbeaks apparently functions in directing small, surface-oriented fishes, crabs, and other invertebrates into the mouth. They capture their prey while swimming in schools near the surface. Many are even herbivorous, but how the beak functions in gathering small prey remains a mystery. Members of the Exocoetidae family are important prey species and popular baitfishes in some areas, and they are especially popular among offshore anglers. They make great whole (rigged) and live bait for billfish, or they can be trolled as dead bait with hooks carefully sewn into the mouth and belly regions. In addition, they make good cut bait for tarpon and king mackerel.

Halfbeaks—Family Hemiramphidae

Halfbeak—*Hyporhamphus unifasciatus*

The halfbeak ranges throughout the gulf to Bermuda and Argentina. The body color is greenish above, the sides and belly are silvery, and three narrow black lines run along the dorsal surface from the head to the origin of the dorsal fin. The tip of the lower jaw and the upper lobe of the caudal fin are yellowish red in color. The body is less deep in profile and more round in cross section than other halfbeaks. They are common in bays and estuaries and less common around coral reefs. In some summers, large numbers have been reported at the B. M. Davis Power Plant in Flour Bluff in the upper Laguna Madre. Lengths to 11 inches have been reported, but the state record for this species is 7.0 inches (Gulf of Mexico, 1995).

Needlefishes—Family Belonidae

Most needlefishes are surface-dwelling fish and are abundant in bays and harbors of warm temperate and tropical coastal waters. A few prefer the open ocean and some live exclusively in fresh water. More than thirty species of needlefishes are known to occur worldwide, and at least six are found along all five gulf state coastlines. Needlefishes are slender and elongate with the jaws of marine

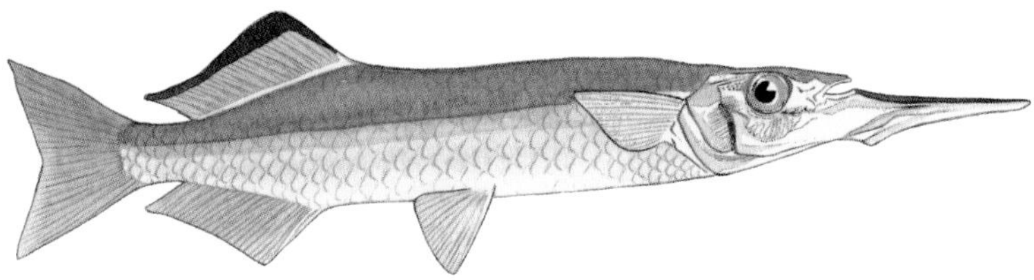

Halfbeak, Hyporhamphus unifasciatus

Atlantic needlefish, Strongylura marina

species formed into a long, beak-like structure equipped with numerous fine teeth. Their scales are tiny, and the lateral line extends along the lower surface of the body, typical of most surface-living fishes. The upper body is greenish in coastal species with white to silvery sides and belly. A fleshy "sunshade" on top of each eye protects it from bright light at the surface. Needlefishes resemble gars without the heavy body armor and are noted for their jumping ability. Schools may scatter with great leaps at the approach of a boat, becoming "living javelins," or they may jump over floating objects as if involved in play.

Despite their fragile appearance, needlefishes are tough, voracious predators. They prowl the surface, attacking small forage fishes like a flash of lightning, the slender jaws slashing with their needle-sharp teeth. Despite their fast swimming ability, many needlefishes are important prey items for large piscine predators. These fish are very curious and will quickly investigate a top water bait, float, or anything else at the water's surface. They are generally regarded as pests by anglers. The largest members of the family may exceed 4.5 feet in length.

Atlantic Needlefish—*Strongylura marina*

Other names: needle gar, guardfish, long-jaws, saltwater gar

The Atlantic needlefish is widely distributed along the Texas coast and usually occurs in schools of two or three dozen in sandy, grassy lagoons, bays, and estuaries. It ranges from Maine to the gulf and south to Brazil, and east to Cuba and Jamaica. It is quite common in the inshore gulf and bays during the spring and summer and may ascend far up rivers. The Atlantic needlefish can be encountered in brackish waters and often travels with alligator gars. This species tolerates salinities from fresh water to 60 ppt during the warmer months of the year and presumably spawns in the bays. Both jaws are nearly equal in length, the side of the head is pale, and the caudal fin is bluish in color. The body is green with a silvery blue stripe running the length of the body, and the belly is silver.

Although it is not eaten, the needlefish has an entertainment value that is well known to inhabitants of tropical islands. The fish have minute parasites that collect on their skin and will jump over anything on the surface that scrapes their belly. They have been "trained" to do this by placing food on the other side of the hurdle. For fishing, this species is easily attracted to moving bright objects, such as spoons or small tandem worm jigs (speck rigs). They are easily startled and become disoriented around artificial light at night, although they are generally attracted to it. The Atlantic needlefish grows to more than 2 feet in length. The state record is 9.0 pounds and 28.8 inches (Gulf of Mexico, 1990).

Killifishes, Sheepshead Minnow, and Live Bearers—Order Cyprinodontiformes

These fishes are widely distributed and occur naturally around all continents except Australia and Antarctica. All species are small and usually found in estuarine or marine environments. Wherever water is too saline, warm, limited in area, or extreme in its fluctuations for most fish, one or more of the killifish species is likely to be present. There are about 670 species in this order, and it includes its fair share of species threatened by pollution or destruction of their habitats. Most are omnivores, although many are efficient predators on insects. Omnivory is one characteristic that allows them to live in harsh environments. Another is their surface-oriented morphology, which enables them to pump the thin, oxygen-rich surface layer of water across their gills to survive. They have small teeth in the jaws and are sometimes referred to as the "tooth-carps." The single dorsal fin is set behind the middle of the back, and the caudal fin is rounded and never forked. The lateral line is usually well developed on the head but is absent from the body.

This family contains the more than one hundred species of egg-laying killifishes or "pupfish," with four occurring in the Gulf of Mexico. Killifishes are renowned for their ability to live under conditions of extreme isolation, temperature, and salinity in North and South American waters and the Mediterranean Sea. Species can live in water ranging from fresh to brine (salinity greater than 80 ppt). Environments, such as desert springs, may have salinities four to five times that of seawater and experience daily temperature fluctuations of 55 to 60°F. All the killifishes, with the exception of *Lucania parva,* are shore fishes. Some species, particularly *Cyprinodon variegatus* and *Fundulus grandis,* respond to small freshwater outflows by seeking out the sources and trying to ascend them. Consequently, they can

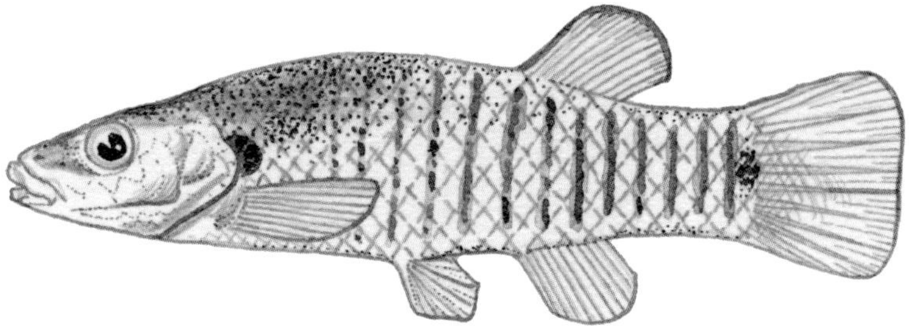

Longnose killifish, Fundulus similis

gain access to most ponds on islands after rainstorms or higher than normal tides. Spineless fins, pectoral fins set low on the body, and a scaled area on the head are characteristic of most species. The eggs laid by members of this group are very large and usually attached to vegetation, and they hatch rapidly. Pupfish get their name from the mistaken notion that the brightly colored males busily engaged in the serious business of reproduction were "playing like puppies." The killifishes are very hardy as a live baitfish and are most in demand by anglers seeking flounder. However, they are rarely available because they can be captured only in minnow traps in very low numbers. Some are being farmed in ponds now on the upper Texas coast, where they are in greater demand as live bate.

Killifishes—Family Fundulidae

Longnose Killifish—*Fundulus similis*

This species is found from the Florida panhandle to the waters off central Mexico. The longnose killifish is one of a dominant group of small estuarine fishes inhabiting the brackish shorelines along the gulf coast. It is most common on unprotected shores or in tidal currents. This fish and the related "livebearers" are distinguished by the absence of stiff spines in the fins and by the positioning of the pectoral fins low on the body. The longnose killifish has eleven to fifteen vertical black bars on each side and a small but distinct black spot on the tail. The snout is long, at least twice as long as the diameter of the eye, and the body is elongate.

This species is a year-round resident, rarely venturing far from shore, and it successfully meets the most rigorous challenges of the coastal environment. This species favors the high-salinity shallows and is rarely found in the less salty marshes. It has a propensity for the inch-deep lagoons no sizable predator would dare invade, along with a physiology enabling it to thrive in the harshest of estuarine habitats. They have been recorded in waters ranging from fresh to salinities of 115 ppt. Very large eggs are laid by the females in sand and mud-sand bottoms beginning in early spring and continuing until the onset of cold weather. They hatch in a few days, and the larvae are much larger than those of other fish species, being capable of foraging and escape behavior upon hatching. Maturity is reached in several months. Thus, the rapid life cycle and enhanced reproductive success ensure their survival. Longnose killifish feed on small crustaceans. This species reaches a maximum size of 6 inches.

Gulf Killifish—*Fundulus grandis*
Other names: mud minnow, mummichug, chub
The gulf killifish ranges from the North Atlantic to Florida, throughout the Gulf of Mexico, and south to eastern Mexico. This species has the same morphological characteristics as the longnose killifish. However, this cigar-shaped fish lacks the distinctive series of bars, although they are sometimes present in the juveniles. The head is blunt with a short snout and the body is dark above and yellowish below, with many small pale spots or mottling. This species does not exhibit the strong schooling behavior of the longnose killifish, and thus it is not always easy to capture them in large numbers. However, it has the ability to survive as wide a salinity range as its relatives. The largest populations are found in brackish water, particularly in shallow tidal marsh channels and ponds. The gulf killifish is found around the shorelines of the Laguna Madre but never in large numbers except in areas or periods of low salinity such as the Laguna Atascosa in the lower lagoon. They are usually 8 inches or less in length and the state record is 6.1 inches (Galveston Bay, 1985).

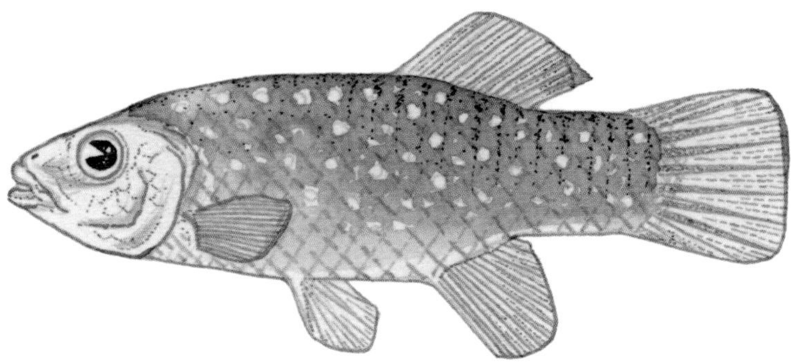

Gulf killifish, Fundulus grandis

Diamond killifish, Adinia xenica

DIAMOND KILLIFISH—*Adinia xenica*
This species is found on the northern gulf coast from Florida to Texas. The head is sharply pointed, and the lower jaw projects outward when viewed from the side. Approximately eight to ten dark bands, each one pale at the center, are present on the male, along with spotted dorsal, anal, and caudal fins. Females have a more slender body shape, with fewer and broader dark bands on the sides, and unmarked fins. Diamond killifish can be found from fresh water to the hypersaline flats. This species is poorly known, but it appears to be a species of the grassy bay margins. There are few records from the Laguna Madre. It may reach 2 inches in length.

RAINWATER KILLIFISH—*Lucania parva*
The rainwater killifish ranges from the waters off Massachusetts throughout the Gulf of Mexico and

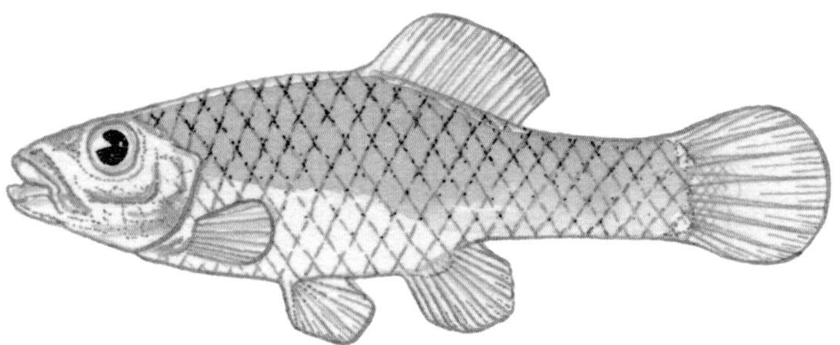

Rainwater killifish, Lucania parva

has been introduced in western North American waters as a means of insect (mosquito) control. The head and body are straw colored, and each scale is darkly outlined, with the sides sometimes showing dark blotches. In the male, the dorsal fin is yellowish, with a dark spot near the base, and the caudal fin is bright yellow. Pelvic and anal fins are orange or yellowish with orange edges. This killifish is generally limited to vegetated areas such as turtle grass flats and algal communities, but it is also found in vegetated areas in coastal fresh waters. It may grow to 2 inches.

Sheepshead Minnows—Family Cyprinodontidae

SHEEPSHEAD MINNOW—*Cyprinodon variegatus*

This species is perhaps the most hardy fish on the Texas coast, having the greatest salinity tolerance of any known fish. It never leaves its estuarine habitat and is abundant in backwater, tidally influenced coastal areas from Maine to Florida, and throughout the gulf. The body depth is nearly one-half the length, and there are five to seven irregular bars on the sides, the widest ones nearer the dorsal fin. There is sometimes a dark spot at the base of the dorsal fin that is especially prominent in the young. Breeding males have a brilliant blue nape (neck area) and orange cheeks, and the lower body may lack dark bands. This species tolerates physical conditions of the most extreme ranges. It has been found in water ranging from 0 to 140 ppt salinity and can spawn in 2-inch deep water so hot a human can barely tolerate standing in it. Few eggs are laid by the female during each spawning encounter, but this species develops very large populations on the wind-tidal flats of the Laguna Madre. It is an important forage fish to certain predators, particularly the reddish egret (*Egretta rufescens*). Sheepshead

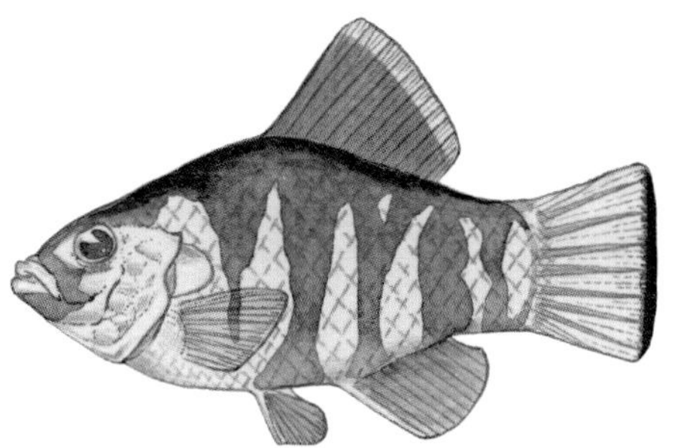

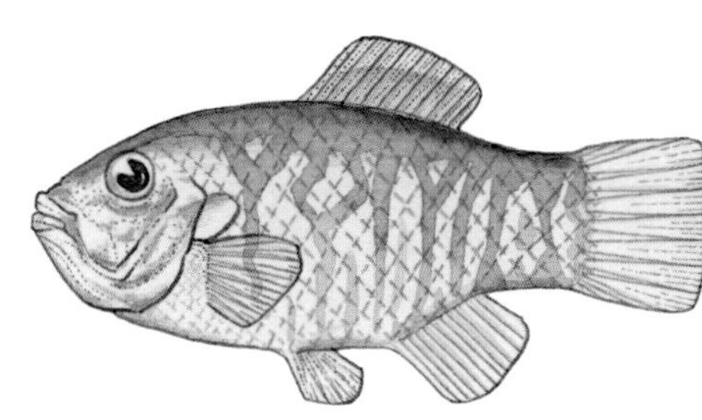

Sheepshead minnow (male and female), Cyprinodon variegatus

minnows feed on almost any food item available, including seagrass, small shelled invertebrates, or even other fish, attacking them with their sharp teeth and eventually consuming them. These fish can grow to 3 inches in length.

Livebearers—Family Poeciliidae

The livebearers (which include mollies, guppies, and swordtails) are a freshwater family with three species that enter the Laguna Madre region. All are common in coastal marshes and are quite tolerant of saltwater. As their group name implies, all species of this family bear living young. The males are easily recognized because they are much smaller than the females and possess an elongated anal fin, which is specialized to function as a reproductive organ (gonopodium) for sperm transfer. The livebearers are small, with most rarely exceeding 2 inches in length. Their small size allows large populations to exist in small areas, where they will eat whatever food is available. Special substrates are not necessary for spawning, and high survival rates are common due to the livebearing mode of birth. Many members of this family, such as the common guppy, are successful aquarium fish and may even establish populations in sewage treatment plants due to the flushing of them by aquarists who tire of their prolific nature.

Members of this family are among the favorites of aquarists. Some have reputations as being "mosquito fish" because of their habit of feeding on insect larvae close to the water's surface. *Gambusia affinis* and *G. holbrooki,* native to U.S. waters, have been introduced to many areas of the world to aid in insect control, but the value of these introductions is considered to be minimal at best because these species tend to compete with, and are predators on, various native fish species. The genus *Poecilia* is noted for the existence of unisexual (female) "species" produced by hybridization or by activation of an egg by a sperm that does not contribute genetic material to the developing egg. The sailfin molly (*P. latipinna*) and the mosquito fish (*G. affinis*) are found in brackish water in the Corpus Christi area and in the vicinity of Port Isabel in the lower Laguna Madre.

Sailfin Molly—*Poecilia latipinna*

This species ranges from Carolina coastal lagoons and throughout the gulf to the tip of the Yucatan Peninsula. They are a common resident of Texas and Louisiana coastal marshes. Males possess a highly modified anal fin specialized as a reproductive organ, but females are difficult to distinguish from members of the closely related killifish family (Fundulidae). Large breeding males have dorsal and caudal fins with a

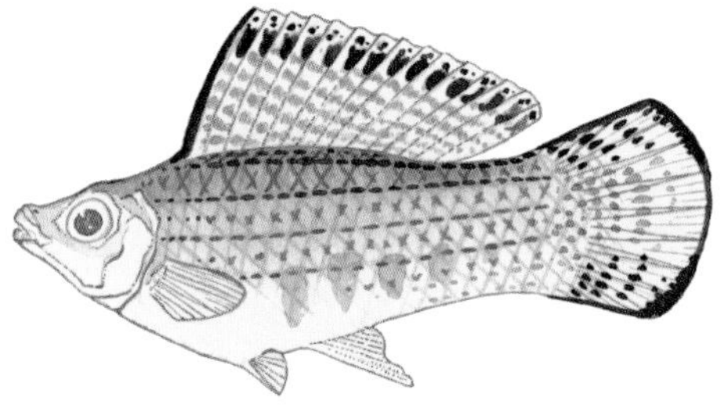

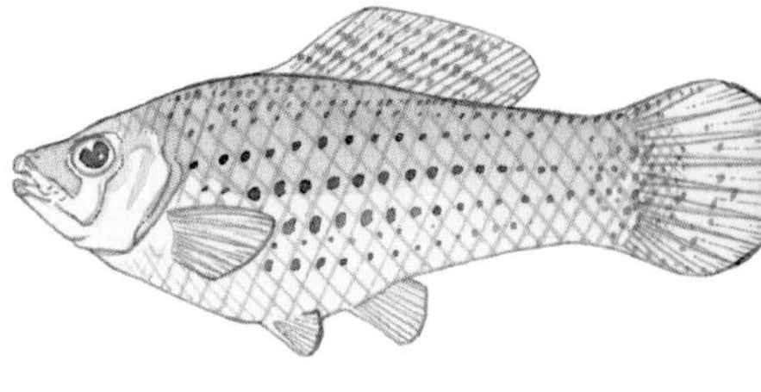

Sailfin molly (male and female), Poecilia latipinna

brilliant blue-green margin and a striking orange color below. Both sexes have rows of dark spots along each scale row, but the females lack bright coloration. The sailfin molly prefers the surface waters of less salty marsh regions and semi-enclosed lagoons. Their diet is oriented toward vegetable material, especially algae covering hard substrate material. The sailfin molly may reach 5 inches in length. About thirty large fry are extruded during birth, and the females need not be refertilized for the next brood as they can store a reservoir of sperm, always ready for the upcoming clutch of eggs. A close relative of the sailfin molly is the Amazon molly (*P. formosa*), which is a most intriguing species. It never requires fertilization of the eggs by males, which is fortunate because all Amazon mollies are female.

MOSQUITO FISH—*Gambusia affinis*
Like others in the family of livebearers, this small species has been widely introduced in the United States as a mosquito control agent and is important in research and, to some extent, as an aquarium fish. The mosquito fish occurs from the western North

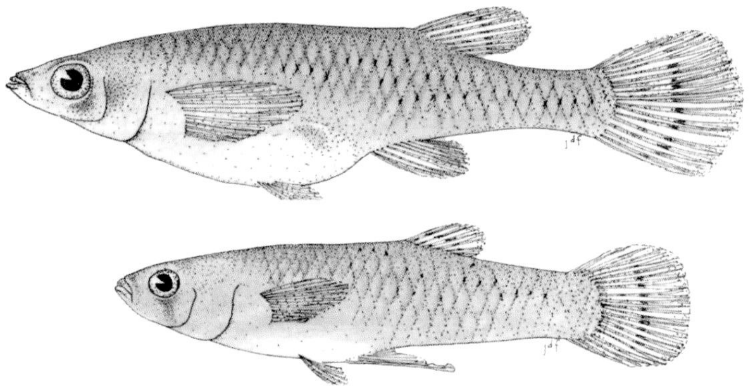

Mosquito fish, Gambusia affinis. *Illustration by Janice D. Fechhelm*

Atlantic throughout the Gulf of Mexico. It is commonly found in freshwater systems between the Mississippi River and the Rio Grande. This is a moderately robust or heavy-bodied fish with a somewhat flattened head and a relatively narrow caudal peduncle. It is distinguished from other species in its family by having a slightly oblique (angled) mouth and a lower jaw that extends slightly beyond the upper jaw. Jaw teeth consist of an outer row of larger recurved teeth and several rows of smaller pointed teeth. The caudal fin is fan-like, and the anal fin of the male is greatly extended as a specialized reproductive organ (gonopodium) for transferring sperm to the female. Body color is light olive to dark greenish brown or silvery yellow dorsally and pale ventrally. The scale margins are dusky in color and form a diamond-shaped pattern from pigmentation along the scale edges. Often rows of small black spots are present on the body and caudal fin, and there is a dark bar below the eye. The dorsal fin has two or three transverse rows of tiny black dots, and the females exhibit a dark spot near the anal fin when carrying eggs.

The mosquito fish prefers areas with dense vegetation and lives in a broad variety of habitats ranging from slow-moving fresh water, protected brackish waters, and full-strength salt water. Like the sailfin molly (*P. latipinna*), this fish is common in low-salinity marshes; however, it is generally found in fresher water than the molly. Its diet consists of surface-occurring insects, insect larvae, and crustaceans. Fecundity rates range from one hundred to more than three hundred fertilized eggs per clutch. Maximum known size is 2 inches for males and about 3.5 inches for females. Recent work has concluded that mosquito fish populations east of Mobile, Alabama, are a different species (*G. holbrooki*).

New World Silversides—Order Atheriniformes

Silversides—Family Atherinidae

The silversides are small fishes found in relatively shallow water along bay margins. They are mostly marine, found along most warm and warm temperate coasts, with some invading fresh water. Populations are highly variable. Of the nearly 160 species, there are two marine and two freshwater species in the Laguna Madre region. Estuarine species are found at low salinities. Members of this family are famous for their interest in surface objects, butting into and jumping over floating debris. Most have a prominent silver band along each side and lack a lateral line. Silversides are slender and elongate with terminal mouths, large eyes, two dorsal fins, and large scales. They are greenish above and pale below. They

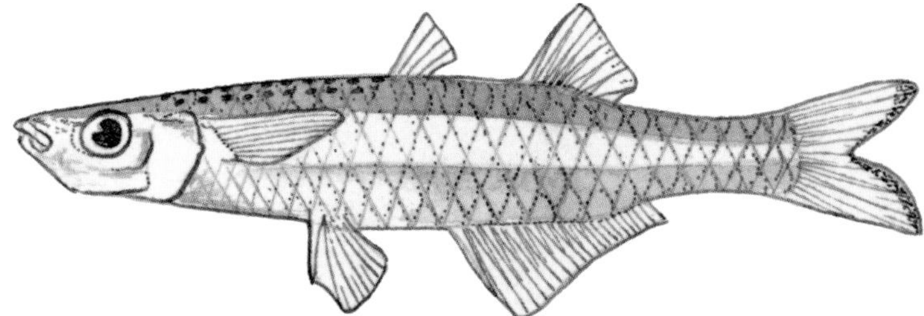

Rough silverside, Membras martinica

are schooling, diurnal planktivores whose supposed potential to control nuisance insects led to the introduction of inland silversides to lakes and reservoirs in California, Oklahoma, and elsewhere. This usually seems to create more problems than it solves, including their replacing native species by preying on their eggs and larvae. They are sometimes used as baitfish and serve as an important prey item. Species usually range from 4 to 6 inches in length.

Rough Silverside—*Membras martinica*

The rough silverside ranges from the waters of New York throughout the Gulf of Mexico to northern Mexico. It lives in saltier areas over the shallow shelf, in the surf zone, and in most Texas bays. It has two rows of small black dots along the back behind the head, and the silver stripe on the side is wider than the eye diameter. The body scales are rough to the touch due to their scalloped edges. It is more abundant in the bays during the summer, and individuals have been collected from the Laguna Madre during most years. The rough silverside may reach a length of 5 inches.

Inland Silverside—*Menidia beryllina*

This species has an extensive distribution in the Mississippi and Rio Grande systems. Its range includes the Atlantic coast from Massachusetts to Florida and throughout the Gulf

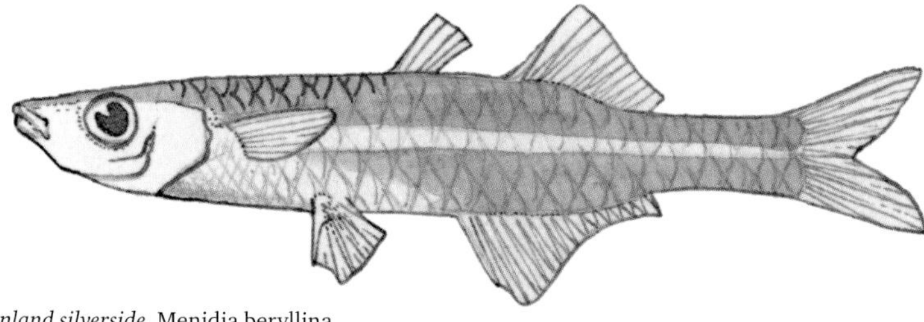

Inland silverside, Menidia beryllina

of Mexico south to Veracruz, Mexico. They are schooling fishes often seen at the surface around piers and along seawalls. Inland silversides are abundant in shallow-water habitats from fresh water to coastal bays, and it is generally more abundant in fresh water than is the tidewater silverside (*M. peninsulae*). The scales are smooth to the touch, and the scales on the dorsal surface are outlined in black. The mouth is somewhat pointed, and its lateral silver stripe is narrower than the diameter of the eye. Silversides are important forage species, and they will flash their reflective lateral stripe and scatter abruptly at the approach of a predator. The inland silverside is one of the few species in the family that spends its entire life cycle in bays. They avoid very salty water and prefer two-thirds strength seawater or less. This species grows to 4 inches in length.

Tidewater Silverside—*Menidia peninsulae*

The tidewater silverside is an abundant species around the shorelines of all Texas bays. It is a deeper-bodied fish than the inland silverside and ranges from northeastern Florida to Veracruz, Mexico. It is difficult to distinguish between the tidewater and inland silverside and usually requires an accounting of specific characteristics such as fin rays and lateral line scales. This species is tolerant of a wide salinity range and is common near the gulf in brackish to full salinity seawater. It is less common in inland waters but can inhabit tidal creeks and marshes. In the Laguna Madre, the tidewater silverside can be abundant on the windward shorelines. Gravid females have been found in the lagoon during every month of the year. This is another important forage fish for large predators. This species may grow to 6 inches.

Tube-Mouths—Order Gasterosteiformes

This group is referred to as the "tubemouths" because many of the fishes have elongate snouts. They also have spines in the dorsal fin. They are

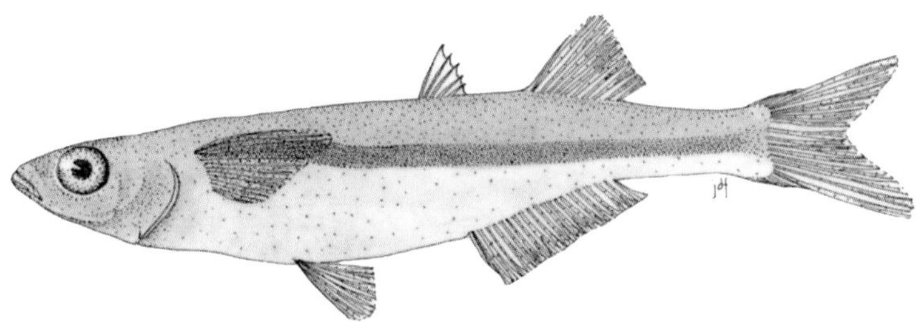

Tidewater silverside, Menidia peninsulae. *Illustration by Janice D. Fechhelm*

mostly warm-water marine species, but a few reside in fresh water. This order is rather small, containing about 260 species of some of the most unusual and best-known fishes, including the seahorses, pipefishes, and sticklebacks. Many are among the favorites of aquarium keepers.

Pipefishes and Seahorses—Family Syngnathidae

The pipefishes and seahorses are among the most interesting of all marine fishes. There are about two hundred species of pipefish and only twenty-five species of seahorses. Family members have sacrificed streamlining and speed for armor, cryptic coloration that conceals them, and secretive behavior; nevertheless, they are a very successful group. All are long and thin, are encased in bony rings, have tube-like snouts with the mouth at the end, and lack pelvic fins. One interesting biological characteristic of the family is that the males carry the fertilized eggs in a special brood pouch. The location and size of this pouch are important in determining species. Individuals are commonly found in vegetated areas, and they closely mimic the vegetation in which they live. These fishes are often well camouflaged in both color and shape. Perhaps the best example is the leafy sea dragon (*Phycodurus eques*) of Australia, which bears numerous leaf-like lobes. The pipefishes and seahorses are found in shallow marine waters throughout the world and occasionally in fresh water. One peculiar and distinctive member of this family, the pipehorse (*Acentronura* sp.), has been collected off the Mississippi coast. It resembles a pipefish but, like a seahorse, has a prehensile tail for holding onto objects.

The seahorses have the head turned downward such that it is at a right angle to the body. They employ the dorsal and pectoral fins primarily for swimming, having converted the tail into a flexible, prehensile appendage for holding onto stationary objects such as submerged vegetation and for some forward movement. Seahorses swim upright in a very slow, unfish-like manner. To compensate for their slow swimming, the specialized mouth allows them to siphon small crustaceans from some distance away after locating their prey with binocular vision. The seahorse makes a great aquarium fish with a couple of drawbacks: it requires live food and may be attacked mercilessly by aggressive tank mates.

CHAIN PIPEFISH—*Syngnathus louisianae*

This is a common pipefish in the Laguna Madre region, especially in the bays near gulf passes. It may also be found in grassbeds a considerable distance from passes. Mature adults

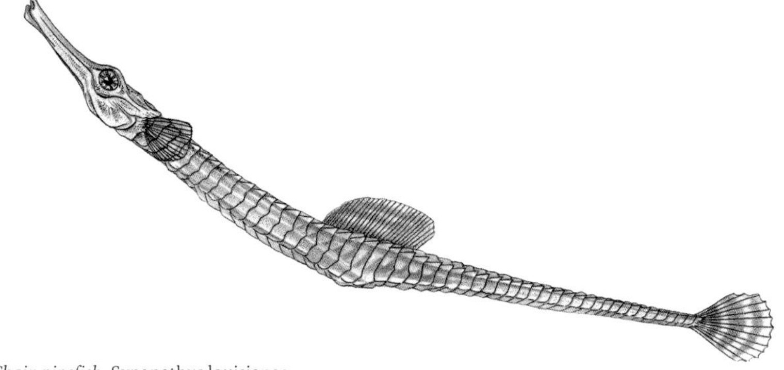

Chain pipefish, Syngnathus louisianae

are reported only from offshore areas. It ranges from the northern gulf to Bermuda and Campeche, Mexico. The lower portion of the trunk has a chain-like row of dark, diamond-shaped marks. The long snout, position of the dorsal fin, and pattern of bands and reticulations on the sides characterize this species. The females are always flat-bellied. It may reach 15 inches in length.

Gulf Pipefish—*Syngnathus scovelli*
The gulf pipefish ranges from Georgia, through the northern gulf, and south to Brazil. This is the most abundant and widely distributed pipefish in Texas bays. It is a shallow-water species occurring in abundance in seagrasses in the upper and lower Laguna Madre. Populations have also been reported from fresh waters in both Louisiana and Texas. It is distinguished by its short snout and dorsal fin length. The dorsal fin is slightly longer and located farther back than that of the chain pipefish (*S. louisianae*). The dorsal fin is usually banded in the females, which also have a V-shaped belly, a deep body, and a silvery bar on each body ring. The males are flat-bellied and uniformly colored. This species grows to 6 inches.

Gulf pipefish, Syngnathus scovelli. *Illustration by Janice D. Fechhelm*

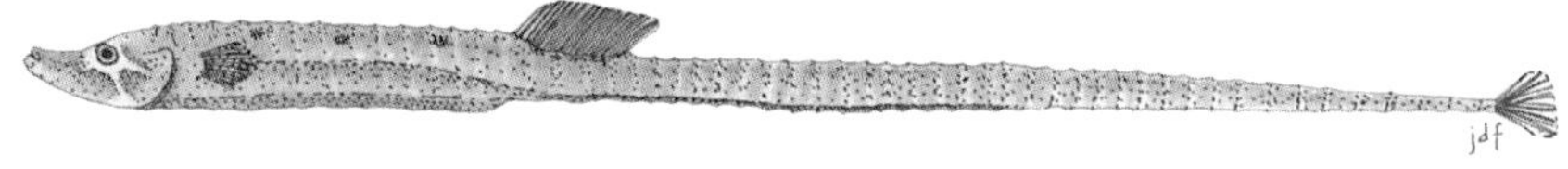

Fringed pipefish, Anarchopterus criniger. *Illustration by Janice D. Fechhelm*

Fringed Pipefish—*Anarchopterus criniger*

The color pattern on the short trunk, a long tail, and the lack of an anal fin are the best traits for distinguishing this species. It also has fleshy tabs on the head and body. There are usually three short whitish bars on each body ring, three black spots set high on the trunk, and three pale streaks radiating from the lower half of each eye. It is thought to range from North Carolina to Florida, throughout the Gulf of Mexico, and south to Brazil. It is a seagrass inhabitant in at least parts of its range. This pipefish may reach 4 inches.

Lined Seahorse—*Hippocampus erectus*

This seahorse is found throughout the gulf to Argentina and is the common larger seahorse of the bays and shallow areas of the Gulf of Mexico. It is especially abundant in seagrass beds in Texas bays near gulf passes. Its coloration is highly variable (olive-brown, orange, or yellow and gold), and it often has large pale blotches and dark lines on the neck and along the back. There are often fleshy lobes or filaments on their bodies, allowing them to mimic vegetation. Those living in sargassum take advantage of these features that provide effective camouflage. They may grow to 6 inches in length.

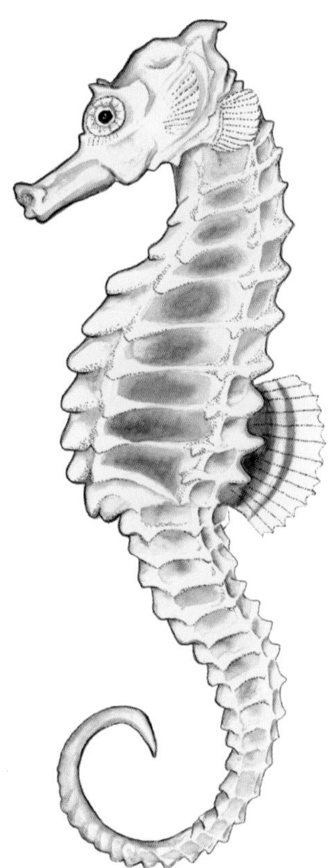

Lined seahorse, Hippocampus erectus

Scorpionfishes and Searobins—Order Scorpaeniformes

With nearly thirteen hundred species in twenty-four families, this is one of the largest orders of fish. Most are associated with the bottom or hard substrate such as rocks and reefs. They have large heads and rounded caudal fins. Members of this order share the common characteristic of a "suborbital stay," which is a bony ridge that runs below the eyes and across the gill covers. As a result, these are sometimes referred to as the "mail-cheeked" fishes. Many also have bony plates and/or spines on the head and body and have large, broad-based pectoral fins; the spines of many species are venomous. Most are marine, shallow-water inhabitants of temperate and tropical waters and occur from the bays out onto the continental shelf. Some species live at considerably greater depths.

Scorpionfishes—Family Scorpaenidae

These are commonly known as "rockfish" in northern waters and as scorpionfishes in tropical waters because of the extreme toxicity of their spines. This family contains nearly four hundred species, with about ninety found in North American waters. They are usually multicolored and many have numerous stout spines and fleshy tabs and appendages, giving them a bizarre, prickly appearance. The color patterns of many inshore species are quite bright, which may serve to advertise their venomous spines, which leave very painful puncture wounds after injection of the venom produced by tissue present on the dorsal, anal, and pelvic fin spines. Scales on the body are either lacking or are very small. Most scorpionfishes are bottom-oriented predators, although many species move up into the water column to feed on schools of fish and squid. Internal fertilization is practiced, and females incubate the eggs in the body cavity after fertilization; the larvae are then released immediately after hatching inside the female.

Spotted Scorpionfish—*Scorpaena plumieri*

This is the most common inshore scorpionfish, and it is not highly venomous. It occurs from the waters of New York to Bermuda and throughout the northern Gulf of Mexico to Brazil. In the Laguna Madre region the spotted scorpionfish is the only scorpionfish species regularly encountered by anglers, and it is considered a dangerous nuisance. It is usually found near jetties, oil platforms, and reefs out to two hundred feet. The body is blotched with shades of brown, the tail stock is pale, and the caudal fin has three dark vertical bars with white separating them. The

Spotted scorpionfish, Scorpaena plumieri

pectoral fins are dark with white or bright yellow spots on the lower surface. It may reach 12 inches in length.

Searobins—Family Triglidae

Nearly one hundred species of searobins are widely distributed and adapted for living on soft bottoms at moderate depths. Searobins are found mostly in tropical coastal waters. They occur throughout bays and estuaries to the middle of the continental shelf. Typically they are brown to reddish in color with large eyes set toward the top of the head. These are peculiar, armored fishes with large pectoral fins resembling and functioning somewhat like wings. Some of the pectoral rays are detached as separate finger-like tactile and chemoreceptive organs that are used as feelers or legs as they "walk" and feed along the bottom. They are usually found at night near the bottom, where they glide along the substrate. They produce sounds, especially during spawning, by vibrating the air bladder, and they are reported to be some of the noisiest fish found along the Atlantic and gulf coasts.

The heads of searobins are bony plated and armed with many spines, some of which become more spiny with age. Because spines are used to distinguish species, spine changes associated with age may make identification difficult; however, most species likely to be encountered are generally easy to identify. Color and the type of habitat where one is collected can also be useful in identifying most species. The mouth is situated just beneath the head and is quite protrusible (capable of being thrust outward), allowing them to feed on a variety of benthic organisms. Most species are regarded as bait stealers and curiosities. At least a dozen species of searobins have been reported from the offshore gulf shrimping grounds.

Bighead Searobin—*Prionotus tribulus*
Other names: docteur
This is the common inshore searobin and the only species whose young have been collected at low salinities. It is also common in saltier bays and estuaries. It ranges from Chesapeake Bay to Florida and throughout the Gulf of Mexico. The head is large and broad, and the caudal fin is blackish with a pale band near the base. The pectoral fins are dark with many narrow crossbands. Adults spawn offshore during the summer and fall, with the young abundant in early spring and congregating at the mouths of bays. They feed on various benthic invertebrates, including small shrimp and polychaete worms. Very young juveniles appear in shrimp trawl catches during October in the upper Laguna Madre. Juveniles and adults are found throughout the lagoon and Baffin Bay in some years. The Texas record is 1.1 pounds, 13.3 inches (Corpus Christi Bay, 1987).

Slender Searobin—*Peristedion gracile*
The body of this searobin, as the name implies, is slender and is straw colored to reddish above and whitish below. There is a dark stripe across the middle of the dorsal fin, and the rear edge of the caudal fin is dark red

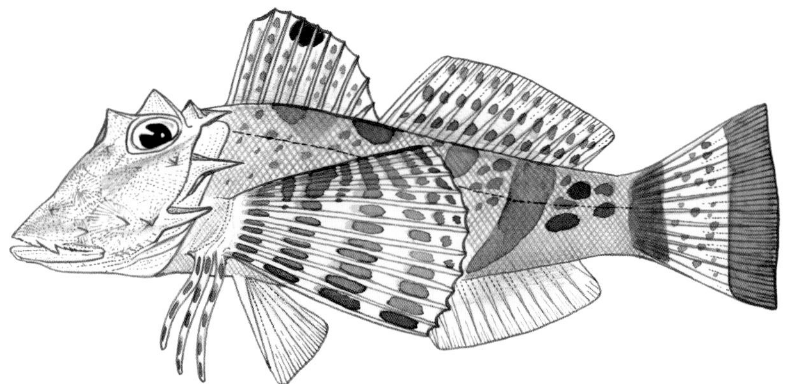

Bighead searobin, Prionotus tribulus

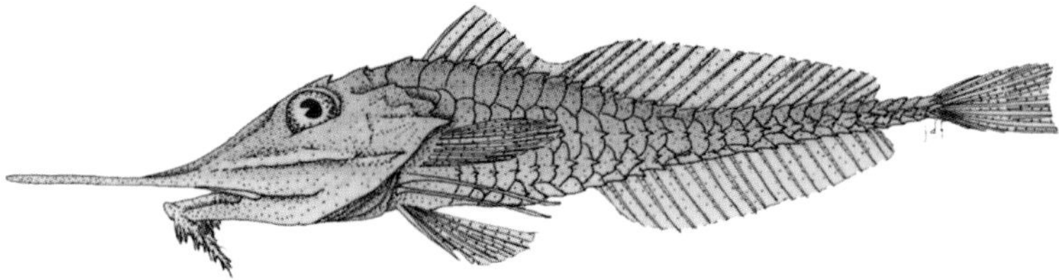

Slender searobin, Peristedion gracile. *Illustration by Janice D. Fechhelm*

in color. Long spines on the snout and barbels on the upper jaw are characteristic of this species. It is a continental slope species with juveniles sometimes found on the outer shelf. It likely ranges throughout the entire Gulf of Mexico and is considered to be rare in Texas bays.

LEOPARD SEAROBIN—*Prionotus scitulus*

A common inshore and shallow bay searobin, this species is not known to occur at low salinities. The upper portion of the body has numerous closely crowded, reddish brown spots, sometimes with diffuse oblique, dark bands on the sides and pectoral fins. There are usually a few dark spots on the first dorsal fin. Individuals reported from the western gulf are generally less well marked than those from elsewhere in its range, which is thought to be from North Carolina to Venezuela. It has been reported from both the upper and lower Laguna Madre. The Texas record is 8.9 inches (Gulf of Mexico, 1993).

BARRED SEAROBIN—*Prionotus martis*

The barred searobin ranges from the northeast Florida coast and the Gulf of Mexico to Campeche, Mexico. It has a black spot between each spine in the second dorsal fin, the body is mottled above, and the caudal and pectoral fins are blackish in color. It may grow to 7 inches in length.

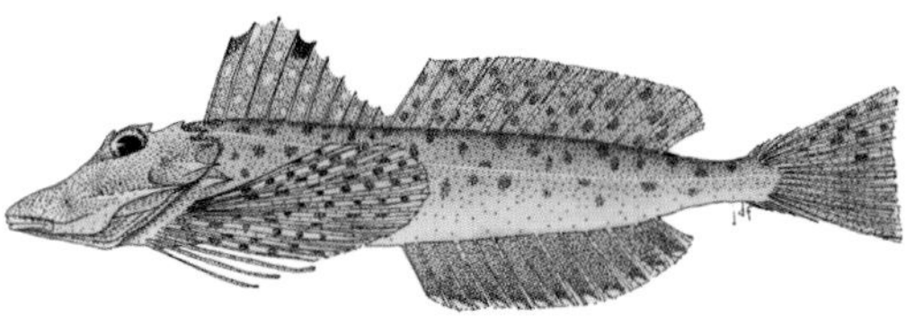

Leopard searobin, Prionotus scitulus. *Illustration by Janice D. Fechhelm*

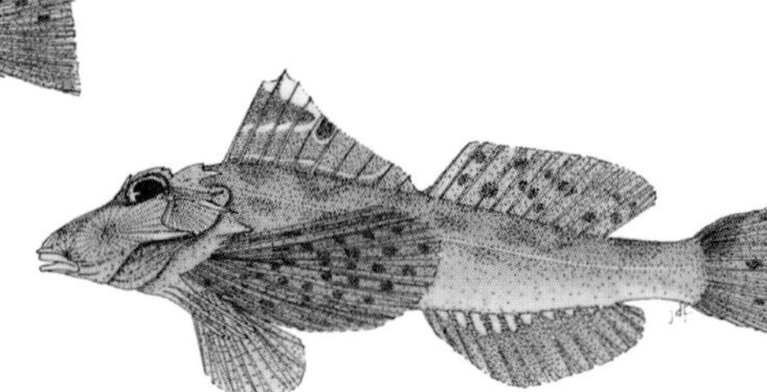

Barred searobin, Prionotus martis. *Illustration by Janice D. Fechhelm*

Perch-like Fishes—Order Perciformes

This is the largest order of fishes and in fact, the largest order of all the vertebrates, with nearly 9,300 species in 148 families. Of this group, 81 families are found in North American waters, including at least 200 species in Mexican waters. Their great diversity in size ranges from tiny gobies and batfish to tunas and swordfishes. Most are adapted for life as predators in the shallow or surface waters of oceans and lakes. They are part of a catch-all category for fishes that do not easily fit elsewhere. This group includes most of the spiny-rayed fishes having stout spines in the anterior part of the dorsal and anal fins. The pelvic fins usually consist of a single spine and five rays, the scales are typically ctenoid (sawtoothed and textured), and a lateral line is almost always present. Small eggs are produced, usually with pelagic larvae for dispersal, and many members have high fecundity rates (produce thousands to millions of eggs). Classification of the order is unsettled; there have been many recent changes and others are certain in the future.

Snooks—Family Centropomidae

The snooks are popular tropical marine game and food fishes with an extended lower jaw like that of the freshwater pikes. At least two species occur in the northwestern Gulf of Mexico. Snooks are silvery on the sides and darker above with vivid yellow fins. Snooks are coastal and brackish water inhabitants often entering fresh waters, especially where limestone outcrops occur in their range. They are generally more common at lower salinities. All species are widely distributed on both coasts of Central America, northern South America, and western Africa, throughout the West Indies, and north to Texas. Three species (the common snook, fat snook, and Mexican snook) have been reported from the Gulf of Mexico. The common snook is the largest and by far the most abundant of the three.

Common Snook—*Centropomus undecimalis*

Other names: snook, saltwater pike, lineside, róbalo, ravillia

This is the largest and most common snook in the Laguna Madre region and one that is highly prized as a food and game fish. This and similar species inhabit tropical waters. Their only occurrence in U.S. waters is southern Florida and the lower Laguna Madre. Their range extends south into Central America and to western Africa. They are most common along mangrove shorelines, brackish pools, freshwater canals, and at the mouths of rivers. Snook are easy to identify because of the solid black line that

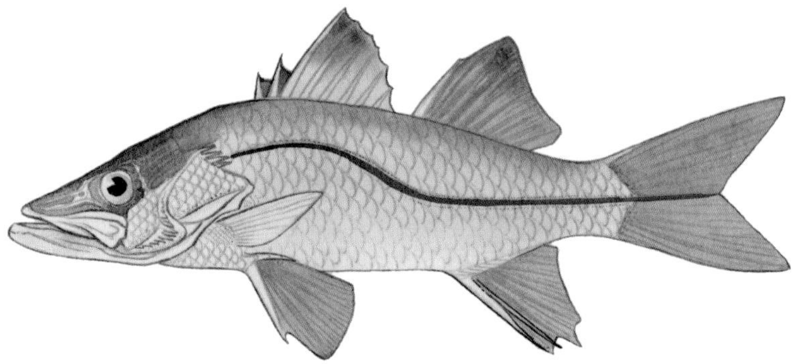

Common snook, Centropomus undecimalis

follows the lateral line from just above the razor-sharp gill cover to the tip of the deeply forked caudal fin. The body is relatively slender, the head is tapered and concave, and the snout is rather long and pointed. The dorsal surface is usually dark green in color, fading to silvery sides, and the belly is white. The less abundant fat snook (*C. parallelus*) is shorter (rarely larger than 14 to 18 inches or 2 pounds) and is much deeper bodied. Even less common is the Mexican snook (*C. poeyi*), which has only recently been reported from the lower Laguna Madre. It is also smaller in size than the common snook.

Snook are known to spawn in June and July around gulf passes, and in Texas they are mainly encountered near passes from the Aransas Pass southward. Until the 1940s, Texas had a considerable commercial fishery for snook, but it has since been uncommon except for a population in South Bay in the lower Laguna Madre. Beginning with the opening of the Fish Pass on Mustang Island, snook were caught beneath the bridge on a regular basis for several years. With the redredging of Packery Channel (connecting the gulf with Corpus Christi Bay), numerous snook have been sighted by divers and are regularly being caught (to 34 inches) along the rock jetties. Interestingly, the still-standing state record (57 pounds, 4 ounces) for snook was taken in the vicinity of this pass in 1937. The fish was caught by the late Louis Rawalt on a cane pole using a strip of white tee shirt for bait. This species is known to reach a weight of 60 pounds, and 10 pounds is usually the maximum size attained for Texas snook.

The snook has long been known as a nocturnally active species, so most serious angling is reserved for the nighttime. It is a structure-oriented species typically lying motionless beneath piers and behind jetty rocks waiting to ambush unsuspecting prey. Fish and large crustaceans (crabs and shrimp) are the preferred food of adults, but they can be taken on a variety of live and artificial baits. Snook are attracted to movement at the water's surface, and top-water and subsurface plugs are a favorite of anglers. An old and specific method of angling for snook called "puddling" was practiced from Bob Hall and Horace Caldwell piers in the gulf into the 1960s, where a top-water lure was swirled in a figure-8 formation around pilings to entice them from the shadows. The strikes are solid and aggressive and the runs long and hard. Small snook will often repeatedly jump free of the water like a ladyfish, and some compare its fight to that of the largemouth bass. The mild and flaky flesh of the snook is excellent, making it one of the finest eating saltwater fish. The yield of fillets is greater than that of most other game fish as well.

The snook appears to be quite tolerant of higher salinities and has likely extended its range north into the upper lagoon since the late 1980s. I caught two adults (26 inches and 30 inches) near Baffin Bay in 1982, and sightings and catches of snook by anglers in the upper Laguna Madre have since increased. In the summer of 2005, TPWD biologists collected two juvenile snook (2 to 3 inches long) during the surveys in the upper reaches of Baffin. These are almost certainly young-of-the-year that were spawned in that bay. Severe freezes on the South Texas coast have long claimed large numbers of the poorly cold-tolerant snook. The similarity of the preferred habitats of the common snook and tarpon has long been used to support the hypotheses of habitat destruction or environmental change as a common cause for the disappearance of both species over the years. However, both appear to be making a rebound in the Laguna Madre region.

For years aquaculturists have attempted to unravel the mysteries of the reproduction of the snook but have met with only limited success. If reports from Packery Channel are an indication of the well-being of South Texas snook, then coastal anglers have a lot to look forward to concerning this premier "tackle buster." Obviously, this area has long been an attraction for this snook. I anticipate that with the continued maintenance of Packery Channel, the snook will be an additional marine target species for coastal anglers to enjoy.

Jacks and Pompanos—Family Carangidae

Jacks and pompanos are rather large, fast-swimming fishes generally found in schools that are constantly on the move. The body shapes of the more than 140 species of jacks and pompanos range from torpedo-like to thin and plate-like. Their habit of continuous movement is reflected in their deeply forked caudal fin and narrow caudal peduncles (body just anterior to the caudal fin), the small cycloid (round and smooth) scales (often absent or modified into bony scutes along the lateral line), the sharply sloping heads (with large eyes and mouth), and laterally compressed bodies. They range in color from silvery to metallic blue or green to bright yellow or gold, and the juveniles of many species have vertical bars on their sides. One of the most distinctive family characteristics is the presence of two "free" (detached) spines found anterior to the anal fin. In young fish, these two spines may be covered by a membrane and not easily seen. In adults these spines, and frequently the anterior-most spines of the dorsal fin, become covered with tissue as well, making their detection difficult. All species are predaceous and several are prized game and food fishes. Identification of some of the smaller species is difficult, but most of the common species can readily be identified. Juveniles of this group make interesting aquarium fishes. Most jacks spawn offshore, and the young of many are free-living in the water and concentrated beneath floating objects, including jellyfish and sargassum. Most jacks feed by making rapid, slashing attacks at schools of small fish such as herrings and anchovies. Some species, like the greater amberjack (*Seriola dumerili*), are reported to cause ciguatera (sickness from eating toxic fish). Adults range in size from approximately 10 inches to 6 feet in length.

Leatherjacket—*Oligoplites saurus*
Other names: leatherjack
This species is one of the few truly estuarine jacks. It prefers nearshore or lower salinity waters around the

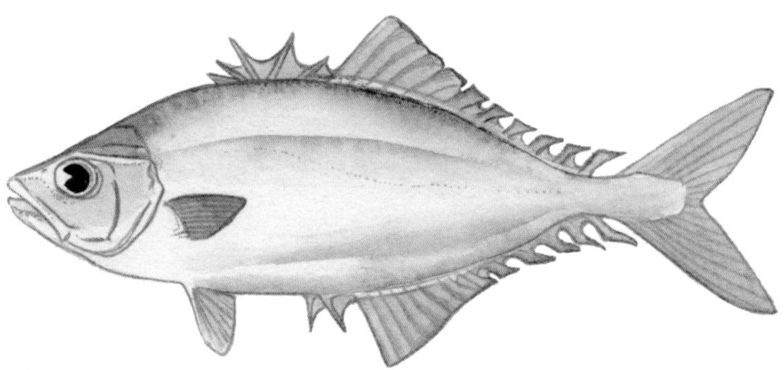

Leatherjacket, Oligoplites saurus

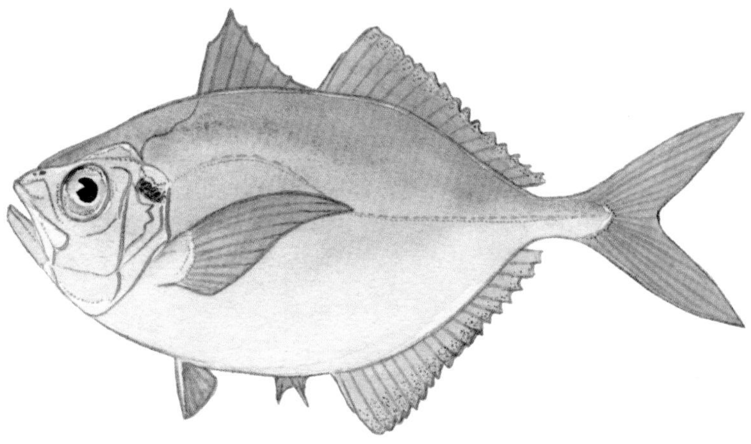

Atlantic bumper, Chloroscombrus chrysurus

mouths of bays and is often found in murky water in large schools. Young-of-the-year (less than 2 inches in length) are present in Texas bays during the late summer and leave for the gulf before the end of November. It has a range from the coast of Maine to Uruguay. The sides are silvery and bluish above and the fins are a vivid yellow. Posterior to the dorsal and anal fins are a series of finlets with the dorsal fin having five nonconnected spines. The lateral line is nearly horizontal and the scales are tiny and embedded, giving the skin a smooth feel and appearance. Like the pompanos, this jack lacks the ridge of scutes along the caudal peduncle. Because of its small size and abundance it is an important intermediate link in the food web between the smaller anchovies and the medium-sized higher predators. The tiny spines of this small jack are extremely sharp, and a puncture from one of them may cause considerable pain for a short while. Although a specific venom has not been identified, there is little doubt that one is present. This species generally attains a length of 4 to 6 inches, but the Texas record is 8.4 inches (Gulf of Mexico, 2002).

Atlantic Bumper—*Chloroscombrus chrysurus*

The Atlantic bumper is one of the most abundant shore fishes in tropical America. It is also very common in the Gulf of Mexico and regularly enters high-salinity bays and estuaries. It ranges from Massachusetts waters to Bermuda and throughout the gulf to Brazil but is apparently absent from the Bahamas. The silvery sides fade to golden below, and the anal and caudal fins are yellow. There is a conspicuous black "saddle" on the caudal peduncle and a small black area (smudge) at the rear edge of the gill cover. The lateral line arches strongly upward near the head.

Like the leatherjacket, the role of this fish in the marine and estuarine environment seems to be one of a low-level carnivore, serving as a link between forage species and larger piscivores (fish eaters). Massive schools can extend across the mouths of bays and passes, making small but snappy strikes at the surface. Such aggregations may be confused with menhaden, which exhibit a similar schooling behavior. They also congregate around rigs and offshore pilings where they can be easily snagged with a series of bare hooks or captured with a cast net for use as live bait. The state record is 9.8 inches (Gulf of Mexico, 2005).

Florida Pompano—*Trachinotus carolinus*

Other names: pompano, cobblerfish, palometa

The Florida pompano is the most popular of all the jacks, sought by both sport anglers and commercial fishermen and is considered by many to be the most delicious of all food fish. The Florida pompano is a shore fish that primarily inhabits the bottom along sandy beaches, although it does enter bays. It ranges from the Massachusetts coast to Brazil but is absent from the clear waters of the Bahamas. The body is relatively deep and almost entirely silvery with a dark, usually bluish back. The belly, anal, and caudal fins are yellow in the juveniles, and this coloration usually persists in

Florida pompano, Trachinotus carolinus

the adults. The anal fin is preceded by two detached spines. The diet of the Florida pompano is composed of molluscs, shrimp, various burrowing crustaceans, and small fish. The species has a long spawning season, and juveniles less than 1 inch long are very abundant in the surf on Mustang and Padre Islands from April through August. All ages usually leave the gulf beaches by the end of December and reportedly migrate to deeper offshore water. A few adults are found in the bays, including the upper Laguna Madre. For at least twenty-five years there has been a sizable population of pompano on the north shore of Baffin Bay. Never leave Starvation Point and head south across Baffin Bay without looking for them. They commonly jump in the wake of a boat, and often they will hit the gunnels of a boat and occasionally jump into it. The general fishing season is late spring through December along gulf beaches and on jetties in the surf zone. November is probably best, although they can be caught year round. In the past, this species was difficult to capture in long (800 to 1200 feet) beach seines because of its propensity for leaping over the top of a net. The state record is 6.3 pounds, 23.3 inches (Gulf of Mexico, 1989), and the world record is 8 pounds, 1 ounce (Florida, 1984).

Jack Crevalle—*Caranx hippos*
Other names: jackfish, horse crevally, tourist tarpon, "bulldog of the sea," jurel, toro
Although it goes by many colorful names, this is the common jack of Texas waters, with both juveniles and adults more commonly found inshore. It is worldwide in distribution in tropical and temperate marine waters and ranges from Cape Cod through the Gulf of Mexico to South

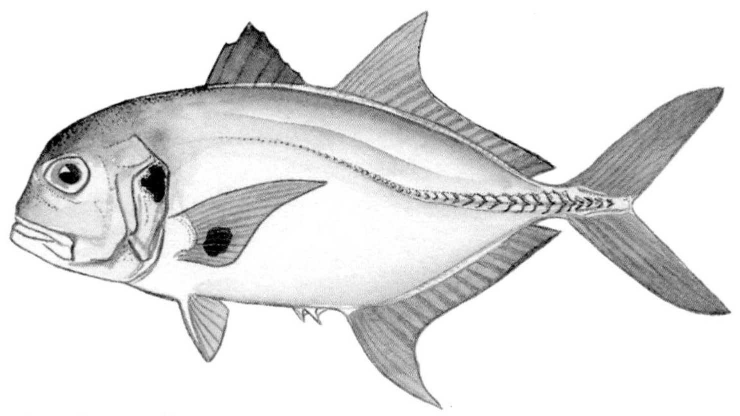

Jack crevalle, Caranx hippos

America. The body is deep, the profile of the head is steep, and the belly and fins are yellow in color. There is a vertically elongate black spot at the rear edge of each gill cover and a broad dark area extending across the lower portion of the pectoral fins. Bony scutes are present on the caudal peduncle anterior to the deeply forked (lunate or half-moon shaped) caudal fin. The young have dark vertical bars on the sides like many other species of jacks. This is a large jack, with adults often exceeding 40 pounds. Although rarely consumed as a food fish due to its oily, strong-tasting flesh, it is most prized as a hard-fighting sport fish. Crevalle are voracious scavengers that follow gulf shrimp boats as they cull their by-catch. Larger individuals tend to congregate around the mouths of passes, but some enter bays. It is not unusual to catch large individuals in the Laguna Madre, especially during the summer months and usually near the Gulf Intracoastal Waterway. Their diet consists of a variety of small fish and crabs. Spawning occurs in the gulf from March through September, and juveniles are abundant in the surf, often moving into bays and roaming in schools around pilings, reefs, and other structures. I have long said that catching one each year was fun but catching two was far too much work. The current state record is 50 pounds, 4 ounces (Port Aransas, 1986). The world record is 57 pounds, 5 ounces (Angola, 1992).

Tripletail—Family Lobotidae

The tripletail is the single representative of this family. This species is a large, odd-looking, grouper-like fish commonly associated with floating debris, pelagic drift-lines, and stationary objects such as channel markers and piers. Individuals of all sizes are sometimes seen floating at the surface, lying on their side in a horizontal position. The dorsal and anal fins have long bases and are well developed, their tips reaching more than halfway to the end of the caudal fin, giving them the appearance of having three tails.

TRIPLETAIL—*Lobotes surinamensis*
Other names: buoyfish, black perch
The tripletail is found worldwide in tropical and warm waters, from Massachusetts and Bermuda to Argentina. The head and body are variously mottled, with backgrounds ranging from tan to dark brown and bronze to yellow. The fins are uniformly black with a pale olive band across the base of the caudal fin. Some individuals have a broad, dark brown bar running from the eye across the cheek to just beneath the gill cover and another from the top of the eye to the dorsal fin. There are also two dark stripes on top of the head, behind the nostrils. The edge of the cheek (preopercle) is

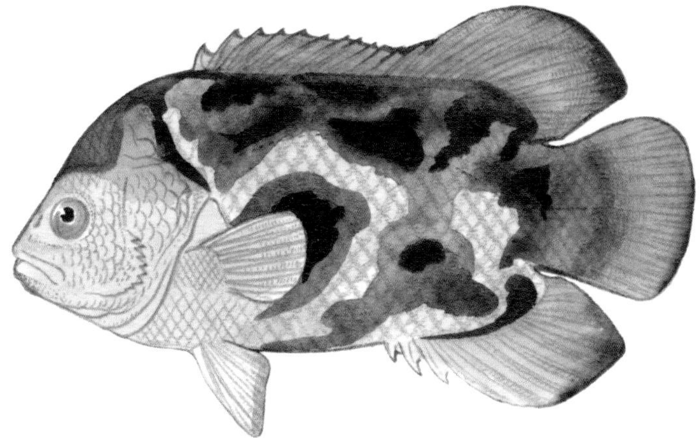

Tripletail, Lobotes surinamensis

strongly serrated or sawtooth shaped. A fish of sluggish behavior, the tripletail often floats horizontally on the surface. Younger individuals associate with floating debris in open waters, around pilings, and beneath bulkheads and piers. This species is not considered to be particularly common in Texas bays and the shallow gulf, but large adults are regularly caught in Matagorda Bay around channel buoys and other structures. Although bony, it is an excellent fish to eat. Its diet consists of shrimp, crabs, and small fish. Spawning occurs in the gulf in spring or early summer, with the young often drifting into the bays. This fish reaches 3.5 feet in length and up to 50 pounds in weight. The state record is 33.5 pounds, 34.0 inches (Matagorda Bay, 1984), and the world record is 42 pounds, 5 ounces (South Africa, 1989).

Mojarras—Family Gerreidae

There are about forty species of mojarras worldwide, with twelve species found off North America and ten species confined to Mexican waters. The mojarras are schooling fishes of great abundance in coastal waters, bays, and estuaries in tropical and warm temperate regions. Some enter fresh water and a few reside there permanently. They are most common over grassy, sandy, and bare bottoms and are rarely found on reefs. They are deep-bodied small fishes with deeply forked caudal fins and greatly protrusible jaws for capturing bottom-dwelling invertebrates. The jaws fit into a sheath that extends along the upper snout when retracted, and when it is extended, the jaws point downward. Mojarras are dull in color, mostly tan or brown, with a metallic silvery background. The head and gill covers are scaled, the body is moderately compressed, and the snout is pointed. Few species reach 12 inches in length and most are generally much smaller. The larger ones in certain areas are considered to be good table fare. In some areas, they are used for bait and are an important prey species.

YELLOWFIN MOJARRA—*Gerres cinereus*
This species is common throughout the Gulf of Mexico and south to Brazil. It inhabits shallow coastal waters over open sand in the surf zone and seagrass beds and mangrove channels in the bays. The head and body are a light tan in color and darker above, often with seven or eight faint brown bars on the sides. The pelvic fins are usually yellow. It is encountered mostly in the fall in the bays and shallow gulf. The Texas record is 12.3 inches (lower Laguna Madre, 1981).

Grunts—Family Haemulidae
These are medium-sized, perch-like fishes of tropical and subtropical coastal waters. The grunts are a family of more than 150 species that closely resemble the snappers but lack the fang-like canines and vomerine teeth (tooth-like patches in the top of the mouth). The common name of the group is derived from the noise made when they grind their pharyngeal teeth (grinding teeth in throat area). However, they are a much more impressive family than their name implies. Schools of grunts with iridescent yellow, blue, and orange stripes are commonly seen over tropical reefs. The young and adults of the many species are quite different in coloration. Only the pigfish (*Orthopristis chrysoptera*) is common inshore, but other species are important predators on offshore reefs. At night, their color patterns are altered

Yellowfin mojarra, Gerres cinereus

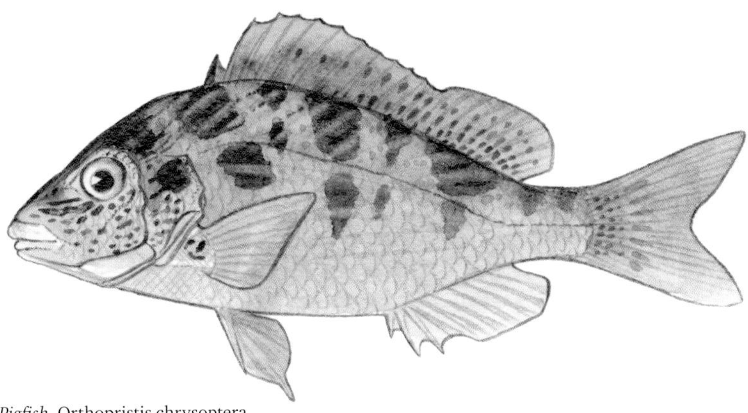

Pigfish, Orthopristis chrysoptera

and the various grunt species leave the reefs to forage on hard-shelled crustaceans living in the surrounding shallow flats. The pharyngeal teeth of grunts form a formidable grinding apparatus. Grunts congregate by day in large numbers around reefs or sheltered areas. The young are often found in seagrass beds in bays and lagoons and along coastal shorelines.

PIGFISH—*Orthopristis chrysoptera*
Other names: piggy perch, piggies, cochon

This species ranges from the New Jersey shore to the Yucatan Peninsula but is most common in the Gulf of Mexico and adjacent bays. They are especially prevalent around piers and jetties and in grassbeds of saltier bays. The largest individuals tend to be found along deep channels and gulf passes. The "piggy" is far less abundant but is commonly confused with the pinfish. Aside from being in different families, piggy perch are deeper bodied, have longer and more pointed snouts, and have eyes that are proportionally much smaller. The scales of the pigfish are each centered with a blue spot and a bronze edge, giving the appearance of having oblique bars on their sides. There are brilliant blue and yellow markings on the cheek. The pigfish is generally very vocal when removed from the water and continually emits loud, pig-like grunts until released. Like other saltwater panfish, the larger ones are excellent when gutted and gilled, scaled, and fried whole. They are very hardy and are an excellent live baitfish for almost all sport and game fish. In the upper Laguna Madre, pigfish enter the fishery as young juveniles in March and most move offshore for the winter. The state record is 1.0 pound and 12.5 inches (Galveston Bay, 1998).

Porgies—Family Sparidae

About 120 species of porgies make up this family of medium-sized fish, several of which closely resemble the grunts. They are best characterized by their anterior-most teeth, which are either flattened incisors or peg-like canines. In the rear of the jaw, the molars are arranged in several rows, giving porgies powerful crushing and grinding abilities. All North American species are deep bodied and have a deep but short head with large eyes and a small mouth. The caudal fin is deeply forked, and the anal and dorsal fins have sharp, stout spines. Many species are predominantly silvery, and most can quickly change to a blotched pattern when stressed or alarmed. Most species are omnivorous, feeding on attached vegetation and invertebrates. Many are important food and sport fishes of warm temperate and tropical coastal waters. They are most common in bays and shallow coastal waters and offshore banks where shellfish and other invertebrates are common.

SHEEPSHEAD—*Archosargus probatocephalus*
Other names: convict fish, bait stealer, sargo raiada, pargo

The sheepshead is a common inshore structure-oriented fish that regularly inhabits rock jetties, pilings of docks and piers, navigation markers, duck blinds, and oyster reefs. It may also be found along the edges of channels and even over grassbeds. Anglers occasionally take this fish in the surf along the gulf beaches. It ranges from

Sheepshead, Archosargus probatocephalus

Cape Cod south through the Gulf of Mexico to Campeche, Mexico. The sheepshead is considered to be a "resident" species because it remains in the same general area from day to day except for the annual spawning movement to the gulf by individuals living within the bays.

The sheepshead or convict fish has six or seven broad black vertical bars over a grayish white background, and because of this coloring they are often confused with the black drum. These bars are often faint and faded in older and larger individuals, but the teeth are a dead giveaway for the sheepshead because they are very prominent, like those of sheep (thus their common name). The sides of both jaws are lined with molar-like teeth, and the front incisors in both jaws are amazingly similar in appearance to human teeth.

The sheepshead is one of the largest members of the porgy family and is deep bodied and narrow through the shoulders, as is their common coastal cousin the pinfish (*Lagodon rhomboides*). When handling the sheepshead, care should be taken because the dorsal and anal fin spines are stout and pointed and the cheek area on the gill covers is razor sharp.

Sheepshead spawn in the near-shore gulf around jetties, rock piles, and reefs during February and March. The larvae are carried by currents into grassbeds in the bays, where they take advantage of abundant food supplies and cover. At about "hand size," the juveniles seek out adult habitats in the bays, especially around the gulf jetties. In some years, the young are very numerous in the grass flats of the Laguna Madre.

The sheepshead diet is somewhat varied but consists largely of shellfish. The powerful jaws and teeth allow them to "graze" very effectively on organisms living on rocks, pilings, and so forth. It is reported to change its diet from algae in the summer to crabs and molluscs in the winter. Baits preferred by anglers include fiddler crabs, pieces of blue crabs, and sea anemones, the latter easily collected from jetty rocks. The best months to catch sheepshead are from December through March, and the rock jetties lining the gulf passes are top spots to find them. Although few anglers target this species, those that do rarely fish for anything else. One of the sheepshead's alternate names is "bait stealer" because they are very adept at doing just that—taking the bait without the angler knowing it. Those experienced at catching them say that "to hook 'em you have to jerk before they bite," while others prefer to keep a tight line and count to three after feeling the first nudge. Even then they are difficult to hook because of the bony mouth and teeth, so strong, sharp hooks are a must. Although gentle with their bite, they

Pinfish, Lagodon rhomboides

are powerful fighters, especially on light tackle. Many jetty anglers prefer the simplicity of long cane or fiberglass poles without reels for catching sheepshead. With large scales, sharp spines, and a very bony rib cage, cleaning a sheepshead is difficult at best and very hard on a knife. Many elect to make a few cuts and skin them with pliers before removing the fillets, avoiding the need to scale and gut them.

The average size of sheepshead is between 1 and 3 pounds, but many are caught each year along the Texas coast weighing between 5 and 8 pounds. The state record is 15 pounds, 4 ounces, and 26.5 inches (lower Laguna Madre, 2002). The U.S. record is 21 pounds, 4 ounces (near New Orleans, 1982).

When commercial fishing in the bays was in full swing in Texas (into the early 1980s), the sheepshead was a target of area netters, especially around Easter. The "strike" netters around Aransas Pass referred to them as "Milton Berle fish" (after the late comedian with the big toothy smile) and said they were the most difficult of all fish to catch by net because they will lie flat on the bottom when a net is pulled over them, thus evading capture.

The flesh of the sheepshead is mild and flavorful, but because of their sharp spines and the difficulty in cleaning them, they are usually passed over as a food fish. Due to the stout ribs and short, thin fillets the yield of meat from one is only about 20 percent of their live weight (about one-half that of other fish).

PINFISH—*Lagodon rhomboides*
Other names: pin perch, sargo, chopa espina, poisson beurre
The common name "pinfish" comes from the presence of numerous spines in both the dorsal and anal

fins. The pinfish is a close relative of the sheepshead, with both having molars on the sides of both jaws and outward-curving incisors on top and bottom giving them a "buck-toothed" appearance. Pinfish range from the southern Atlantic states throughout the Gulf of Mexico. They are of stunning coloration, with blue and yellow horizontal stripes and vague vertical bars on their sides. There is usually a dark spot (less distinct on larger individuals) behind the gill cover. The pinfish is widespread throughout all bays and nearshore gulf waters. It is especially common around structures, including piers and wharfs, and is the dominant species in the grass flats. No fish is more characteristic of the Laguna Madre than the pinfish. It is one of the more famous saltwater "bait stealers," quickly destroying or removing a dead or live shrimp from a fish hook. It has little value as a sport fish or as table fare due to its small size, but its flesh is considered to be quite good when the larger individuals are cleaned and fried whole and thus it qualifies as a saltwater "panfish." The Texas record is 2.8 pounds (upper Laguna Madre, 2000), but the average size is usually 0.25 to 0.5 pound. The largest individuals are generally taken from deeper water such as channels, boat basins, and passes. Growth is relatively slow, with average lengths of 3 and 5 inches for one- and two-year-old individuals, respectively. The offshore spawning period is of long duration, but the greatest influx of juveniles into the grassbeds is in late winter and early spring. The highlight of many youngsters' first fishing trip to the coast is catching dozens of these eager and feisty fighters on small hooks and cane poles. The pinfish is a favorite cut bait among bottom anglers and is one of the best, most available, and hardiest live baits for game fish such as speckled trout, redfish, and tarpon. Care should be taken when removing these wiggly and prickly fish from a hook because an angler can easily be "finned" by their sharp spines.

Drums or "Croakers"—Family Sciaenidae

The "croakers" or drums are a group of noisy, bottom-oriented fish with many consuming a crunchy diet of invertebrates, and they are perhaps the most characteristic group of large northern gulf inshore fishes. They are warm temperate and tropical in distribution. In numbers of marine species, they exceed those of all other families, with 270 species, 34 of which are found in North American waters. In numbers of individuals, or biomass, in the Laguna Madre region they are among the top three species, the others being mullet and the much smaller anchovies. This family is generally characterized by a deeply notched dorsal fin, rounded caudal fin (rather than forked or straight), and one or two spines in the anal fin. Members are generally various shades of brown, black, and silver, the mouth is often set low on the head, and many species possess chin barbels. Internally, they are notable for their multibranched air bladder and huge otoliths (ear stones). Both features presumably relate to the fact that this group produces loud sounds (and can hear them as well), especially during the spawning season, by vibrating muscles attached to the air bladder. The well-developed lateral line (extending into the caudal fin rays) is indicative of their capabilities in murky habitats.

Several species in this family grow to a large size and are important commercial and game fish. The three most important food and sports fishes in the Laguna Madre region are members of this family. Most spawn in the shallow gulf, with the larvae entering the bays where they spend their early lives. Most are carnivorous, fast growing, and short lived, but the larger species are long lived. Although most species are adapted to living over muddy bottoms, a few are common to sandy and rocky habitats. Individuals may move from soft, muddy substrates to harder ones as they grow older. Because they are often inhabitants of turbid estuaries, bays, and even rivers, their elaborate sound-producing and sound-receiving systems undoubtedly assist them in communicating with one another. Members of the croaker family are popular with bay anglers and with gulf surfcasters and pier fishermen and some species are even popular aquarium fishes.

RED DRUM—*Sciaenops ocellatus*
Other names: redfish, channel bass, spot tail, saltwater carp, "rat" red, "bull" red, pescado colorado, poisson rouge

The red drum is one of the most sought-after coastal marine fishes in U.S. waters. They are always available to anglers in the bays, and during the fall the larger, sexually mature adults prowl the surf zone and gulf passes in massive schools. In the Laguna Madre, as along the remainder of the Texas coast, the red drum and the spotted seatrout are the most prized shallow-water game fish. At one time, commercial fishermen took great numbers of red drum in the Laguna Madre with nets and trotlines, but since 1981 the red drum has enjoyed game fish–only status, making it available only to recreational anglers.

The redfish is somewhat similar in shape to its cousin the black drum but is more streamlined and lacks the black bars and barbels. They generally have a coppery hue while in the bays and during the spawning season

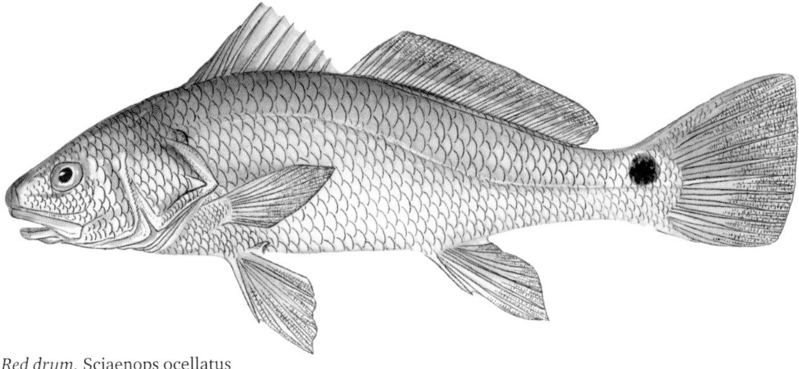

Red drum, Sciaenops ocellatus

but are usually silvery when taken from the surf during the remainder of the year. One of its more distinctive features is the presence of an ocellus or ocelli (one or more black spots) on each side of the upper portion of the caudal peduncle or tail stock. Most of these fish have spots, but on rare occasions individuals will have no spots or have their entire sides covered with them. One often hears that multispotted individuals are hatchery-released fish. While this can be true, wild fish show this trait as well.

Red drum adults begin schooling in the bays in late summer and work their way to the gulf through the passes during the fall period. This migration usually consists of fish that are at least three to five years of age and 26 to 30 inches in length. These fish mature once they reach the gulf and then spawn in the vicinity of the passes on incoming tides during the September to November period. The red drum spawns multiple times in a season and a 3-foot redfish may spawn as many as 20 million eggs during the spawning period. The developing larvae are carried into the bays, where they settle in the seagrass beds (or even on bare or shell bottoms), take advantage of the abundant food supplies, and find refuge from predators. Little movement of red drum occurs except for the adult spawning migration to the gulf. Tagging of red drum and their cousin, the spotted seatrout (*Cynoscion nebulosus*), has generally shown 80 percent of them to move less than five miles from the tagging site, regardless of the length of time between tagging and capture.

Juveniles consume mainly shrimp, but as adults a large portion of their diet is fish and crabs. Young red drum grow very fast, reaching 12 to 14 inches at the end of their first year, 18 to 20 inches after the second year, and 25 to 28 inches by the end of the third year. All are sexually mature at the end of four or five years. Old reports state that "ripe" (ready-to-spawn) adults were sometimes taken in Texas bays, but there are no recorded instances of such catches today.

Red drum individuals are known to reach forty years of age, and the current Texas record is 59.5 pounds, 54.3 inches (Sabine Pass jetty, 2000). The U.S. record is 94.0 pounds for an individual coming from the cooler Atlantic waters off North Carolina in 1984. Fish living in colder waters generally grow much slower than their counterparts at warmer latitudes but live much longer, thus attaining much larger sizes. Those between 3 and 5 pounds make the best table fare. The larger ones (more than 12 to 15 pounds) are rather oily and fishy tasting, but this can be remedied somewhat by trimming the red muscle away from the fillets before cooking.

Red drum, like the black drum, tolerate fluctuations in temperature and salinity quite well. Rarely are they found in abundance in the Laguna Madre when salinities are above 50 ppt, but they regularly invade fresh water. As with the striped mullet (*Mugil cephalus*), it is common to find them many miles upriver from a bay. Killing freezes in the Laguna Madre, like those in 1983 and 1989, claim many red drum, but since the larger individuals are in the gulf at that time of year, most casualties are the smaller, younger individuals. Thus, the spawning gulf population is not affected by these catastrophic events.

Red drum are great shallow-water gamesters on light tackle and also offer the surf angler some real excitement on long rods with their strong and determined fights. They readily take live, dead, and cut bait as well as a variety of artificials, including soft plastics, topwater lures, and the gold spoon, a longtime lure of choice on the bay flats. Sight casting artificials to reds on the flats is one of the most exciting methods of fishing known to anglers. The red drum is also a favorite of fly fishermen who work to make perfect presentations to tailing reds and take great care not to "spook" them in the clear, shallow water. In the Laguna Madre, there are generally always hungry reds to 28 inches ready to take almost anything thrown at them. One of the premier spots on the Texas coast for catching red drum is the Nine Mile Hole east of the Land Cut in the upper Laguna Madre. This isolated shallow-water area is generally "gin" clear and shallow, and during late summer it is filled with enormous schools of large reds "staging" for their spawning migration to the gulf.

TPWD has been stocking the Laguna Madre with fry and fingerling red drum (since 1979) and spotted seatrout (since 1984) primarily to replace those lost to freezes. Most stocking has occurred in the upper lagoon, with more than 600 million red drum and 200 million trout fry having been stocked to date. Although the effect of the stocking enhancement program on recreational catches is only recently being documented, estimates are that a significant number of the red drum landed in the upper Laguna Madre began life in the TPWD hatchery in Flour Bluff, Texas. Additionally, at least nine freshwater lakes in Texas have been stocked with red drum since 1987, with Calaveras Lake, Braunig Lake, and Tradinghouse Creek receiving the lion's share. This stocking program ensures that freshwater and coastal anglers alike can enjoy the thrill of latching into one of the strongest-fighting and best-tasting fish the Texas coast has to offer.

BLACK DRUM—*Pogonias cromis*
Other names: drum, drumfish, "puppy" drum, "bull" drum, tambour

The black drum reaches the greatest size of any member of the economically important drum/croaker family, with some historic reports of individuals reaching weights of 150 pounds. The current Texas record is 81.0 pounds and 51.2 inches (Gulf of Mexico, 1988). It is also the most abundant food fish on the Texas coast but one that is not regularly consumed and is rarely sought out by recreational anglers. In the upper Laguna Madre, 90 percent of all fish species caught by TPWD in spring and fall gill net samples are black drum. Its range extends from the waters of Maine to southern Florida and it is common in the Gulf of Mexico, but its abundance declines rapidly south of the Rio Grande. It is plentiful in all Texas bays but is most abundant from Corpus Christi Bay south through the lower Laguna Madre.

The black drum is easily recognized by the four or five broad vertical bars on each side and the conspicuous barbels on the chin. In larger individuals, the bars are often faded and far less evident. The only other inshore Texas fish with similar vertical markings is the sheepshead, which sports six or seven vertical bars and lacks the chin barbels. The black drum has an excellent sense of smell and nearly all of its food is found on the bottom. Bivalve molluscs, crabs, and shrimp are preferred prey organisms. In some areas, persistent schools are known to cause damage to oyster reefs. They are opportunistic in their feeding behavior, consuming a wide variety of both dead material and living organisms. In the Laguna Madre, the black drum regularly exhibits the practice of "grubbing" in a head-down, tail-up posture on the mud flats and seagrass beds, indiscriminately ingesting bottom material, including pieces of broken shell colonized by a thick film of algae and various microorganisms. When

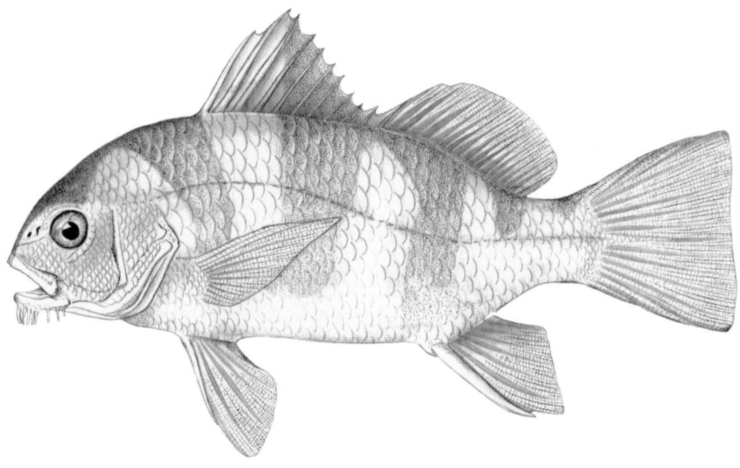

Black drum, Pogonias cromis

the southeast onshore sea breeze increases in strength in the afternoon and moves the water over the algal mats of the wind-tidal flats in the bays, black drum follow the rising water. They "noodle" through the mats searching for food and retreat to deeper water when the wind drops and the water recedes from the flats during the night. It is not easy to determine what they are eating because there is difficulty in separating food taken from the flats from that obtained in deeper water. A unique characteristic of the black drum is the presence of heavy and powerful plate-like pharyngeal teeth in the throat, which allow them to easily crush clams, oysters, crabs, and other shellfish seldom eaten by other fish. Anglers should think twice before sticking their fingers into the throat of a large black drum to remove a fishhook because the fingers are far more easily crushed than an oyster.

Like its cousins, the red drum and spotted seatrout, the black drum is euryhaline, having a broad tolerance to a wide range of salinities. It will travel considerable distances up creeks and rivers and will remain in bays when salinities exceed 80 ppt, which surpasses the salinity tolerance of any other member of the drum family.

While the black drum is also tolerant of a wide range in temperature, it is among the species most commonly killed during severe freezes in the Laguna Madre. However, this likely has as much to do with their great abundance in the lagoon during the winter period as it does with their limited tolerance to low water temperatures.

Spawning occurs in all Texas bays and the gulf from December to June with a peak in February and March. There is generally a second spawning period in May and June that sometimes lasts until November. Like its cousins, the black drum females do not spawn all of their eggs at once but do so incrementally over several months. In the upper Laguna Madre, black drum mature and spawn at a much smaller size than anywhere else on the Texas coast. Males as small as 0.5 pound and females as small as 0.75 pound are capable of spawning. Spawning generally occurs at salinities below 45 ppt, but the upper lagoon is often at or above this level. Both bay- and gulf-spawned black drum larvae utilize the estuarine areas to benefit from an abundant food supply and to seek protection from predators in the seagrass beds. In the Laguna Madre, all sizes and ages of drum can be found throughout the year, but during the summer months the larger individuals are noticeably less abundant, with most apparently having moved to the gulf. Black drum juveniles grow relatively fast and are between 6 and 10 inches at the end of their first year, 12 to 15 inches after the second year, and 17 to 20 inches after the third year of life. Thereafter, this long-lived fish (some determined to be more than fifty years old) grows at a rate of about 2 inches per year. Results from tag returns reveal that the greatest movement of black drum is among those older than four years of age, but individuals of all ages will move considerable distances during times of adverse environmental conditions and sparse food supplies.

Abundant black drum populations in the Laguna Madre (especially in the upper Laguna Madre and Baffin Bay) have long supported an active and highly productive commercial fishery. Black drum commercial landings have always comprised a large portion of the total finfish landings on the Texas coast. As of 2006 these landings were averaging 3 million pounds per year, with 50 percent (1.5 million pounds) coming from the Laguna Madre (and nearly 90 percent of that from Baffin and Alazan Bays alone). Trotlines with circle hooks baited with an array of natural baits such as carrot pieces, oak leaves, crab parts, and even pieces of wooden dowel are used to catch them. Along with the gig, these are the only commercial gears allowed in this coastwide fishery (any nongame species of fish can be taken legally with a gig). In years past, biologists and commercial fishermen told of the thunderous and eerie "booming" or "drumming" sounds produced by ready-to-spawn black drum as they crowded into the shallow upper reaches of Alazan Bay at night to spawn. They reported that the bay bottom and boat hulls would resonate from the deafening courtship sounds produced by thousands of adults pushed up onto the tidal flats with their backs above the water's surface.

Although the black drum is rarely the target of recreational anglers, many are caught incidentally each year by those fishing for redfish and trout. The large, mature "bulls" (almost always females) are regularly caught from piers and boats in the deeper channels and passes as the fish head to the gulf on their spawning migration. While the flesh of the small "puppy" drum is of exceptional quality as table fare, that of the larger individuals is of poor quality and is rarely eaten because of its coarse, oily texture and because the flesh is often full of parasitic "spaghetti" worms (which are known to occur in red drum and spotted seatrout as well). This parasitic worm is actually an intermediate stage of a tapeworm found in sharks. Although unsightly, these worms are otherwise harmless when the fish is cooked. Because a single female may produce up to 5 million eggs per year, it has long been suggested by fishery managers that the larger fish be released. In the upper Laguna Madre, the average black drum caught in February and March is considerably larger than those caught in the warmer months, and individuals weighing 40 to 50 pounds are frequently caught in the Land Cut during the late winter and early spring period. Overall, some of the best fishing for black drum is the February to April period, with shrimp, crabs, squid, and cut fish being prime bait when fishing on the bottom. It is not uncommon to catch black drum on artificial lures at any time of the year, especially on scented soft plastic lures and crab-imitation flies during the spring and summer months. Sight casting for puppy drum is becoming a new angling experience for Laguna Madre anglers.

By the mid-1990s the black drum population had increased by 200 percent coastwide (from the late 1980s) following the banning of gill nets, reduced bag and increased size limits, and no killing freezes since 1997 (no major freezes at all since 1989). With the Laguna Madre having more black drum than any other Texas bay system, the angling outlook is excellent for this seldom targeted recreational species even while it supports a strong commercial fishery.

Spotted Seatrout—*Cynoscion nebulosus*

Other names: speckled trout, speck, weakfish, squeteague, yellowmouth, truite gris, trucha de mar

The spotted seatrout is the most important game fish on the Texas coast because it is the recreational angler's most frequently sought after and most frequently caught sport fish. Bay fishing guides rely on this species

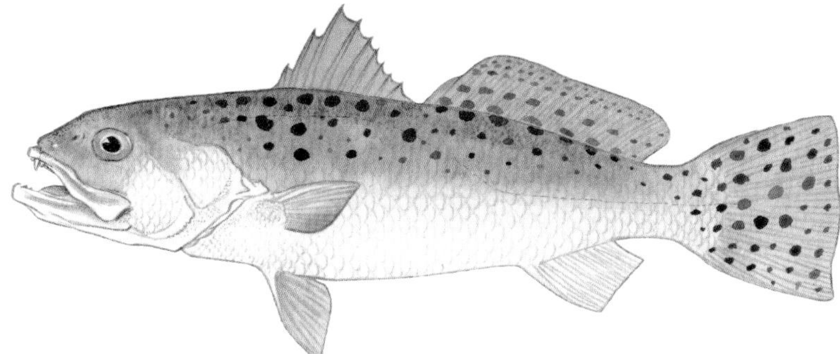

Spotted seatrout, Cynoscion nebulosus

for their livelihood and refer to it as the "bread and butter" and the mainstay of their industry. A great deal is known about the biology of the spotted seatrout because of its overall great economic importance.

The "speck" ranges from the waters of New York to Tampico, Mexico, but is most abundant in the coastal bays of the Gulf of Mexico. It is available to anglers throughout the year in all Texas bays and around gulf passes. They are present in the surf during much of the year. Specks are commonly found in shallow, clear, grassy areas in bays, especially near the edges of sandspots and grassbeds and on the deeper edges (dropoffs) of sand flats. Trout are considered to serve an important role in structuring prey species in grassbed communities in all Texas bay systems.

Except for a winter migration to the gulf by some of the larger trout, the entire life cycle of this species occurs within the bays of Texas. Most of them probably spend their entire lives in an area of no more than a few square miles. Spawning generally begins in April when water temperatures reach 70°F and lasts through October, with a peak between April and June. Females can spawn and redevelop eggs multiple times during this warm weather period. Trout have high fecundity rates and are prolific spawners, with the larger females capable of producing more than 1 million eggs per spawn. Males mature sooner than the females and can be sexually mature at 8 to 10 inches (two years of age). Females generally do not mature before two or three years of age (12 to 14 inches). Spawning is generally at dusk in shallow, grassy areas of bays with moderate to high salinity levels. Although large trout are present in the gulf at all times of the year, there is no indication that they spawn there because the gonads of the adults are rarely fully developed ("ripe") and no fry or fingerlings have been collected in the surf zone at any great distance from the gulf passes. In summer 2007 numerous females taken from the surf zone on Padre Island National Seashore (thirty-plus) were examined, with most showing advanced egg development many miles (thirty-plus) from the nearest pass (Port Mansfield).

Female trout grow faster than the males and to much larger sizes. Few males are longer than 20 inches (generally less than 16 inches). Trout average 12 to 13 inches after the first year and 14 to 16 inches after the second year when they enter the sport fishery (for which the current minimum size is 15 inches). By the end of the third year they range between 16 and 19 inches in length. Trout are known to live at least ten years, with females reported to average 32 inches in length at that age. Interestingly, the state rod and reel record trout from the upper Laguna Madre (1996), weighing 13 pounds, 11 ounces, and 33.1 inches in length, was determined to be only six years of age, demonstrating that growth can be very rapid and highly variable.

The spotted seatrout is truly a beautiful fish, with silvery sides fading to a metallic blue sheen on the upper body. They are covered with small black spots of varying density on the sides and on the dorsal and caudal fins. They have prominent canine teeth (fangs), and in juveniles the interior of the mouth is a deep yellow in color. These top-level, visual predators feed primarily on free-swimming organisms living near the surface and mid-water. Juveniles eat mostly shrimp and small fish, but those 20 inches and longer are almost exclusively piscivorous, with mullet comprising as much as 60 percent of their diet. Trout are gluttonous and aggressive in their feeding habits. It is not uncommon to catch a 22-inch trout with the tail of a 14-inch mullet or trout protruding from its mouth.

Like the red and the black drums, the spotted seatrout is euryhaline and can be found some distance up river mouths and also thriving in highly saline bays. However, they do not tolerate low water temperatures well and are among the more commonly killed fish during freeze events (48°F water temperature persisting for twenty-four hours can be lethal). Younger individuals of warm water species tend to be more tolerant of lethal low water temperatures than are the adults, and in the case of trout the larger (older) individuals are more frequently killed during the freezes. Trout, red drum, and black drum populations can rebound rather quickly following killing freezes, usually reaching their pre-freeze population levels within four to five years. Following the catastrophic freeze of January 1951, in March 1952 TPWD biologists set a gill net near the Land Cut and caught three trout that weighed 15 pounds each. Without a doubt some of the larger trout survived the freeze or were recruited from the lower lagoon or the gulf. During the winter, smaller trout seek out deeper water in the bays and at least some of the larger ones go into the gulf, where they remain until spring. Trips to the Land Cut between February and May for these large, silvery, and aggressive "tiderunners" returning from the gulf produce some of the best fishing action to be experienced in the entire Laguna Madre.

The trout is a very determined and showy fighter, usually thrashing about at the surface, with the smaller ones commonly jumping free of the water when hooked. The larger ones frequently come quickly to the surface trying to dislodge the hook by a violent shaking of the head, showing that gaping yellow mouth.

Live shrimp suspended beneath a popping cork or rattling float is the most common method of fishing for trout, but they readily take soft plastics jigged off the bottom or fished under a float, spoons (silver being a universal favorite), all types and sizes of topwater lures, and even flies and popping bugs offered by fly casters. Any dropoff or depression ("pothole"), however slight, or edges of channels, sandspots, and seagrass beds are prime areas to find them. Baffin Bay contains an estimated ten square miles of "worm rock" (serpulid worm reefs) that offers superb trout fishing year round. The Laguna Madre is also famous for its trout fishing under generator-powered lights at night from piers. While the smaller "school" trout are most often caught at night, many large female ("sow") trout are landed at night as well. Locating trout feeding beneath diving gulls and casting to the upwind side of recently surfacing fish "slicks" are other tactics that can be very productive. These oily, floating slicks (which smell like watermelon or cantaloupe) are often the result of trout (but also drum and catfish) regurgitating after gluttonous feeding. In the Laguna Madre, unlike other bay systems, trout feeding beneath diving gulls does not always mean "school" trout. Often the schools are made up of hungry trout weighing between 8 and 10 pounds each.

The mild and flaky flesh of same-day-caught trout is some of the finest seafood that salt water has to offer. No commercial fishing for this species is allowed in Texas (as with the red drum), so seafood aficionados must catch their own in order to sample the succulent flesh. Current regulations are aimed at increasing the number of large trout available to anglers. Recent work at TAMU–CC shows that released trout show very high survival rates (greater than 90 percent) when handled carefully. Fishing ethics are changing, and many anglers are starting to release most of their fish so they can live to fight another day. A recent phrase says "practice CPR," meaning "catch 'em, photograph 'em, and release 'em!" Some are even promoting a "just keep five" bag limit. This new bag limit in the lower lagoon will be enforced in September 2007. This view is in contrast to times past when most anglers kept all that they could legally take home. The Troutmasters tournaments award bonus points to contestants bringing in their fish alive and subtract points for those weighed in dead. Other tournaments are starting to adopt the "catch-and-release" format, with a few now requiring that all fish entered be digitally photographed on site and released.

The Laguna Madre is definitely the hotspot for large "sow" trout (trophies are generally considered to be those longer than 25 inches and above 5 or 6 pounds). Many anglers consider those more than 30 inches long and caught on artificials to be the ultimate shallow-water trophy, and I fall into the ranks of that group. The Texas state rod and reel record has been held by an upper Laguna Madre trout since 1975. The first record was held for 21 years. A trout caught by a fly caster in the lower Laguna Madre in 2002 (15.6 pounds) currently holds the Texas fly fishing state record. The U.S. record (17 pounds, 7 ounces) was caught in Fort Pierce, Florida (1995), but this record could eventually be broken by a Laguna Madre trout if sufficient time occurs between catastrophic freezes.

The Texas "lagoon" has always produced phenomenal numbers of trout of all sizes. Few fish are more beautiful, and no game fish is as abundant and accessible year round to coastal anglers. Few fish fight more deliberately and make as fine a meal. Without a doubt, the Laguna Madre offers vast and prime habitat and some of the very best fishing opportunities for spotted seatrout anywhere on the gulf coast.

Sand Trout—*Cynoscion arenarius*

Other names: sandy, sand sea trout, white trout, trucha blanca

Of the three marine trout species, the sand trout and the spotted seatrout are found in both the shallow gulf and Texas bays. The center of abundance for the sand trout is in the offshore waters, but adults do occur in fishable quantities in the larger, more open bays and in deeper channels. The "sandy" is far less numerous than the spotted seatrout and also lacks spots but has a pinkish to greenish sheen on its dorsal surface. It ranges from the lower Atlantic states south to Campeche, Mexico. Spawning is during the spring in the gulf or in

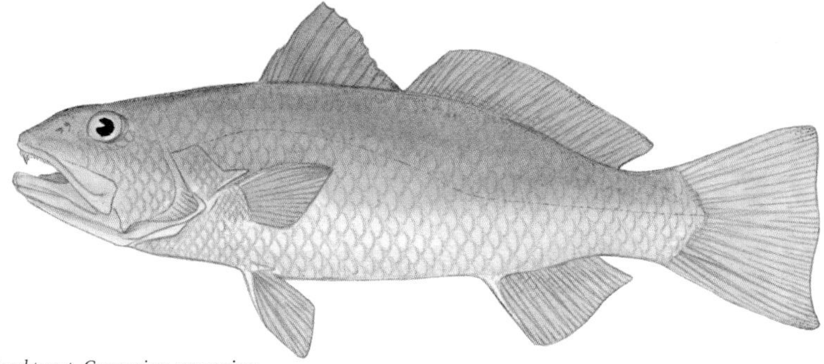

Sand trout, Cynoscion arenarius

the deeper, more saline areas of the bays, and it is thought to migrate to the gulf for the winter when water temperatures drop. An estuarine nursery ground is not obligatory for the species because it can complete its entire life cycle on the offshore shelf. Today sand trout rarely exceed 14 to 16 inches (1 pound), but the state record is 6 pounds, 4 ounces (near Texas City, 1972). Cut fish and whole squid fished on the bottom work well as bait. Sand trout are schooling fish and can at times be caught in fairly large numbers. For this reason they have always been popular with party boat operators in Texas bays. Anglers land more of them in Galveston Bay than on the remainder of the coast. In fact, in Galveston Bay they generally rank second behind the spotted seatrout in total landings. The flesh is quite good but only if iced quickly because it turns mushy soon after death. The flesh does not lend itself to freezing either and must be consumed fresh. Although this species is rarely the target of Texas anglers, it is fairly abundant and available year round in most bays. It is believed that this is a nonspotted relative of the Atlantic weakfish (*C. regalis*) common along the eastern U.S. coast. Even into the 1970s, sand trout in the 3- to 4-pound range were regularly caught in the deeper, muddy areas of Corpus Christi Bay, especially during the fall and winter. Like various other sport fish species, their overall abundance and average size has decreased noticeably over the last twenty to thirty years. Today, a 2-pound fish is considered large.

Silver Trout—*Cynoscion nothus*

Other names: gulf trout

The silver trout is generally found only in the gulf (at depths from 20 to 120 feet), and its range tends to be seaward of the sand trout. It occurs from the Maryland coast south and throughout the gulf and reaches

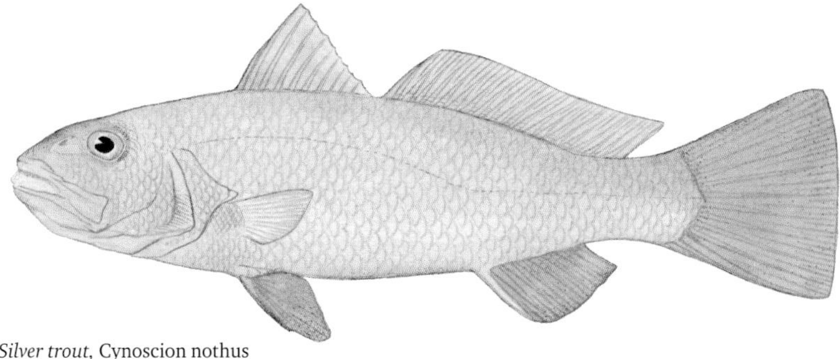

Silver trout, Cynoscion nothus

a slightly larger average size than its close cousin, the sand trout. The two species are best distinguished by counting the rays in the anal fin (the sand trout having eleven and the silver trout having eight or nine). This summer spawner tends to be uniformly silver, lacking any pinkish or yellowish coloration. The current record is 6.9 pounds (Gulf of Mexico, 1992), and the largest individuals tend to be caught on the bottom using cut bait near offshore oil platforms during the late summer and early fall. They will sometimes be taken during the winter in deep bay waters near gulf passes. Like the sand trout, the silver trout has an orange-colored mouth internally, unlike the yellow-colored mouth of the spotted seatrout. While good to eat, its flesh is said to be even "weaker" than that of the sand trout and must be iced and eaten quickly. Like the sand trout, these are regarded as "slow biters but hard pullers."

Silver perch, Bairdiella chrysoura

Silver Perch—*Bairdiella chrysoura*
Other names: yellowtail, sugar trout, poisson blanche

Unlike their common name implies, this fish is not really a perch but rather another member of the drum/croaker family. Although very common and quite abundant in the gulf and bays of Texas, this tasty and scrappy panfish commonly falls into the category of "trash" fish. Because of their small size they generally attract no attention as either food or sport fish. More often, they are caught on small hooks or by cast net and quickly converted into bait by anglers. They make excellent live bait for tarpon and king mackerel when free-lined or fished beneath a float in the gulf. The sides are a brilliant silver and the fins a vivid yellow in color. They tend to feed near the bottom on small fish, crustaceans, and worms. The silver perch or yellowtail occurs in the coastal waters of all five gulf states and into northern Mexico and is especially common along the Texas coast. They spawn in both the bays and the gulf, and their abundance can vary greatly from year to year. The young reside in the grass flats and also in the open muddy bays. Adult silver perch are most abundant in the saltier bays but leave them during the coldest months of the year. The state record is 0.3 pound and 8.0 inches (Galveston Bay, 1987).

Atlantic Croaker—*Micropogonias undulatus*
Other names: croaker, golden croaker, grunter, crocus, rocodina

All members of the family Sciaenidae are quite vocal, especially the males during the spawning season. These fish vibrate their inflated air bladders, producing sounds similar to those made when a tightly inflated balloon is rubbed. Of all the species, the Atlantic croaker is likely the most vociferous of them all.

The Atlantic croaker is similar in

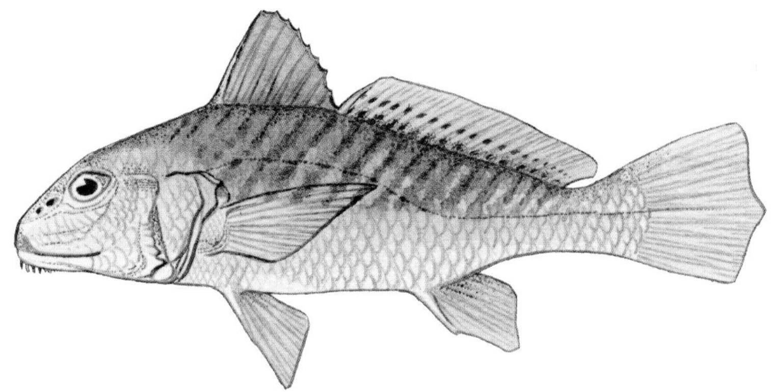

Atlantic croaker, Micropogonias undulatus

shape to the red drum and has smaller barbels on the chin than the black drum. The presence of "whiskers" on any fish indicates its bottom-feeding behavior, and this species has a preference for crustaceans, shellfish, and worms. It is most commonly confused with the spot croaker (*Leiostomus xanthurus*) but is less robust in body shape and lacks the prominent shoulder spot. Across the middle of the body it has short, vertical but irregular brown streaks formed from spots on the scales. The juveniles are silvery in color but take on a brassy yellow color as adults (thus the alternate name golden croaker). This is most pronounced in the larger individuals.

The Atlantic croaker ranges from the waters of Massachusetts south throughout the Gulf of Mexico to the Yucatan Peninsula. They are generally found over sandy, shelly bottoms in the bays and surf zone and are perhaps the most common bottom-dwelling estuarine species in Texas waters. The croaker generally averages 1 pound or less, but the Texas record is 5.5 pounds and 29.0 inches (Gulf of Mexico, 2002).

The croaker is by far the most commonly sought after panfish on the Texas coast, with most taken by anglers in Galveston Bay. They are available year round in all bays, but most are caught from gulf piers and jetties during October and November when the adults are leaving the bays for the gulf to spawn. The spawning period may extend into February before the adults return to the bays. The flesh is mild and fine grained and is of excellent quality.

It is a common prey species for numerous predatory fish, and many are taken "intentionally" (as a baitfish to sell) and "incidentally" (by the bay and gulf shrimp fleets as by-catch) each year. As a result, it is rare to find individuals more than three years of age. As recently as the 1970s, individuals in excess of four or five years of age were common along the Texas coast. From coastal Karankawa habitation sites, it is known that the Atlantic croaker was widely utilized as a food source and that it grew to much larger sizes than seen today.

Until the late 1970s, the annual golden croaker run was a much-anticipated and highly predictable event in the Port Aransas area, and many anglers would target the adults during their fall migration to the gulf. I witnessed perhaps the last major fall run of Atlantic croaker in 1978 at the south jetty in Port Aransas. Late on a November afternoon, thousands upon thousands of large adults were nervously milling around the jetties, most weighing between 2 and 3 pounds, but many were considerably larger (4 to 5 pounds). They were so concentrated around the edges of the rocks in both the channel and on the gulf side that many were being stranded on the lower pink granite rocks with each wave surge. The golden "grunting" and "croaking" fish had bellies that were swollen with eggs and milt (sperm). To my knowledge this phenomenon has not been observed to this degree at Port Aransas since then. It is doubtful that this once common fall event is seen anywhere on the Texas coast today. The species has a long spawning period and there may be some spawning during every month of the year. The postlarval croaker are most abundant from November to January in the surf zone. Young croakers are abundant in the bays at precisely the times when the populations of large predatory fishes are at their lowest level of the year.

Since the mid-1990s the use of croakers as live bait has grown dramatically, especially along the southern coast of Texas. TPWD landings data show the croaker to be a very effective natural bait. Demand for them is high, and most bait stands offer them for sale regularly (usually seven to eight dollars per dozen but as much as twelve dollars per dozen during times of short supply or when there are few available of the desired bait size). Anglers using them (dubbed "croaker soakers") swear by them as a bait and believe that trout cannot resist the distress call the croaker emits when hooked and cast into the water. There is much controversy among anglers (especially from those who use only artificials) over the "ethics" and "conservation" aspects of using croaker as bait. Without a doubt they are effective, and many fish (especially trout) are caught using them. The Port Mansfield Chamber of Commerce recently banned the use of croaker as a live bait in their annual tournament because many believe they offer an unfair advantage to those using them. According to the growing anti-croaker contingency, the "croaker wars" are just beginning. It will be interesting to see over time how the croaker fares as a baitfish along the Texas coast.

SPOT—*Leiostomus xanthurus*
Other names: spot croaker, Lafayette
The spot is another of the so-called "trash fish" along the Texas coast, mainly because of its small size. Along the Atlantic coast, where it grows to a considerably larger size, it is especially popular as both a sport and commercial species. The spot ranges from Cape Cod south to the Rio Grande. It is commonly confused with the Atlantic croaker, but closer inspection reveals a more blunt snout, a deeper body profile, no chin barbels, a forked caudal fin, and a distinct shoulder spot just behind the gill cover. Although rare in grassbeds, it is abundant in all Texas bays during the warmer months and in the surf where it apparently spawns during the fall. The presence of spot postlarvae in

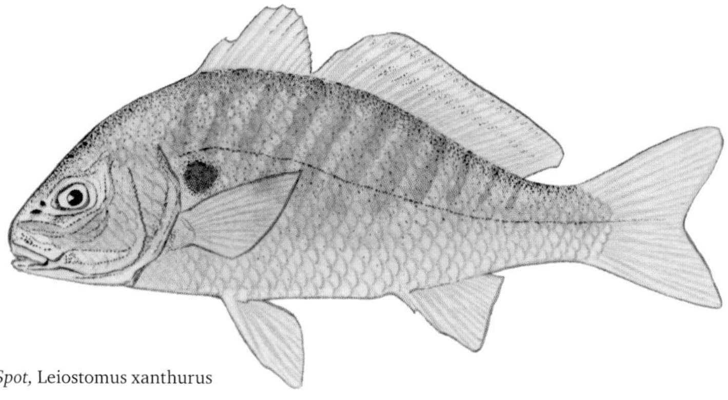

Spot, Leiostomus xanthurus

the surf overlaps that of the croaker, but its peak occurrence is later in the season. It is an extremely abundant species, and in total biomass in Texas bays and estuaries the spot ranks very high overall. Like juvenile Atlantic croakers, spots are taken incidentally in great numbers as by-catch by the shrimp fleet and discarded. Unlike the Atlantic croaker, they hold little value as a live baitfish because they are quite fragile and far less hardy. In fact, few are alive when removed from shrimp trawls even after tows of short duration. Like the Atlantic croaker, the spot has a short life span and very few are thought to live beyond one year of age.

Southern Kingfish—*Menticirrhus americanus*

Other names: whiting, sea mullet

Two of the three kingfish species that inhabit the Laguna Madre region range from Chesapeake Bay south to Texas. The southern kingfish is silver-gray to brown in color and is easily distinguished by the dark bars or mottled coloration on the back and sides. All three species have a single thick barbel at the tip of the lower jaw that, at times, may be minute and easily overlooked. Both the northern kingfish and gulf kingfish are more common in the surf zone, but the southern kingfish is commonly found in the deeper Texas bays. This species has a nearly flat belly and is somewhat triangular in cross section when viewed head on. Like some of its cousins, it has an inferior (shorter) lower jaw and feeds on or near the bottom, preferring small invertebrates. Rarely are kingfish targeted by bay anglers. The average size is usually less than 1 pound, but the state record is 3.6 pounds (Gulf of Mexico, 1972).

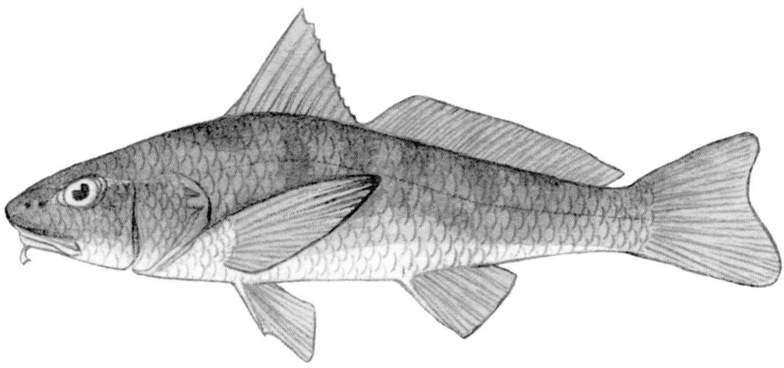

Southern kingfish, Menticirrhus americanus

Gulf Kingfish—*Menticirrhus littoralis*

Other names: gulf whiting

Although this species occasionally enters the bays, it is primarily a resident of the gulf, especially the surf zone, where it is one of the four dominant species present. It has the most restricted habitat requirement of any of its family members present on the Texas coast. It is mostly silver in color, lacks the mottled pattern on the sides, and is the most abundant of the three species of kingfish or whiting. All three species make excellent table fare and can be caught in great numbers, especially during the summer months. Because of their great availability, many campers on gulf beaches have utilized this whiting as a staple for both the table and as fish bait. It has been reported to have an iodine-like flavor, but I have never noticed this despite having eaten it many times over the years. Kingfish are the classic "bait stealers" in the surf zone, with one

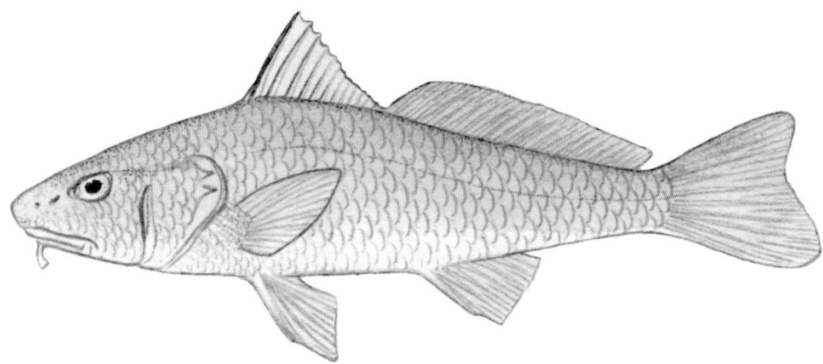

Gulf kingfish, Menticirrhus littoralis

after another hitting the bait as it rolls along the bottom. For this reason, small jigs tipped with strips of cut fish and Fish Bites® (canvas impregnated with fish scent) are good, durable choices for bait. Because of their small size, whiting get little respect as sport fish. However, they are solid fighters on light tackle and are readily available to anglers during most of the year. Many fishless forays to the gulf beach are avoided because of the cooperative whitings (kingfish). The state record for the gulf kingfish is 2.4 pounds (Gulf of Mexico, 1995).

NORTHERN KINGFISH—*Menticirrhus saxatilis*

This is a less common but characteristic species best known from the inshore shelf and shallow coastal waters. It is dusky gray above and sometimes blackish. The sides and back have distinct dark oblique bars, with a diagonal bar on the neck forming a V-shaped pattern with the first bar on the body. The longest dorsal fin spine on the adults reaches well beyond the beginning of the second dorsal fin. This species ranges from Cape Cod to Florida and throughout the Gulf of Mexico and may grow to 12 inches in length.

BANDED DRUM—*Larimus fasciatus*

This small drum occurs mainly in the shallow gulf and rarely enters the bays. It is more common off Louisiana but ranges from the waters of Massachusetts to northern Mexico. The body coloration is brownish above, becoming pale below, and seven to nine conspicuous vertical black bands are present on the sides. The body shape is fairly deep, and the mouth is very oblique and angled upward. The fins are generally yellowish in color. It has no commercial value, and larger individuals can be a nuisance to anglers in some areas. It may attain 10 inches in length.

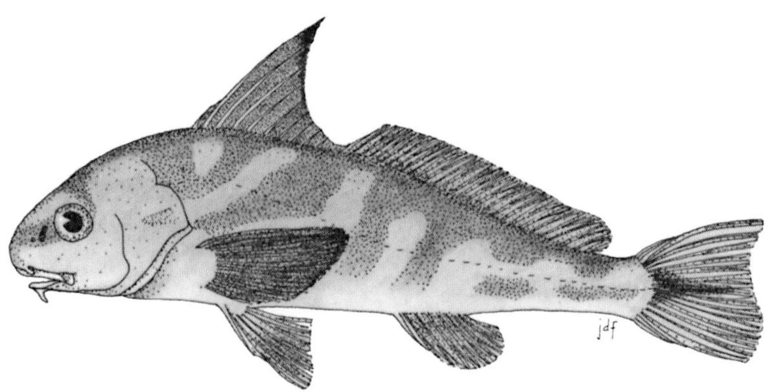

Northern kingfish, Menticirrhus saxatilis. *Illustration by Janice D. Fechhelm*

Banded drum, Larimus fasciatus. *Illustration by Janice D. Fechhelm*

Mullets—Family Mugilidae

The mullets are a large family of fairly similar fishes. They are small to medium-sized and live in coastal waters and estuaries and warm temperate to tropical regions of the world. The eighty species of mullet (two in the Gulf of Mexico) are readily recognizable by their rather thick but sleek bodies, forked tails, hard-angled mouths, large cycloid (round and smooth) or moderately ctenoid scales, low-set pelvic fins, and two widely separated dorsal fins. The streamlined body shape is advantageous in helping them to avoid the wide range of predators that attack their schools as they move through shallow inshore waters and to speed them along on their spawning migrations. Many mullet species have adipose eyelids. The body is rounded (in cross section) in front and compressed toward the rear, and the mouth is small, terminal, and triangular in shape.

Adult mullets usually live in small groups or schools. Most show a tolerance or even an affinity for fresh water, and some species may regularly enter or spend considerable parts of their life cycles in inland lakes or rivers. Some live almost exclusively in fresh water. Mullets feed largely on organic detritus (an array of live and dead material on the bottom) and small algal cells they capture while swimming at an angle to the bottom, running their mouths along and through the sediment. They can disturb large volumes of bottom material while feeding, and their "trails" can be visible from some distance. They also graze vegetation and surface film from hard substrates. Larger particles are retained by their fine gill rakers and pulverized by their gizzard-like stomachs. Digestion takes place in an extraordinarily long intestine (five to eight times the body length), which is necessary because much of the

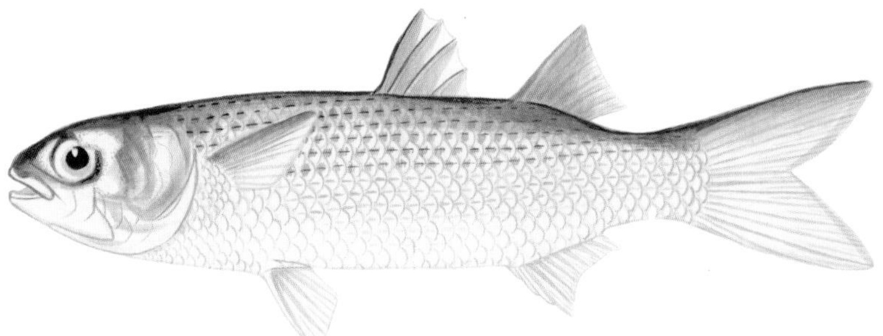

Striped mullet, Mugil cephalus

ingested material is poorly digestible and requires a long retention time in the gut. Mullets are cultured for food in Africa, the Middle East, and much of the Orient and are marketed east, but not west, of the Mississippi Delta. They are important food fishes because they are highly abundant and very accessible.

Striped Mullet—*Mugil cephalus*
Other names: black mullet, Biloxi bacon, lisa pardete

Most anglers know that in order to locate game fish you need to first "find the baitfish," and jumping, surface-schooling mullet are the most frequently observed fish in coastal waters. Although there are two species of mullet in Texas waters, the striped mullet is far more abundant and occurs worldwide between 42° N and 42° S latitude in warm temperate and subtropical waters. This mullet is one of the most abundant fishes along the Atlantic and gulf coasts and ranks first in fish biomass (total weight) in the Laguna Madre. Because of this, the lagoon has long been termed a "mullet-dominated" bay. It has been noted that this mullet is rivaled in numbers, but not biomass, by the sheepshead minnow (*Cyprinodon variegatus*) in the Laguna Madre.

The body of the striped mullet is silvery, the back is bluish, and the sides have dark longitudinal stripes. There is a large bluish spot at the base of the pectoral fin, and the dorsal and anal fins lack scales. The pigment in the eye is more dispersed and more brownish than that of the white mullet (*M. curema*). The striped mullet is well adapted to the wide range in temperature and salinity common to coastal environments, tolerating salinities from fresh to greater than 80 ppt (the latter being nearly three times the salinity of the Gulf of Mexico). In the past, mullet were the last large fish to succumb as salinities rose to hypersaline levels in the Laguna Madre. They commonly enter river mouths and creeks and have been found inland as far as one hundred miles. However, mullet are especially sensitive to cold temperatures, and following severe winter freezes the striped mullet has accounted for nearly one-third of all marine fishes killed on the Texas coast. The mullet is also one of the fishes most affected by red tides. The striped mullet is widely distributed throughout Texas bays during the warmer months, with the smaller individuals moving to deeper water and concentrating in channels and boat basins during the winter. The sexually mature adults begin leaving the bays in September and head to the gulf to spawn. Extensive floating schools or "rafts" of mullet that can extend for many miles comprise untold hundreds of thousands of individuals. These can be seen in the gulf passes and in the surf zone during the fall migrations. The channel at Port Aransas can appear to be filled from bank to bank with mullet. When they are migrating, I refer to them as "chirping" mullet because of their whimsical behavior of rhythmically opening and closing their mouths in unison at the water's surface. After assembling in the surf zone and nearshore gulf, they travel six to twenty miles offshore to spawn during the period from October to March, with a peak in November and December. Each female produces 0.5 to 2.5 million eggs, with the developing larvae transported inshore through gulf passes by the prevailing winds, currents, and tides and into the nurseries of the back bays.

The larvae are carnivorous, but the juveniles and adults are primarily herbivores and opportunistic omnivores, with their primary food sources being detritus and phytoplankton. All ages have the added ability to filter microscopic plankton from the water using the comb-like rakers on the gills. Mullet are one of the few fishes to have a true gizzard, which is needed to pulverize and digest cellulose in the plant matter they consume. By January, small mullet (about 1 inch in length) are abundant in all Texas bays and quickly adopt the behavior, seen in all ages and sizes, of schooling and milling around the margins of bays. Adults that survive and don't become dinner for gulf predators return to the bays in the spring. Mullet are relatively fast growing, reaching 4 to 6 inches after the first year. They become sexually mature at two or three years of age (8 to 12 inches) and live another two or three years, repeating the annual migration to and from the gulf each fall.

Mullet are economically important to humans and serve as valuable forage for a wide variety of aquatic predators. They can be purchased fresh or frozen from most bait and tackle shops and are easily captured with a cast net. Anglers use them as dead bait or fish them live. Individuals in the 4- to 6-inch range are referred to as "finger" mullet and are fished whole or cut into chunks for bottom fishing. Larger mullet are generally always used as cut bait. Those 8 to 12 inches long are called "pony" mullet, while the largest ones are known as "horse" mullet. The average adult size is usually 1 pound or less, but individuals weighing 4 to 5 pounds are not uncommon in Texas waters. I photographed a 10-pound mullet taken from a cooling lake off the upper Laguna Madre in the late 1970s. The current Texas record is 7.2 pounds, 24.9 inches (lower Laguna Madre, 1999).

In Texas, mullet are rarely consumed as table fare, as the more murky, turbid waters tend to impart a muddy flavor to the somewhat oily flesh. However, in Florida mullet are smoked and fried and the roe (eggs) is considered a true delicacy, the latter fetching four to five dollars per pound. In the 1980s, a commercial fishing operation applied for permits to harvest mullet in the Port Aransas area primarily for export. TPWD was quick to deny the application based on the vast numbers of mullet that could easily and quickly be netted while making their fall migration to the gulf and because of their great overall value to the bays of Texas. TPWD regulations prevent anyone from possessing mullet more than 12 inches in length during the period from October to January.

Many marine fish exploit the striped mullet regularly as a primary food source. Gut analysis of juvenile and adult southern flounder, spotted seatrout, and red drum show the mullet to be a large portion of their diets, and mullet comprise as much as 80 percent of the diet of Atlantic bottlenose dolphins; various water birds also eat the smaller mullet with great regularity. Mullet are considered to be a major pathway in the flow of energy in coastal bays because they feed near the bottom of the food web, are so abundant, and are consumed by such a wide variety of aquatic predators. It might be argued that the great abundance of red drum and large "sow" trout in the Laguna Madre is largely attributable to the endless availability of striped mullet.

WHITE OR SILVER MULLET—*Mugil curema*

Other names: lisa blanca

The white or silver mullet is difficult to distinguish from the striped mullet, but it is far less common on the Texas coast. The white mullet is generally silvery in color with less distinct or no stripes on the sides and often has a golden spot on the gill cover. The caudal fin is generally edged in black. The second (soft) dorsal and anal fins of the white mullet are covered in dense scales, whereas those fins are without scales on their close cousin. The white mullet tends to be more tropical in its distribution and is not well suited to the temperature and salinity fluctua-

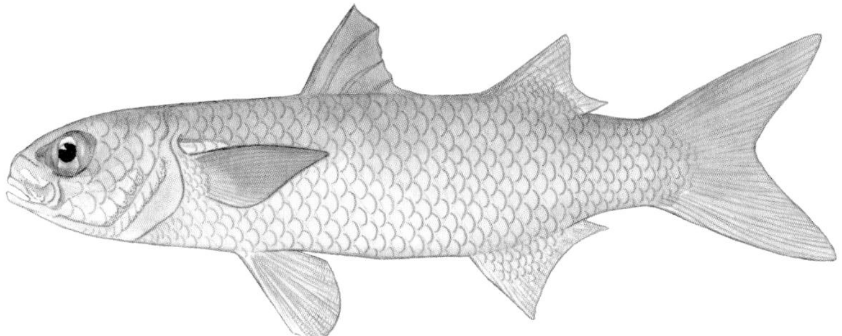

White or silver mullet, Mugil curema

tions common in Texas bays. Thus the white mullet is more common in the Gulf of Mexico and around its passes. However, it can occasionally be found in tidal ponds and inlets on the mainland shore of the Laguna Madre. The spawning season appears to be during the spring and early summer in the gulf. Larval stages have been taken as far offshore as the 55-fathom (330 feet) contour. The adult white mullet rarely grows as large as the striped mullet. In Florida the white mullet is a highly prized food fish; because of its preference for cleaner water it has a clean and less muddy-tasting flesh than the striped mullet.

Stargazers—Family Uranoscopidae

Stargazers lurk along the bottom and lie partially buried in the sediment as they wait to ambush unsuspecting prey. About thirty species are known, all occurring in the coastal waters of tropical and temperate latitudes. They are medium-sized, burrowing, heavy-bodied marine fishes with electric organs capable of delivering a mild shock. Their eyes are set directly on top of the head. Juvenile stargazers have considerably larger heads relative to body size than do adults and have several projecting bones on the skull. Two species of stargazers are found inside the 100-fathom (600 feet) curve in the Gulf of Mexico.

Stargazers have venomous spines on the edges of the gill covers, and specialized glands at their bases can deliver venom through grooves in the spine to inflict painful injuries to swimmers and waders. Some species have on the floor of the nearly vertical mouth a worm-like "lure" that can be twitched to attract prey.

Southern Stargazer—*Astroscopus y-graecum*

This species has electric organs located on a naked area on top of the head. These organs are derived from

Southern stargazer, Astroscopus y-graecum

muscles behind the eyes capable of discharging 50 volts. Although of low amperage, the electric charge is likely delivered only for defensive purposes. This species is present from the Carolina coasts throughout the gulf and south to northern Brazil. The top of the head and body are dark olive-brown with uniformly distributed large white spots of equal size. Two large blackish areas are present in the soft (second) dorsal fin, and the caudal fin has three horizontal blackish brown streaks. The body is fully scaled, and a fleshy keel, or ridge, extends down the center of the belly. The bones on top of the head form a Y shape. The southern stargazer's habits guarantee a certain degree of seclusion, and thus it should not be considered a rare species. This species has been recorded from the Laguna Madre and Baffin Bay. The state record for the southern stargazer is 3.3 pounds, 15.8 inches (Gulf of Mexico, 1993).

Combtooth Blennies and Scaleless Blennies—Family Blenniidae

Blennies are small fishes that live in and around rocks, reefs, and other hard substrates. Six families contain nearly 700 species, and this family alone comprises 345 species. Blennies tend to be secretive in their behavior but more outgoing when feeding, with some consuming invertebrates, such as tiny crustaceans, while others scrape off and consume algae. They are ferociously territorial, and watching their bluffs and antics in an aquarium can be most entertaining. Blennies are common in the intertidal zone, and one group is known to leap from one tide pool to another when alarmed. They are an important part of the rocky inshore marine fauna in much of the world, especially in tropical and subtropical regions. Many species have pelagic larvae, enabling them to quickly and effectively colonize disturbed coastlines. They are commonly found at or near the water's edge along rocky shorelines, shelly areas, and jetties, but some prefer seagrass beds. Blennies are hole dwellers, frequently nesting in cans, oyster shells, or in empty burrows. Their "combtooth" common name stems from the numerous closely packed teeth present in the jaws, although a few species also possess dagger-like teeth on each side of the lower jaw. Most are rather elongate and may be brown to olive in color and variously barred or mottled, although some are brightly colored. Gobies have blunt heads, which are usually topped by fleshy knobs (cirri), and their bodies are scaleless. The pelvic fins, each with only two to four visible rays, are situated in front of the pectoral fins.

Molly Miller—*Scartella cristata*

This species is a very common blenny on South Texas and western Florida jetties. In Texas, they are usually a plain brownish gray to purple with reddish branched cirri above the eyes. Pearly white spots may be present on the body, and the caudal fin is usually barred. This species is largely herbivorous. Their average size is 4 inches.

Striped Blenny—*Chasmodes bosquianus*

This is a common blenny species, especially on grass flats, among clumps of oysters, on mangrove roots, and along seawalls. The striped blenny ranges from the waters of New York to the entire gulf, from Pensacola to Veracruz, Mexico. The mouth is large and the teeth in the lower jaw are slender, pointed, and recurved. The snout is rather long and pointed, and the head lacks cirri. Stripes are present on the sides and on the dorsal and anal fins. The body is brown with dark wavy lines. They are often mottled or spotted, which allows them to blend well with their surroundings.

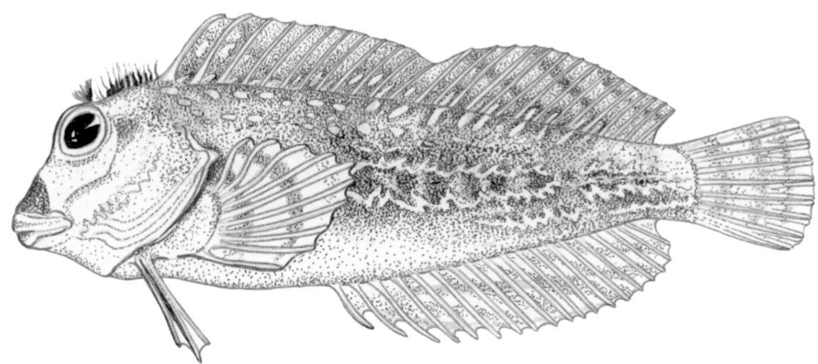

Molly miller, Scartella cristata

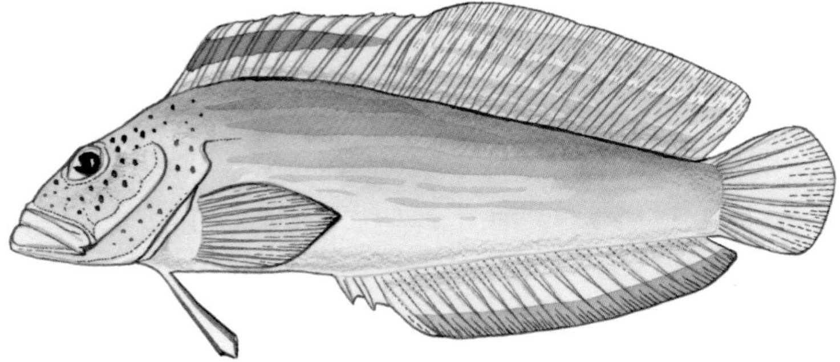

Striped blenny, Chasmodes bosquianus

The females are variously mottled, and the anterior portion of the dorsal fin is blue in the males. The striped blenny has been recorded from both the lower lagoon near Port Isabel and from the upper lagoon. The average size is 4 to 6 inches.

CRESTED BLENNY—*Hypleurochilus geminatus*
This is the most common blenny on the southern Texas jetties and oil platforms and in the shallow gulf and the saltier bays. Males are dark brown with a faint pattern of blotches. The females and young have bands or patches on the body and four square-shaped spots with white centers. A supraorbital (above the eyes) cirrus is present and is long in males but short in females; there is usually a cluster of four or five small cirri at the base of the primary cirrus. The crested blenny may grow to a length of 4 inches.

FEATHER BLENNY—*Hypsoblennius hentz*
Feather blennies are often found on oyster reefs and along rocky shores but seem to prefer a softer, muddy-bottomed habitat in higher salinity

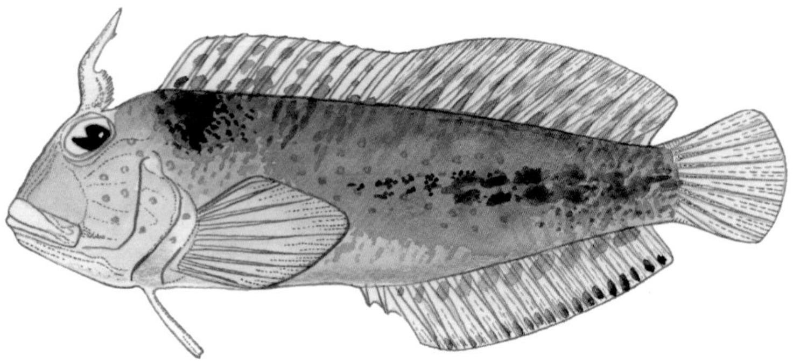

Crested blenny, Hypleurochilus geminatus

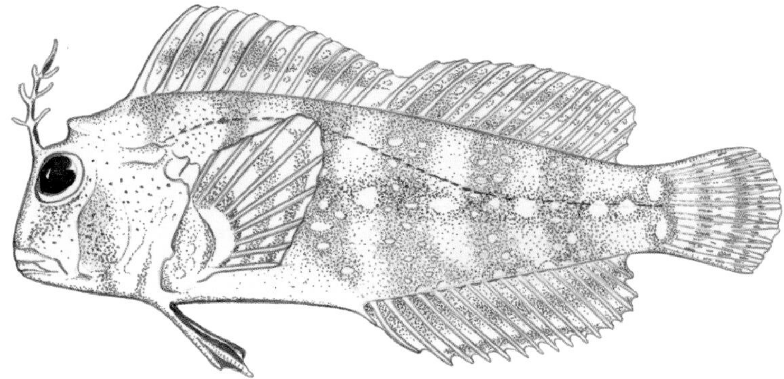

Feather blenny, Hypsoblennius hentz

bays. The prominent cirri above the eyes have numerous short side branches. The body is usually yellowish brown above and whitish below, with many dark brown spots and five or six oblique dark bars. It may reach 4 inches in length.

Gobies—Family Gobiidae

Gobies are generally small, secretive fishes that are very common in certain habitats; many are restricted to specific areas. Although common, they either remain hidden or have such effective protective coloration that the average coastal resident rarely observes them. They are usually inactive, resting on the bottom until disturbed, then quickly darting for cover. They often participate in symbiotic relationships with other animals (hosts), such as serving as "cleaners" that remove parasites from other fishes. This is perhaps the largest family of fishes, with more than two thousand species, including representatives from all warm seas, some tropical fresh waters, and a few temperate marine and estuarine localities. Gobies are generally less than 4 inches long, and some are among the smallest of all vertebrates. They are a readily recognizable group. Members are characterized by a small, round sucking disk created by the pelvic fins, two dorsal fins, a blunt head with large eyes, and a rounded caudal fin. Most species are camouflaged to match their backgrounds. The fins of the males are often strikingly flashy during the breeding season, and during the incubation period they guard the nest. Reef gobies are usually more colorful than their estuarine relatives. A few lack any color, being transparent, and some are important as aquarium fishes.

Their success seems to be best explained by their remarkable ability to adapt to habitats or microhabitats that most other fishes find inaccessible, such as cracks and crevices in coral reefs, inside large sponges, in the burrows of certain invertebrates (e.g., shrimp), mud flats, mangrove swamps, fresh water on oceanic islands, and inland seas and estuaries. On tidal flats, some gobies manage to survive by breathing air and "walking" across mud bottoms.

FRILLFIN GOBY—*Bathygobius soporator*

This tropical species has been reported from the Port Aransas jetties and from Port Isabel in the lower Laguna Madre. It ranges from the North Carolina coast to Florida and throughout the Gulf of Mexico, with subspecies throughout the Caribbean. It can be expected in any rocky area and along the water's edge, especially along the South Texas coast. The body is brown with darker bars and blotches, the back is often crossed by four or five black saddles, and the fins are densely spotted with brown. The upper three to five pectoral fin rays are filamentous and free from the membrane connecting the remainder of the fin rays. It grows to a length of about 3 inches.

CODE GOBY—*Gobiosoma robustum*

The code goby is a characteristic and abundant fish in the submerged grassbeds of the South Texas coast. It ranges from Chesapeake Bay to Florida, through the Gulf of Mexico to the Yucatan Peninsula. It has many irregular and interconnected dark bands or series of black dots and dashes along the sides, with pale spots that make the pattern appear somewhat chainlike. They prefer seagrass beds (turtle grass and shoal grass) and algal mats, especially in shallow, protected areas of moderately high salinity. The code goby grows to 2 inches in length.

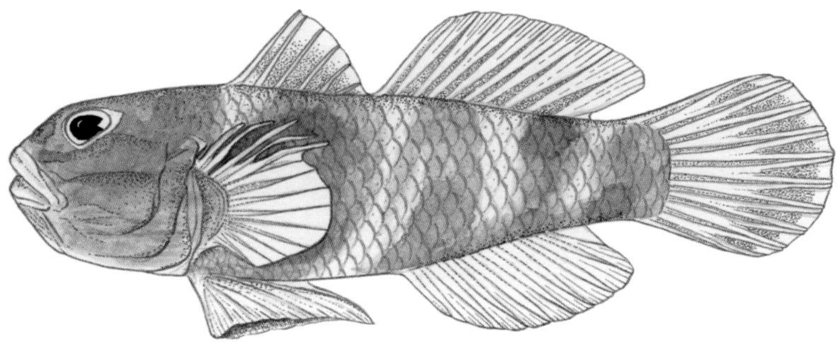

Frillfin goby, Bathygobius soporator

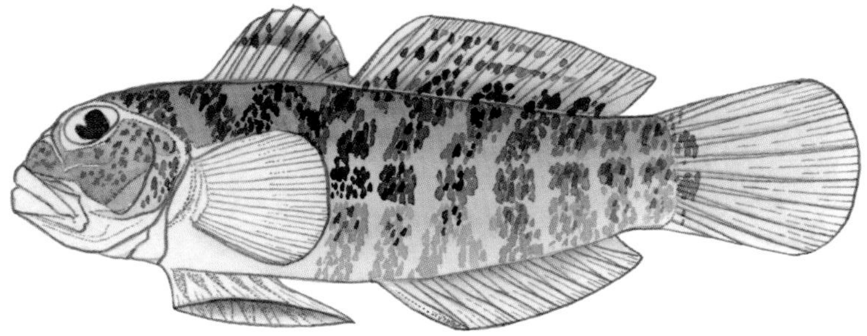

Code goby, Gobiosoma robustum

NAKED GOBY—*Gobiosoma bosc*
The naked goby is normally associated with hard estuarine substrates such as oyster reefs, which hide this species so well that it is not usually seen. Large populations sometimes develop in marsh ponds. It has been recorded from a number of sites in Baffin Bay and the remaining Laguna Madre, but it is far less common than the code goby. It is found from Long Island Sound southward and throughout the Gulf of Mexico to the Bay of Campeche, Mexico. The unscaled body has nine to eleven dark brown vertical bars separated by narrow light-colored areas. They may grow to 2.5 inches.

GREEN GOBY—*Microgobius thalassinus*
The green goby ranges from Chesapeake Bay to the Texas coast at Corpus Christi. This species is uniformly a dusky greenish or bluish with metallic specks, especially on the head. Females have a few prominent dark spots on the tip of the first dorsal fin, and the males have a row of small black spots near the margin of the anal fin. This goby is considered to be rare in the Laguna Madre region and

Naked goby, Gobiosoma bosc

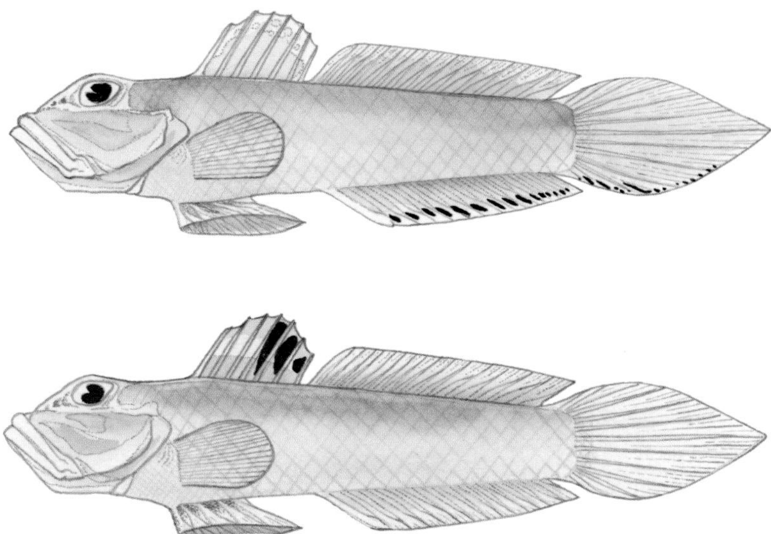

Green goby (male, top, and female, bottom), Microgobius thalassinus

is common nowhere, probably because of its habitat preference. They are known to live within sponges and in muddy tide pools. It has been collected sporadically in the grass flats in both the upper and lower lagoons. The green goby may reach 2.5 inches in length.

LYRE GOBY—*Evorthodus lyricus*

This species is found from Chesapeake Bay to the Gulf of Mexico and in the West Indies. The body color is tan or gray with five or six irregular, narrow dark vertical bars. The caudal fin has two distinctive dark square blotches; it is irregularly banded on

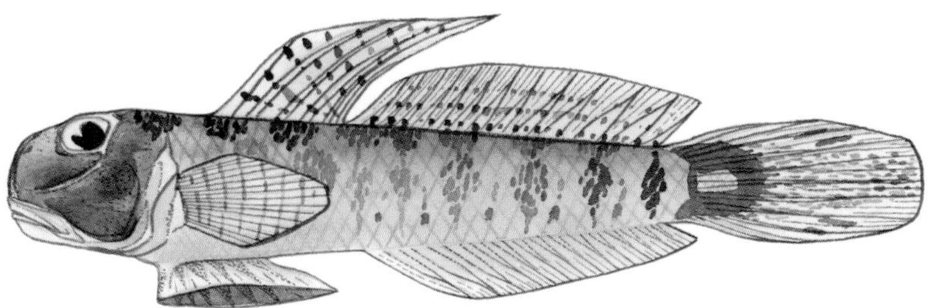

Lyre goby, Evorthodus lyricus

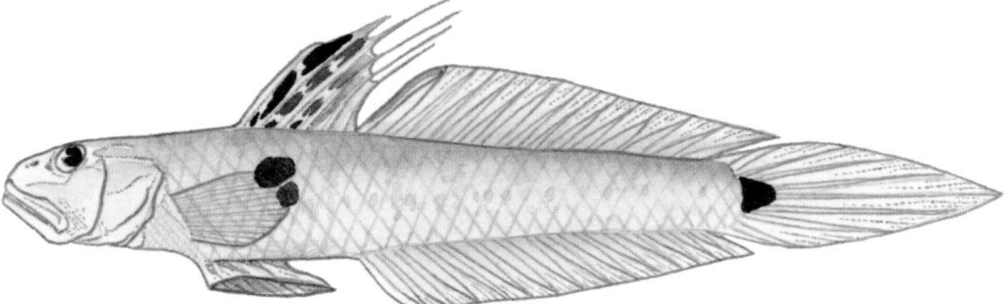

Sharptail goby, Gobionellus hastatus

the females and is striped with pink in the males. This goby is found mainly in the muddy backwaters of bays and estuaries, often in areas of poor water quality and high turbidity. It has been reported from the extreme northern and southern ends of the Laguna Madre. It grows to 3.5 inches.

SHARPTAIL GOBY—*Gobionellus hastatus*

This goby ranges from the inland bays to at least the 30-fathom (180 feet) contour in the gulf. The body is relatively elongate with dark brown oval spots above the pectoral fins. It has been reported from Corpus Christi Bay, Cayo del Oso, and the upper Laguna Madre. It may reach 9 inches in length.

DARTER GOBY—*Ctenogobius boleosoma*

This fish has a blackish oval spot above the base of the pectoral fins and a large black spot on the base of the caudal fin. The body is tan with four or five narrow, longitudinal bars and distinct V-shaped markings on the upper portion of the body. Males have fins that may be orange colored on the upper half with a yellow stripe below. Darter gobies are the most widespread of the gobies, found in quiet waters of bays and estuaries, in grassy and muddy areas, but generally not on reefs. It is considered to

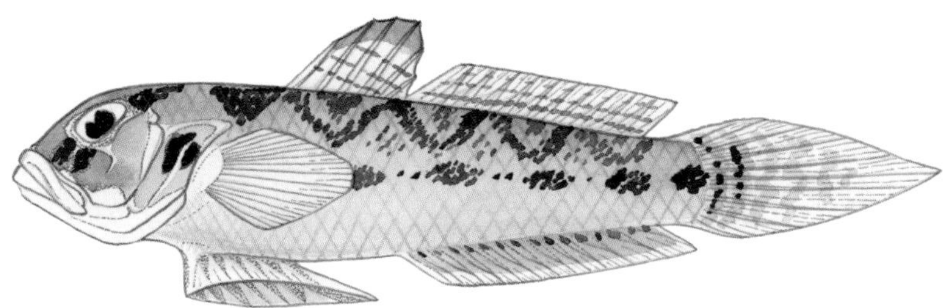

Darter goby, Ctenogobius boleosoma

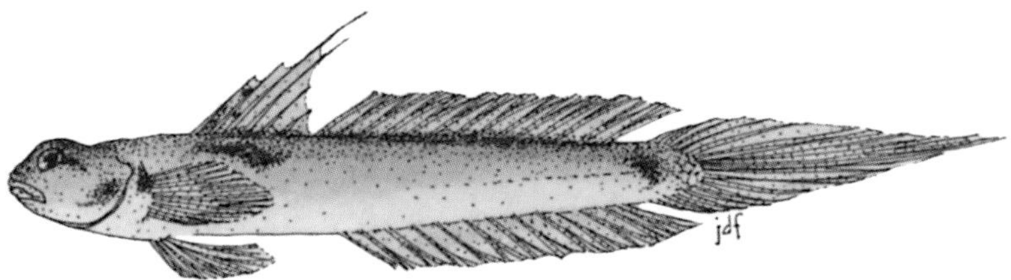

Highfin goby, Gobionellus oceanicus. *Illustration by Janice D. Fechhelm*

be common in the Laguna Madre, except during hypersaline conditions. This species may reach a length of 3 inches.

HIGHFIN GOBY—*Gobionellus oceanicus*
This large goby is a wide-ranging species found on muddy bottoms of low salinity bays to the middle of the continental shelf. This fish is silvery in color with a dark shoulder spot and a dark spot at the base of the caudal fin. It ranges from coastal North Carolina to the Bay of Campeche, Mexico, and is known to reach 8 inches in length.

FLATFISHES (FLOUNDERS AND SOLES)—ORDER PLEURONECTIFORMES

The flatfishes have acquired the habit of swimming with the laterally compressed body oriented horizontally instead of vertically. More than eleven families and 570 species of flatfishes are known. They are mostly marine and common in temperate and tropical coastal waters, but some inhabit polar, deep sea, and freshwater environments. Most flatfishes live on the soft bottoms of bays and continental shelves, on which they have worldwide distribution. Flatfishes are favored as food and sport fishes, so a great deal is known about select species.

Interestingly, adult flatfishes are not bilaterally symmetrical. Early in their development (thirty to forty days after hatching) one eye migrates from the bottom side to the "upper" side during the free-swimming, pelagic larval stage. Eye migration requires about five days, and the side turned toward the bottom is called the "blind" side and is lacking in pigmentation. The top or upper side is often cryptically colored and capable of color change, making flounder nearly invisible to predators or prey. They are usually aided in camouflage by the bottom sediments whose texture and color they mimic and in which they partially bury themselves.

The pectoral fin of the "eyed" side is better developed, but the teeth are more prominent on the lower side. Almost all are bottom dwellers and lie in wait for their prey, which they ambush with a sudden rush.

Most flatfishes remain close to the bottom even while swimming. Presumably, the efficiency of this type of swimming is improved by their spineless, flexible dorsal and anal fins that almost completely encircle the body.

"Left-Eyed" Flatfishes—Family Paralichthyidae

Species in this group are known as the "left-eyed" flatfishes because their eyes and coloration are on the left side. There are nearly 120 species, only a few of which are found in North America. All commercial flounders that occur south of Cape Hatteras through the gulf are in the genus *Paralichthys.* Most other species are of a small, noncommercial size, even when fully grown. Various small species of flatfishes occur regularly in shrimp boat by-catch and are often incorrectly assumed to be young southern flounder (*Paralichthys lethostigma*).

When the larvae are less than an inch long, the right eye migrates to the left side and the mouth usually shifts to that side as well. In addition, a rearrangement of the internal organs and the gills takes place. Occasionally "reversed" individuals are found in which the external features are on the opposite (right) side. Ambicoloration and partial or complete albinism (whitish and without color) are other abnormalities seen in flatfishes.

Ocellated Flounder—*Ancyclopsetta quadrocellata*

This flounder has on its side four large spots (ocelli) that usually have white centers; one is above the anterior curve of the lateral line and the other three are arranged in a triangle mid-body. This flounder is common in bays and the shallow gulf, with the largest individuals found in deeper water. This species is often trawled in small numbers in the larger, saltier bays, including the Laguna Madre. It may reach a length of 10 inches. The state record is 16.6 inches (Galveston Bay, 2001).

Southern Flounder—*Paralichthys lethostigma*

Other names: southern fluke, mud flounder, door mats, saddle blankets, plie, lenguad,

Mention the southern flounder and one immediately envisions a malevolent-looking fish lying totally concealed on the bottom waiting for unsuspecting prey to venture by. This species is the largest and most abundant of the twenty-five different flatfishes found in the Gulf of Mexico and adjacent waters. It is also one of

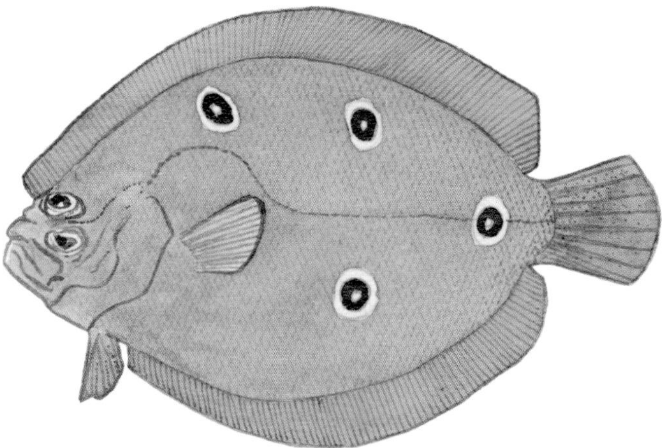

Ocellated flounder, Ancyclopsetta quadrocellata

the most highly demanded food fishes in the United States. Like the black drum, the southern flounder is both a sport and commercial species in Texas waters. The fine-grained, mild-tasting flesh is universally considered to be among the "best of the best" when it comes to quality table fare.

Soon after the right eye migrates to the left side, southern flounder develop the characteristic habit of "side-swimming" in the horizontal rather than the vertical position. The upper surface has an olive- to brown-colored background overlain with dark blotches and white spots. The body is laterally compressed (rather than dorso-ventrally compressed like the skates and rays), with the lower or "blind side" being completely white and lacking any pigmentation. The southern flounder exhibits cryptic coloration, meaning that they are chameleon-like and can change the color and pattern of their upper surface to mimic almost any substrate or bottom type. The mouth is lined with rows of dangerously sharp, fang-like teeth designed to grab and hold on to anything that comes within range. Flounder are "ambush" feeders and lie in wait for unsuspecting prey to come to them rather than actively swimming about searching for their next meal as do most fish.

The southern flounder ranges from Cape Hatteras on the Atlantic coast south throughout the Gulf of Mexico into northern Mexico. They are most abundant between April and October in bays with low to moderate salinity and are most commonly found on soft bottoms (sandy and silty) and along the edges of grassbeds, channels, and passes. As the first cold fronts approach in September or October, the adults begin a mass exodus toward the gulf to spawn. This much-anticipated annual event is known as the flounder "run," and many anglers and giggers target them near gulf passes as they leave the bays. The larvae are carried into the bays, where the young grow very rapidly. The juveniles eat crustaceans, but the adults are strictly fish eaters, feeding on any type of fish that strays too close. Adults return to the bays during early spring, but the individuals do not concentrate into such large groups as they do during the fall migration. As with many fishes, the females grow faster than the males and attain much larger sizes. Rarely do males exceed 12 inches, but females reach lengths of 25 to 28 inches. Flounder have been aged to nine years, but few are thought to live beyond three or four years today. Incidental by-catch by the bay shrimp fleet takes a heavy toll on young flounder, especially on the smaller, easier-to-catch males. After the first year, flounder are between 12 and 14 inches long, and by the end of the second year they range in length from 14 to 18 inches. After the third year they are between 19 and 22 inches in length. The long-standing Texas record is 13.0 pounds and 28.0 inches (Sabine Lake, 1976). The U.S. record stands at 20 pounds, 9 ounces (Florida, 1983).

Flounder are taken by rod and reel using a variety of natural and artificial baits. Red and white worm jigs dressed with strips of cut bait or peeled shrimp bumped slowly along the bottom are very effective, as are live mud minnows (killifish) and finger mullet. They are quite gentle on the bite, and both skill and patience are required to consistently hook

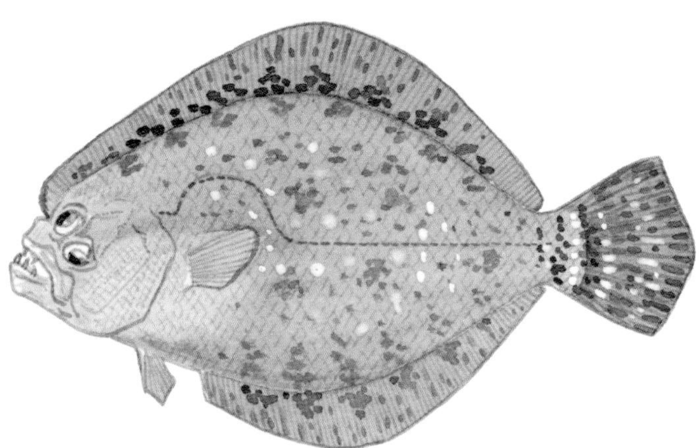

Southern flounder, Paralichthys lethostigma

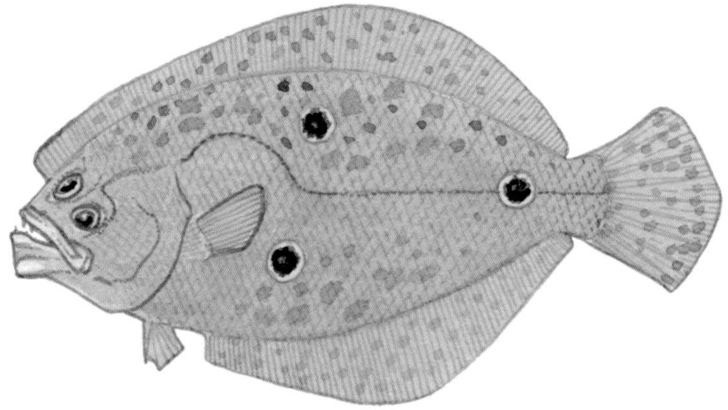

Gulf flounder, Paralichthys albigutta

them. Flounder are the most difficult of all fish to grab and hold on to as they "have no handles"; as a result, many are lost at the moment they are ready to be landed. Landing nets are definitely required for successful flounder fishing trips. However, the greatest numbers of flounder are taken with a gig on calm, windless nights (allowing good viewing in clear, shallow water) using the old stand-by kerosene lantern or submersible lights during flood tides when the fish are buried high on the flats. Adult gulf flounder (*P. albigutta*) reach comparable sizes but are less abundant than the southern flounder and relatively few show up in catches. With a coastwide decline in populations, there has been considerable discussion about the possible reasons. By-catch of spawning adults in the gulf is a frequent focus of the discussions.

GULF FLOUNDER—*Paralichthys albigutta*

Other names: doormat, plie, lenguad

The gulf flounder ranges from the coast of North Carolina, along the gulf states to Texas, and into northern Mexico. Three distinctive ocelli with dark centers are present on its upper surface; one is situated on the lateral line near the tail, with the other two above and below the front curve of the lateral line along the middle of the body. Most gulf flounder are caught around wrecks, and they are frequently found near bridges, docks, and pier pilings. With the onset of cold weather, adults begin a movement from the bays to the gulf, where they remain until spring. There does not seem to be a clear distinction between the habitat of this species and the southern flounder. It is much less abundant than the southern flounder, and most records are from the saltier bays. Average size is 1 to 3 pounds.

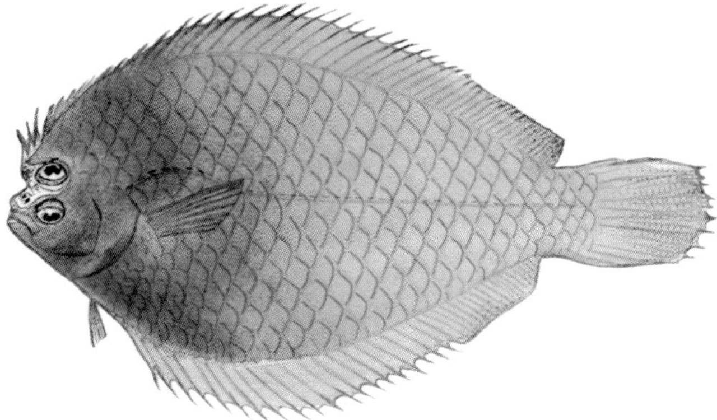

Fringed flounder, Etropus crossotus

FRINGED FLOUNDER—*Etropus crossotus*

This species ranges from Chesapeake Bay to the Gulf of Mexico and throughout the Caribbean. It is brown in color on the eyed side and lacks spotting on the body. The pelvic fins are asymmetrical, with the one on the eyed side located on the midline of the belly, and the mouth is very small. The jaws on the blind side are quite arched, and the lateral line is nearly straight throughout its length. The fringed flounder is found in water up to 100 feet deep and may occur in bays and lagoons throughout the year. This species may not spawn in the bays, however, because it is very rarely found in the bays during the winter. Maximum length is about 6 inches.

BAY WHIFF—*Citharichthys spilopterus*

Other names: dab

In sheer numbers of individuals, this small flounder leads all other flatfish

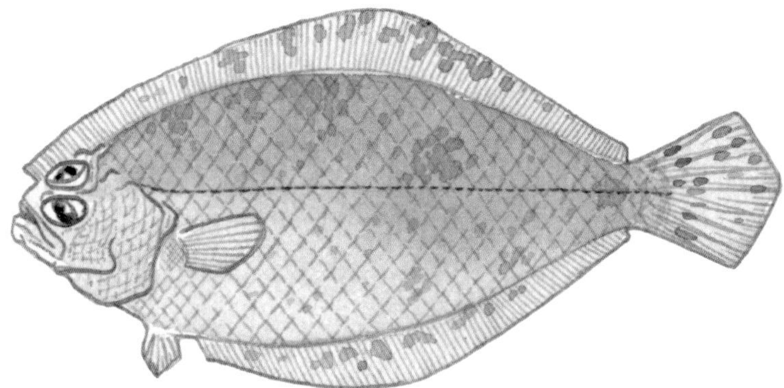

Bay whiff, Citharichthys spilopterus

species. The bay whiff is found from the New Jersey shore south and throughout the Gulf of Mexico. It is uniformly tan to brown on the upper surface and white or yellowish on the underside and is seldom larger than 6 to 8 inches. There are usually two spots on the caudal peduncle and a light spot under the pectoral fin. The body and fins may not always have spotting. Despite the limitation apparently imposed by its name, the bay whiff frequents a great variety of environments, from bay shorelines out to the continental shelf. In the bays, it is found mainly on muddy bottoms. It occurs in the bays throughout the year, but the adults are most abundant there during the summer months.

American Soles—Family Achiridae

Of the sixty species of soles worldwide, a large majority are short-bodied, nearly round fish with their eyes and coloration on the right side. Most are found in the tropic and subtropic seas, but only three species are found in the Texas Laguna Madre. Because these fishes are generally quite small, few of them have any commercial value. Recent work has shown them to be closely related to the left-eyed flatfishes. Their eyes are small, the head is rounded at the front, and the snout is not prominent. Soles can use their blind side to adhere to hard objects such as aquarium walls.

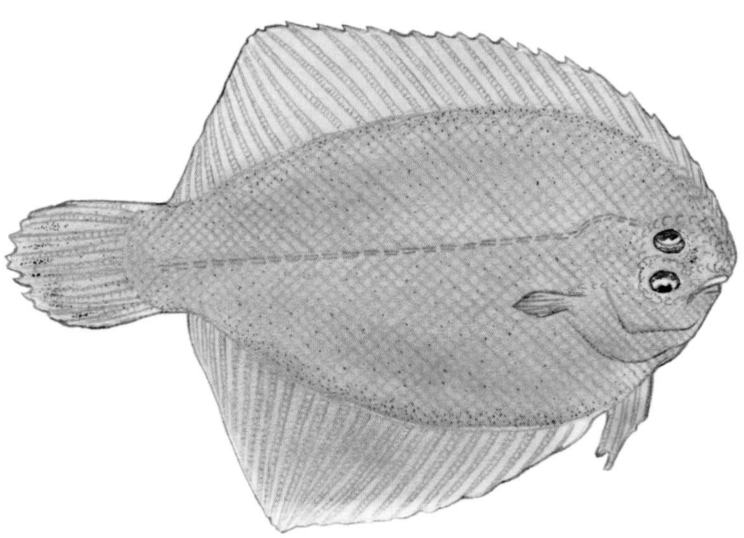

Lined sole, Achirus lineatus

LINED SOLE—*Achirus lineatus*

The lined sole ranges from the South Carolina coast to Uruguay. It is olive to brown in color and has eight narrow bands that fade with age. It is fairly common in the shallow gulf and bays, especially during the summer, and is rarely found in waters of less than 15 ppt salinity. Juveniles have been collected in small numbers in the Cayo del Oso and the Laguna Madre during the warmer months of the year. It reaches 5 inches in length.

HOGCHOKER—*Trinectes maculatus*

This species ranges from Massachusetts to Panama and is extremely common on most shallow bay bottoms along the gulf coast. It is dark gray-green to brown with seven or eight darker vertical bars. It lacks spots and pectoral fins, and the snout is rounded. It is tolerant of low salinity (brackish) waters. Smaller individuals can be found some distance up rivers and larger ones, farther downstream. It occurs sporadically in the Laguna Madre. Young hogchokers are frequently sold in aquarium stores as "freshwater flounder." Their ability to adhere to hard objects is said to have once choked a hog and thus earned them their name. They range from 3 to 7 inches in length.

Tongue Fishes—Family Cynoglossidae

BLACKCHEEK TONGUEFISH—*Symphurus plagiusa*

Other names: patch

This fish ranges from New England, around Florida, and throughout the gulf to the Yucatan Peninsula. It is generally dark brown, and some

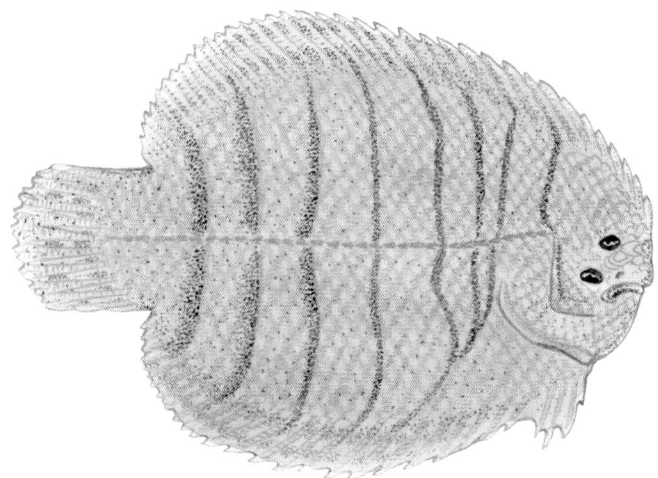

Hogchoker, Trinectes maculatus

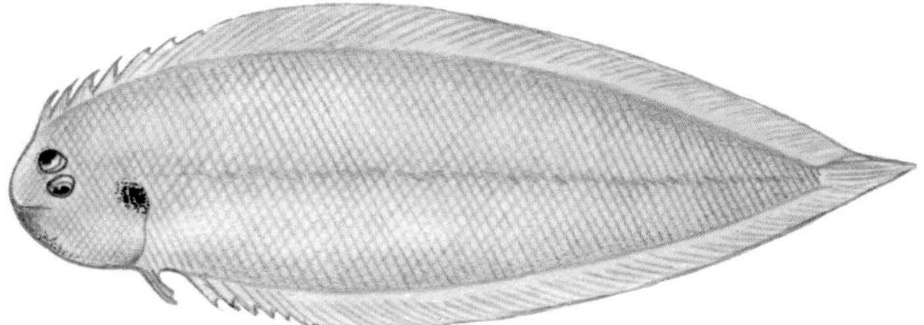

Blackcheek tonguefish, Symphurus plagiusa

individuals may have crossbands. A large dark blotch is present on the gill cover (hence the common name and the alternate name, "patch"), and the caudal fin is continuous with the dorsal and anal fins. The mouth is very small, and the lower jaw is partially equipped with small teeth, attesting to their diet of small worms and other soft-bodied, bottom-dwelling invertebrates. This species is common on the bottoms of bays and is rarely found in water deeper than 120 feet. It is found in the deeper channels throughout the year. Young juveniles enter shrimp trawl catches in the upper Laguna Madre during the winter and leave the shallow areas by the summer. It reaches a length of 8 inches.

Triggerfishes, Filefishes, Boxfishes, Puffers, Porcupinefishes and Molas—Order Tetraodontiformes

This group has a distinguishing small mouth with incisors or fused, tooth-like bones modified into a sharp beak powered by strong jaw muscles. The jaws contain either two or four teeth total (one or two per jaw), which determines the family to which the different species belong. The scales are usually modified into plates or spines. There are about 340 species in this order, and they comprise a variety of body shapes, ranging from globular to triangular to very laterally compressed. All are slow swimmers, and they propel themselves through the water with a rounded caudal fin, by "sculling" with the pectoral fins, and/or by movements of the dorsal and anal fins. All fins are typically placed far back on the body. Most species possess some form of anatomical defensive weaponry such as inflatable and spine-covered bodies, body armor, stout fin spines that can be locked into an erect position, tough leathery skin, or poisonous flesh. Their diet generally consists of invertebrates that other fishes cannot eat, mostly because of their heavy shells, spines, or other body armor.

The triggerfish and filefish families include around forty species and have been given the common name "leatherjackets" in reference to their external covering. These fishes have laterally compressed bodies, lack pelvic fins, and have separate, well-defined teeth. They have a long, file-like dorsal spine and sandpaper-like skin, and the gill opening is reduced to a small diagonal slit in front of the pectoral fin. They are well armored and most are slow-moving, solitary, and often brightly colored reef dwellers. Most species range from Bermuda, through the Gulf of Mexico to Brazil, inhabiting warm temperate and tropical waters. They occur in all coastal habitats from inshore seagrass beds to coral reefs and deeper rocky slopes.

The triggerfish is so named because of the stout first dorsal fin spine that can be locked rigidly in place when the second spine (the "trigger") is depressed. Most triggerfish produce sounds by grunting or grinding their teeth together. The young of many species associate with sargassum and other floating debris. Most adults live around hard substrates, and their tiny mouths are well adapted to browsing for small organisms attached to these substrates. Triggerfishes prefer food items such as crabs, octopus, shellfish, sea urchins, and corals, and their hard mouths make them resistant to capture with hook and line.

Because they do not move away from danger and are apparently very clumsy, filefishes are often called "foolfish." Young filefish are well camouflaged and omnivorous, eating sponges, sea whips, hydroids, and soft-bodied invertebrates. All members can distend the belly by ingesting water and/or air, which presumably discourages predators by making them appear larger and also by enabling them to wedge themselves into tight places. These fish swim by undulating the long second dorsal and anal fin, while the caudal fin is used little for locomotion. Some species are displayed in public aquaria.

Filefishes—Family Monacanthidae

Orange Filefish—*Aluterus schoepfi*

The orange filefish is found in waters throughout the Gulf of Mexico, the Atlantic and Caribbean, and from Bermuda to Brazil. The color and pattern of this species is variable. It is usually brown with an orange cast due to many tiny orange spots uniformly scattered over the body, which fade soon after death. The body is deep in profile in adults, and the snout is generally flattened. It has a squarish caudal fin and an elongated spine on the head. Adults are widespread on offshore reefs while the young are common inshore. This fish has been observed to spend hours with its head down and tail up in the water. With a very small mouth

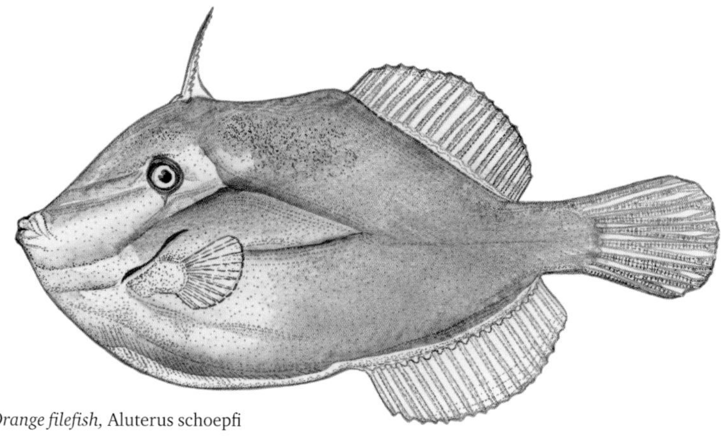

Orange filefish, Aluterus schoepfi

equipped with sharp teeth, this species easily snaps off barnacles that are firmly attached to pilings. Although considered to be a rather common species, observing one may be a rare event. They are drifters and lethargic in behavior but fascinating to watch. They congregate around floating debris or sargassum, orienting their laterally compressed bodies into the current. Their long, undulating dorsal and anal fins propel them, and like lightning they strike out at prey. They may be captured anywhere that floating debris provides cover or refuge. Quite a few large individuals have been reported from the northern end of the upper Laguna Madre. The average size is 12 inches.

PLANEHEAD FILEFISH—*Stephanolepis hispidus*

This is the most common inshore filefish over the continental shelf, with the young often entering the bays. It ranges from the tropical and warm temperate Atlantic Ocean from Nova Scotia and Bermuda to Brazil, including the Gulf of Mexico and Bahamas. The planehead filefish is the most strikingly marked of all the filefishes. It is generally tan to brown or greenish in color but can be brown with darker brown blotches, spots, and lines. There are usually two dark areas along the bases of the anal and dorsal fins and a darker blotch on the upper sides, below the anterior portion of the dorsal fin. It is distinguished from its relatives by a distinct spine projecting downward from the chest. It often floats in sargassum and is the only common filefish in the grass flats of the saltier bays. It relies on camouflage and its tough skin to escape predators. Though of no commercial value, they make fascinating aquarium fish, easily captured with a net in the hands of a child. The planehead filefish rarely exceeds 6 inches but has been reported to reach 10 inches in length.

Puffers—Family Tetraodontidae

The puffers differ from the porcupinefishes and burrfishes (Diodontidae) in that they possess a median division in the upper and lower jaws and have small spines on the body. These fishes have no true teeth; instead the sharp edges of the jaws serve as teeth. Both puffers and porcupinefishes are capable of inflating their stomachs with either air or water and increasing their buoyancy. When alarmed, they will inflate themselves, causing the spines to become more prominent and thus protecting themselves from predators.

Puffers produce a strong poison called tetradotoxin, produced mainly in the viscera and skin, which can be fatal to humans. The flesh of the puffer is considered a delicacy in Japan, and extracts from puffer skin are used in the Caribbean Islands to induce "zombie-like" behavior. Most puffers are marine pelagics found in tropical and subtropical shore waters of the Indian, Pacific, and Atlantic Oceans. They are slow swimmers and hover over stationary prey, striking with precision. Puffers primarily feed on large crabs and other hard-shelled invertebrates. Body color and pattern, presence and distribution of fleshy tabs, and the extent of body spines are used to distinguish the different species.

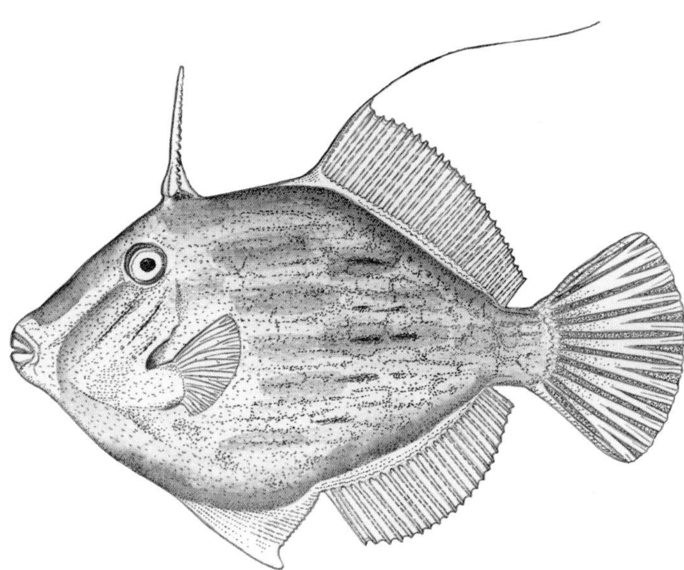

Planehead filefish, Stephanolepis hispidus

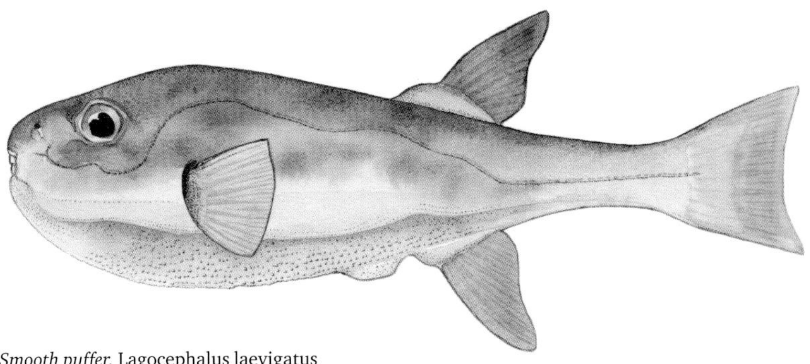

Smooth puffer, Lagocephalus laevigatus

Smooth Puffer—*Lagocephalus laevigatus*

Other names: rabbitfish, silver puffer

This is the largest puffer in the region, and it is generally found on the inner and middle shelf, although it is known to frequent saltier bays. It is silvery gray to olive-gray in color, darker above than below. The caudal fin is slightly forked, and the body lacks scales except on the prickly belly and the throat area. There is a fleshy fold of skin extending from behind the base of the pectoral fin to the caudal fin. The smooth puffer inhabits the warm temperate Atlantic Ocean from Massachusetts to Brazil, including the Gulf of Mexico and Bahamas. Adults are pelagic and usually found near continental margins, while the young are common on coastal and offshore banks. Juveniles may be present in the bays and around passes and channels, but adults are rare in the bays. Large individuals have been reported from Corpus Christi Bay and the upper Laguna Madre. Although this is not a common species, it is routinely captured in shrimp trawls and occasionally caught by anglers. Because of its size and powerful jaws, the smooth puffer is one of the most formidable browsers in the sea. It is sufficiently swift to chase down mobile prey, including squid. This species approaches 2 feet in length and weighs 2 to 4 pounds. The Texas record is 10.8 pounds and 30.0 inches in length (Gulf of Mexico, 2001).

Least Puffer—*Sphoeroides parvus*

This is the puffer most common in the bays and inshore areas off the Louisiana and Texas coasts. It is found in shallow, turbid coastal gulf and bay waters from Florida to the Bay of Campeche, Mexico. It is small in size, and the body is tan to dark olive-gray in color above with numerous small pale green spots; black spots are often present on the cheeks. There are

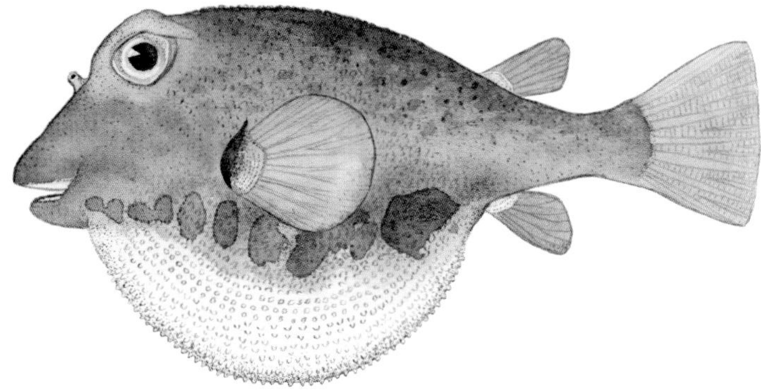

Least puffer, Sphoeroides parvus

irregular dark and light markings on the sides and dorsal surface as well. Juveniles are common in all bays, but all ages are most abundant in the more saline bays. Adult size is usually less than 4 inches. The current state record is 6.0 inches (Galveston Bay, 1990).

Southern Puffer—*Sphoeroides nephelus*

This is the common puffer in the northeastern gulf, where it inhabits bays and protected coastal waters. It ranges from the east coast of Florida to the Yucatan Peninsula of Mexico and perhaps as far as South America. The body is brown with numerous pale tan rings, semicircles, and blotches on the sides and a distinct dark spot at the corner of each pectoral fin. Dark slashes are often present on the lower half of the cheeks. It may reach 12 inches in length.

Porcupinefishes and Burrfishes—Family Diodontidae

Porcupinefishes and burrfishes occur worldwide in shallow waters of tropical to warm temperate seas. The group consists of nineteen species in six genera, with seven species

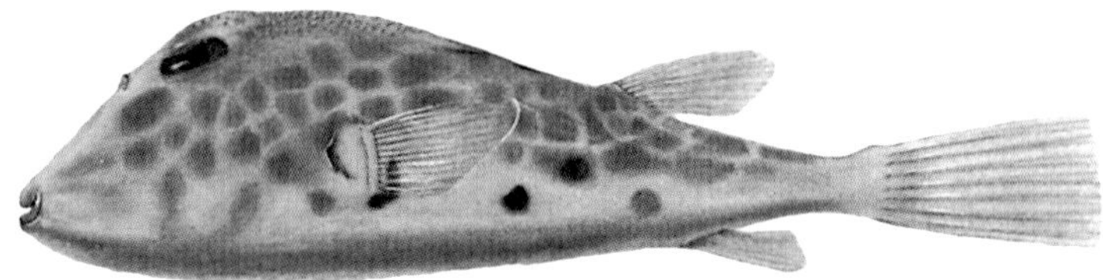

Southern puffer, Sphoeroides nephelus. *Illustration by Janice D. Fechhelm*

found in the Gulf of Mexico. These are highly inflatable fishes, like the puffers, but they have longer spines and strong beaks with one tooth in each jaw for crushing armored prey. They are globular in shape, with a head that is broad and blunt and a mouth that is very small and situated at the most anterior point of the head. The gill opening is slit-like and lies immediately in front of the pectoral fin base. The lateral line is inconspicuous, and the body and head are covered with large spine-like scales. Members of this group are benthic or associated with floating seaweed. Their food consists of sea urchins, molluscs, and crustaceans. They are often dried and sold as curiosities. Other tropical species are thought to occur offshore.

Striped Burrfish—*Chilomycterus schoepfi*
Other names: spiny boxfish, porcupine fish
The striped burrfish has sides that are yellowish brown above with dark brown wavy and parallel stripes, and the lower body varies from white to yellowish or even dark in color. Dark stripes on the dorsal fin may be wide or narrow. Large individuals often have large dark spots on the body and fins. The very young are gaudily colored in oranges and yellows, with cartoon-like black spots and rings. Striped burrfish are ubiquitous coastal residents, found in a wide variety of habitats. They are common in the bays and the shallow gulf, especially during the summer. Individuals are most commonly found

Striped burrfish, Chilomycterus schoepfi

in seagrass beds in saltier bays and coastal lagoons. These fish are generally found as solitary individuals and do not appear to be particularly abundant, although nowhere in their range are they considered uncommon. Because this species is so well armored and "fearless," striped burrfish make little effort to flee or hide from divers. Thus, they are likely to be one of the first fishes spotted by a snorkeler entering the water. This species is very hardy and thus makes an excellent aquarium fish. Most individuals will soon learn to accept food from the hand. This fish is very sensitive to low temperatures, however, and some are killed nearly every winter. One individual was reported to weigh 33 pounds when landed and it still weighed 20 pounds after being drained of the water it had ingested. However, the Texas state record is only 0.9 pound and 8.5 inches long (Gulf of Mexico, January 1995).

Visitor Contact Information

The contact information below for visitor centers, chambers of commerce, and Web sites related to the Laguna Madre area is subject to change, but updates should be easily accessible via Internet search engines.

Brownsville Convention & Visitors Bureau
650 FM 802
Brownsville, Texas 78520
800-626-2639, 956-546-3721
http://www.brownsville.org

Corpus Christi Area Convention & Visitors Bureau
1201 North Shoreline
Corpus Christi, Texas 78401
800-766-2322, 361-881-1800
http://www.corpuschristi-tx-cvb.org

Harlingen Chamber of Commerce
311 East Tyler Street
Harlingen, Texas 78550
800-531-7346, 956-423-5440
http://www.harlingen.com

Laguna Atascosa National Wildlife Refuge
FM 106
Rio Hondo, Texas 78583
956-748-3607

Port Isabel Chamber of Commerce
421 Queen Isabella Boulevard
Port Isabel, Texas 78578
800-556-7678, 956-943-2262
http://www.portisabel.org

Port Mansfield Chamber of Commerce
800 Bayshore Drive
Bayshore, Texas 78598
956-944-2354

Raymondville Chamber of Commerce
142 S. Seventh St.
P.O. Box 746
Raymondville, Texas 78580
956-689-3171
http://www.raymondvillechamber.com

South Padre Island Convention & Visitors Bureau
600 Padre Boulevard
South Padre Island, Texas 78597
800-767-2373, 956-761-6433
http://www.sopadre.com

Coastal Conservation Association:
http://coastalconservationassocia tion.org

National Marine Fisheries:
http://nmfs.noaa.gov

National Parks Service:
http://nps.gov

The Nature Conservancy:
http://nature.org

Padre Island National Seashore:
http://nps.gov/pais

Texas General Land Office:
http://glo.state.tx.us

Texas Parks and Wildlife Department:
http://www.tpwd.state.tx.us

U.S. Army Corps of Engineers:
http://www.usace.army.mil

U.S. Fish and Wildlife Service:
http://fws.gov

Upper Laguna Madre

Name	Location	Boat Ramp	Boat Dock	Pier
Kaufer-Hubert Memorial Park	FM 628, Loyola Beach, Kleberg Co.	*	*	*
Padre Island National Seashore	Park Road 22, Corpus Christi, Kleberg Co., 361-949-8068	*		
Riviera Beach Pier	County Road 2360E, Riviera, Kleberg Co.			*
Philip Dimitt Municipal Fishing Pier	End of Jester St., Port Aransas, Nueces Co.			*
C&W Bait Stand	3909 Laguna Shores Rd., Corpus Christi, Nueces Co., 361-939-7776	*	*	
Catchin Connection	Laguna Shores Rd. & Wyndale Street, Corpus Christi, Nueces Co.	*	*	
JFK Causeway	At Humble Channel, Corpus Christi, Nueces Co.	*	*	*
JFK Causeway	At the Gulf Intracoastal Waterway, Corpus Christi, Nueces Co.	*	*	*
Laguna Shores Resort & Marina	Laguna Shores Rd., Corpus Christi, Nueces Co., 361-949-1881	*	*	
Marker 37	South Padre Island Dr., JFK Causeway, Nueces Co.	*		*
Cosway Bait & Tackle	South Padre Island Dr., JFK Causeway, Nueces Co.		*	*
Padre Island Investment	White Cap and Caravel, Corpus Christi, Nueces Co.	*		
Padre Island Investment	End of Cobo de Caba, Corpus Christi, Nueces Co.	*		
Padre Island Investment	Gypsy and Bounty, Corpus Christi, Nueces Co.	*		
Padre Island Investment	Fortuna Bay and Monte Pelle, Corpus Christi, Nueces Co.	*		
Padre Island Investment	Encantada and Cruiser, Corpus Christi, Nueces Co.	*		

Padre Island Investment	Cartagena, Corpus Christi, Nueces Co.	*		
Bird Island Basin	Padre Island National Seashore, Park Road 22, Corpus Christi, Nueces Co., 361-949-8068	*		
Willamson's	Laguna Salada access, Kleberg Co.	*		

Lower Laguna Madre

Name	Location	Boat Ramp	Boat Dock	Pier
Ted's Restaurant	5717 Padre Blvd., South Padre Island, Cameron Co., 956-943-6161	*		
South Padre Marina	6101 Padre Blvd., South Padre Island, Cameron Co., 956-761-9457	*	*	
Destination South Padre Island RV Park	1 Padre Blvd., South of Queen Isabella Causeway, South Padre Island, Cameron Co., 956-761-5665	*	*	*
Jim's Pier	209 West Whiting, South Padre Island, Cameron Co., 956-761-2865	*	*	
Sea Ranch Marine Center	1 Padre Blvd., South of Queen Isabella Causeway, South Padre Island, Cameron Co., 956-761-7777	*	*	
South Point Marina	500 South Point Dr., Port Isabel, Cameron Co., 956-761-5327	*	*	
Park Center	702 Champion, Port Isabel, Cameron Co.	*		
City Park	End of Pompano, Port Isabel, Cameron Co.	*	*	
White Sands Motor Lodge & Marina	418 West Highway 100, Port Isabel, Cameron Co., 956-943-6161	*	*	
Anchor Marina	40 Tarpon Ave., Port Isabel, Cameron Co., 956-943-9323	*	*	
Pirates Fishing Pier	204 North Garcia, Port Isabel, Cameron Co., 956-761-5327	*	*	*
Fred Stone Park	End of North Shore Dr., Port Mansfield, Willacy Co.		*	*
Willacy County Navigation District	Laguna St., Port Mansfield, Willacy Co.	*	*	

Laguna Marine Ramp	Port Mansfield, Willacy Co., 956-944-2428	*		
Adolph Thomae Jr. County Park	End of FM 2925, Arroyo City, Cameron Co.	*		*
Sanchez Bait Stand	36405 Marshall Hutts, Arroyo City, Cameron Co.	*	*	*

Glossary

ADIPOSE FIN—a fleshy median dorsal fin without spines or rays.

AMBICOLORATION—in the flatfishes, part or all of the blind side having the same or similar pigment as the side with the eyes.

ANADROMOUS—living in salt water but migrating to fresh water to spawn.

ASTRONOMICAL TIDES—tides resulting from the gravitational pull of the sun and moon.

ASYMMETRICAL—lacking symmetry or correspondence of anatomical features, patterns, or coloration on both sides; not equal on both sides.

BARBEL—fleshy, tentacle-like structures situated on the head and sensitive to tactile and/or chemical stimuli.

BENTHIC—referring to the bottom or substrate or to organisms that live on the substrate in the marine habitat.

BILATERAL SYMMETRY—when structures and their location are identical on both halves of the body.

CANINES—large, conical, pointed teeth in the upper jaw.

CATADROMOUS—living in fresh water but migrating to the sea to spawn.

CAUDAL PEDUNCLE—that region of the body between the most posterior ray of the anal fin and the base of the caudal fin or tail.

CEPHALIC OR "HEAD" FINS—fin-like structure on both sides of the head formed by the pectoral fins and rostral cartilage.

CIGUATERA—a disease of the nervous system caused by eating certain tropical fishes.

CIRRUS (PL., CIRRI)—a fleshy appendage, usually on the head or fin tips.

CRYPTIC COLORATION—coloring that disguises or conceals an animal's shape or pattern by blending with the surrounding environment.

CTENOID—scale type having a comb-like margin of tiny spines (ctenii) on the exposed posterior section; the ctenii cause the scales to feel rough to the touch.

CYCLOID—thin, smooth-edged scales of soft-rayed fishes having an evenly curved posterior border without any spines or ctenii.

DERMAL DENTICLES—plate-like scales of cartilaginous fishes that do not grow after formation; present on fishes such as sharks and rays.

DETRITUS—loose material resulting from the wearing away or breakdown of a material or tissue, such as inorganic sand and gravel or organic plant and animal tissue.

DORSAL—the back or upper surface of the body.

DORSO-VENTRAL COMPRESSION—condition of being flattened from top (dorsal) to bottom (ventral), as seen in rays, skates, and mantas.

EPIPELAGIC—upper region of the water column, generally between the surface and 200 meters (660 feet).

ESTUARINE DEPENDENT—organisms that require an estuarine environment during their early stages of development to survive.

ESTUARY—the lower end or mouth of a river where fresh water mixes with salt water, creating a low-salinity or brackish environment.

EURYHALINE—organisms capable of withstanding wide variations in salinity.

GILL RAKERS—the combtooth, or knob-like projections on the posterior margins of the gill arches used for straining food from the water.

GONOPODIUM—in certain male fish species, the modified anal fin used for sperm transfer; it is analogous to the mammalian penis.

HERBIVORY—diet consisting of only plant or algal material.

HYPERSALINE—water with salinity exceeding that of normal seawater (greater than 35 ppt).

INTERTIDAL ZONE—the zone which is alternately flooded and exposed by rising and falling tides.

LATERAL COMPRESSION—condition of being flattened from side to side (as seen in the flounders and soles).

LATERAL LINE—a series of sensory pores along the sides of the body from behind the gill opening to the base of the caudal fin responding to certain frequency sounds or water particle movement.

LEPTOCEPHALUS—a laterally compressed, transparent larval stage of eels, bonefish, tarpon, and ladyfish.

METEOROLOGICAL TIDES—tides resulting from wind and storm activity creating waves and an increase in water height.

MILT—fish sperm and seminal fluid, or the reproductive glands of male fishes when filled with this fluid.

OCELLUS (PL., OCELLI)—round spot or "eye" surrounded by a lighter area located on the caudal region of certain fishes.

OPERCULUM OR OPERCLE—the flat, thin bones that cover the gills on each side of the head of fishes (also called gill cover).

OSMOREGULATION—the maintenance of a certain water and salt balance, regardless of the salinity of the water a fish is in.

OTOLITHS—calcium carbonate ear "stones" within the chambers of the skull of certain fishes that transmit vibrations from the surface of the fish to the inner ear.

PALATAL (PALATINE) TEETH—teeth situated in the most anterior region of the upper jaw (palate).

PELAGIC—refers to the water column or the organisms living there.

PH—measure of the concentration of acids or bases; pH in water ranges from 0 (very acidic), to 7 (neutral), to 14 (very basic).

PHARYNGEAL TEETH—teeth situated in the throat or gill region.

PISCINE—of, or relating to, or characteristic of a fish.

PISCIVOROUS—organisms whose diets consist of fish.

PREHENSILE TAIL—a tail adapted for adhering to or holding, especially by wrapping around an object, such as the tails of seahorses.

PROTRUSIBLE—capable of being projected or thrust forward, as in the mouth of certain fishes.

RECURVED—curved inward or backward, as in the teeth of certain fishes.

SCUTES—modified scales found along the midline of some fish species (e.g., herring) and along the lateral line on others (e.g., leatherjacket).

SERRATED—referring to a surface or margin bearing sawblade-like spines or notches.

SPIRACLES—openings behind the eyes of rays and some sharks where water is drawn into the gills.

STENOHALINE—tolerance to only a narrow range in salinity.

SUBORBITAL—situated below or beneath the eye.

SUBTERMINAL—indicating the mouth is located just below the tip of the snout, with the upper jaw projecting slightly beyond the lower jaw.

SUPRAORBITAL—area above the eye.

SYMBIOTIC RELATIONSHIP—a relationship between individuals of two species in which both species may benefit, or one species benefits at the other's expense (i.e., a parasite), or neither species benefits.

TERMINAL MOUTH—indicates that the mouth is situated at the end or most anterior portion of the head.

TRUNK OR BODY RINGS—in pipefish and seahorses, the raised body sections situated anterior to the anus.

VENTRAL—the lower surface or belly of the body.

VOMERINE (VOMER)—the hard upper (roof) part of the mouth that often bears teeth.

Bibliography

Allyn, R. 1967. *A Dictionary of Fishes.* 11th ed. St. Petersburg, Fla.: Great Outdoors Publishing. 134 pp.

Andrews, P. B. 1964. Serpulid reefs, Baffin Bay, Southeast Texas. Pp. 101–20 in *Depositional Environments of South-Central Texas Coast* (field trip guidebook). Gulf Coast Association of Geological Societies Annual Meeting, Corpus Christi, Tex.

Barton, M. 2007. *Bond's Biology of Fishes.* 3rd ed. Belmont, Calif.: Thomson Brooks/Cole. 891 pp.

Beebe, W., and J. Tee-Van. 1933. *Field Book of the Shore Fishes of Bermuda.* New York: G. P. Putnam's Sons. 337 pp.

Behrens, E. W. 1966. Surface salinities for Baffin Bay and Laguna Madre, Texas, April 1964–March 1966. *Publications of the Institute of Marine Science,* 11:168–73.

———. 1968. Cyclic and current structures in a serpulid reef. *Contributions in Marine Science,* 13:21–27.

Bond, C. E. 1996. *Biology of Fishes.* 2nd ed. Fort Worth, Tex.: Saunders College Publishing. 750 pp.

Bortone, S. A. 2002. *Biology of the Spotted Seatrout.* New York: CRC Press. 328 pp.

Breder, C. M., Jr., 1948. *Field Book of Marine Fishes of the Atlantic Coast.* New York: G. P. Putnam's Sons. 332 pp.

Breuer, J. P. 1957. An ecological survey of Baffin and Alazan Bays, Texas. *Contributions in Marine Science,* 4(2): 134–55.

———. 1962. An ecological survey of the lower Laguna Madre of Texas, 1953–1959. *Publications of the Institute of Marine Science,* 8:153–83.

Britton, J. C., and B. Morton. 1989. *Shore Ecology of the Gulf of Mexico.* Austin: University of Texas Press. 387 pp.

Brown-Peterson, N., P. Thomas, and C. R. Arnold. 1988. Reproductive biology of the spotted seatrout, *Cynoscion nebulosus,* in south Texas. *Fishery Bulletin,* 86(2): 373–88.

Bryan, C. E. 1971. *An Ecological Survey of the Arroyo Colorado, Texas 1966–1969.* TPWD Technical Series No. 10. Austin: Texas Parks and Wildlife Department. 28 pp.

Burr, J. G. 1930. A sail down the

Laguna. *Year Book on Texas Conservation of Wildlife,* 1929–1930:54–58.

———. 1945a. Adventure on Laguna Madre. *Texas Game and Fish,* 4(4): 8–9, 17–20.

———. 1945b. Nature wins. *Texas Game and Fish,* 4(9): 16–17, 25–26.

———. 1947. The Laguna Madre sphinx. *Texas Game and Fish,* 6(5): 4, 21–22.

———. 1950. Pass cutting on Padre Island. *Texas Game and Fish,* 9(3): 22–23.

Buskey, E. J., B. Wysor, and C. Hyatt. 1998. The role of hypersalinity in the persistence of the Texas "brown tide" in the Laguna Madre. *Journal of Plankton Research,* 20:1553–65.

Carpelan, E. G., R. I. Lonard, and D. B. Fenn. 1967. Invertebrates in relation to hypersaline habitats. *Contributions in Marine Science,* 12:219–29.

Castro, J. I. 1983. *The Sharks of North American Waters.* College Station: Texas A&M University Press. 180 pp.

Chin, J. L. 1978. Distribution of marine grasses in southern Laguna Madre. Report to Texas Parks and Wildlife Department on file at Texas A&M University–Corpus Christi, Center for Coastal Studies Library. 45 pp.

Coffen, C. 1975. *Specks and Redfish and How to Catch 'Em.* Houston: Double C Productions. 169 pp.

Cole, R. M. 1981. The serpulid reefs of Baffin Bay, Texas. Pp. 63–74 in *Geology of Clay Dunes, Baffin Bay, and the South Texas Sand Sheet,* ed. J. L. Russell and R. W. Shum (field trip guidebook). 83rd Annual Meeting, Texas Academy of Science, Austin.

Collins, M. R. 1985a. Species profiles: life histories and environmental requirements of coastal fishes and invertebrates (south Florida): striped mullet. U.S. Fish and Wildlife Service Biological Report 82 (11.34). U.S. Army Corps of Engineers, TR EL-82-4. 11 pp.

———. 1985b. Species profiles: life histories and environmental requirements of coastal fishes and invertebrates (south Florida): white mullet. U.S. Fish and Wildlife Service Biological Report 82 (11.39). U.S. Army Corps of Engineers, TR EL-82-4. 7 pp.

Compagno, L., M. Dando, and S. Fowler. 2005. *Collins Field Guide to Sharks of the World.* London: HarperCollins. 368 pp.

Copeland, B. J. 1967. Environmental characteristics of hypersaline lagoons. *Contributions in Marine Science,* 12:207–18.

Copeland, B. J., and R. S. Jones. 1965. Community metabolism in some hypersaline waters. *Texas Journal of Science,* 17:188–205.

Copeland, B. J., J. H. Thompson Jr., and W. Ogletree. 1968. Effects of wind on water levels in the Texas Laguna Madre. *Texas Journal of Science,* 20:196–99.

Cornelius, S. E. 1984a. *An Ecological Survey of Alazan Bay, Texas.* Technical Bulletin No. 5, Caesar Kleberg Wildlife Research Institute, Kingsville, Tex. 163 pp.

———. 1984b. *Contribution to the Life History of Black Drum and Analysis of the Commercial Fishery of Baffin Bay,* volume 2. Technical Bulletin No. 6, Caesar Kleberg Wildlife Research Institute, Kingsville, Tex. 53 pp.

Diana, J. S. 2004. *Biology and Ecology of Fishes.* 2nd ed. Traverse City, Mich.: Cooper Publishing. 498 pp.

Dunaway, V. 2002. *Sport Fish of the Gulf of Mexico.* Stuart, Fla.: Florida Sportsman. 261 pp.

Dunham, David. 2005. *Texas Parks and Wildlife Outdoor Annual Hunting and Fishing Regulations.* Austin: Texas Monthly Custom Publishing. 112 pp.

Felder, T. 1978. Fishing the Texas surf. Texas A&M University Sea Grant College Program. TAMU-SG-79–605. 13 pp.

Fishes and Fishing in Louisiana. 1965. Bulletin 23, Louisiana Department of Conservation. 701 pp.

Fuls, G. E. 1974. Further ecological studies on the macroichthyofauna of the Laguna Salada, Texas. MS thesis, Texas A&I University, Kingsville. 106 pp.

Gilbert, C. R., and J. D. Williams. 2002. *National Audubon Society Field Guide to the Fishes, North America.* New York: Chanticleer Press. 607 pp.

Guest, W. C., and G. Gunter. 1958. *The Sea Trout or Weakfishes (Genus Cynoscion) of the Gulf of Mexico.* Ocean Springs, Miss.: Gulf States Marine Fisheries Commission. 40 pp.

Gunter, G. 1941. Death of fishes due to cold on the Texas Coast, January, 1940. *Ecology,* 22:203–208.

———. 1945a. Some characteristics of ocean waters and Laguna Madre. *Texas Game and Fish,* 3(10): 7, 19–22.

———. 1945b. Studies on marine fishes of Texas. *Publications of the Institute of Marine Science,* 1(1): 1–90.

———. 1946. Problems of the Texas coast. *Texas Game and Fish,* 5(12): 9, 25–28.

———. 1952. The importance of catastrophic mortalities for marine fisheries along the Texas coast. *Journal of Wildlife Management,* 16(1): 63–69.

———. 1961. Salinity and size in marine fishes. *Copeia,* 1961:234–35.

———. 1967. Vertebrates in hypersaline waters. *Contributions in Marine Science,* 12:230–41.

Gunter, G., and H. H. Hildebrand. 1951. Destruction of fishes and other organisms on the south Texas coast by the cold wave of January 28–February 3, 1951. *Ecology,* 32(4): 731–35.

Hardegree, B. 1997. Biological productivity associated with the serpulid reefs of Baffin Bay, Texas. MS thesis, Texas A&M University–Corpus Christi. 130 pp.

Hedgpeth, J.W. 1947. The Laguna Madre of Texas. Pp. 367–80 in Transactions of the 12th North American Wildlife Conference, Austin, Tex..

———. 1967. Ecological aspects of the Laguna Madre, a hypersaline estuary. Pp. 408–19 in *Estuaries,* ed. G. H. Lauff. Publication No. 83. Washington, D.C.: American Association for the Advancement of Science.

Helfman, G. S., B. B. Collette, and D. E. Facey. 1997. *The Diversity of Fishes.* Malden, Mass.: Blackwell Science. 528 pp.

Hellier, Jr., T. R. 1962. Fish production and biomass studies in relation to photosynthesis in the Laguna Madre of Texas. *Publications of the Institute of Marine Science,* 8:1–22.

Hensley, R. A., and B. E. Fuls. 1998. *Trends in Relative Abundance and Size of Selected Finfishes and Shellfishes along the Texas Coast: November 1975–December 1996.* Management Data Series No. 159. Austin: Texas Parks and Wildlife Department. 88 pp.

Hildebrand, H. H. 1969. Laguna Madre, Tamaulipas: observations on its hydrography and fisheries. Pp. 679–86 in *Lagunas costeras, un simposio: Memoir of the International Symposium on coastal lagoons (origin, dynamics and productivity) UNAM-UNESCO. Mexico, D.F., November 28–30, 1967,* ed. A. Ayala-Castanares and F. B. Phleger. Mexico City: Universidad Nacional Autónoma de Mexico.

Hildebrand, H. H., and D. King. 1979. *A Biological Study of the Cayo del Oso and Pita Island Area of the Laguna Madre.* 2 vols. Final Report to Central Power and Light Company, Corpus Christi, Texas. 243 pp. (vol. 1), 235 pp. (vol. 2).

Hoese, H. D. 1958. The case of the pass. *Texas Game and Fish,* 16(6): 16–18, 30–31.

Hoese, H. D., and R. H. Moore. 1998. *Fishes of the Gulf of Mexico: Texas, Louisiana, and Adjacent Waters.* 2nd ed. College Station: Texas A&M University Press. 422 pp.

Husak, A. 1979. *Fishing the Bays of Texas.* Houston: Cordovan. 162 pp.

King Ranch and Kenedy Trust. 1993. *Environmental Impacts of the Plan to Dump Dredged Spoil from the Gulf Intracoastal Waterway on Lands Bordering the Laguna Madre.* Kingsville, Tex.: King Ranch and John G. Kenedy Charitable Trust. 108 pp.

Krull, R. M. 1976. The small fish fauna of a disturbed hypersaline environment. MS thesis, Texas A&I University, Kingsville. 112 pp.

Leard, R., B. Mahmoudi, H. Blanchet, H. Lazauski, K. Spiller, M. Buchanan,

C. Dyer, and W. Keithly. 1995. *The Striped Mullet Fishery of the Gulf of Mexico, United States: A Regional Management Plan, No. 33.* Ocean Springs, Miss.: Gulf States Marine Fisheries Commission. 19 pp.

Lutz, P. L. 2003. Biology of the spotted seatrout. *Fish and Fisheries,* 4(4): 374.

Marine Resources of the Atlantic Coast Leaflet No. 13: Spotted Seatrout, Shallow Water Sportfish. 1970. Atlantic States Marine Fisheries Commission, Florida. 4 pp.

Martin, J. H. 1979. A study of the feeding habits of the black drum in Alazan Bay and the Laguna Salada, Texas. MS thesis, Texas A&I University, Kingsville. 103 pp.

Martin, J. H., and L. W. McEachron. 1996. *Historical Annotated Review of Winter Kills of Marine Organisms in Texas Bays.* Coastal Fisheries Branch, Management Data Series No. 50. Austin: Texas Parks and Wildlife Department. 20 pp.

Matlock, G. C. 1983. Stomach contents of selected fishes from Texas bays. *Contributions in Marine Science,* 26:95–110.

McEachran, J. D., and J. D. Fechhelm. 1998. *Fishes of the Gulf of Mexico.* Vol. 1. Austin: University of Texas Press. 1120 pp.

———. 2005. *Fishes of the Gulf of Mexico.* Vol. 2. Austin: University of Texas Press. 1014 pp.

McEachron, L.W., G. C. Matlock, C. E. Bryan, P. Unger, T. J. Cody, and J. H. Martin. 1994. Winter mass mortality of animals in Texas bays. *Northeast Gulf Science,* 13(2): 121–38.

Migdalski, E.C. 1958. *Angler's Guide to the Salt Water Game Fishes, Atlantic and Pacific.* New York: Ronald Press. 506 pp.

Miles, D. W. 1950. The life histories of the spotted sea trout, *Cynoscion nebulosus,* and the redfish, *Sciaenops ocellatus.* Annual Report to the Texas Parks and Wildlife Department, 1949–1950. 38 pp.

———. 1951. The life histories of the spotted sea trout, *Cynoscion nebulosus,* and the redfish, *Sciaenops ocellatus,* sexual development. Annual Report to the Texas Parks and Wildlife Department, 1950–1951. 13 pp.

Moffett, A. W., L. W. McEachron, and J. G. Key. 1979. Observations on the biology of sand seatrout (*Cynoscion arenarius*) in Galveston and Trinity Bays, Texas. *Contributions in Marine Science,* 22:163–72.

Moore, R. H. 1974. General ecology, distribution and relative abundance of *Mugil cephalus* and *Mugil curema* on the south Texas Coast. *Contributions in Marine Science,* 18:241–55.

Moyle, P. B., and J. J. Cech Jr. 2004. *Fishes: An Introduction to Ichthyology.* 5th ed. Upper Saddle River, N.J.: Prentice Hall. 726 pp.

Murdy, E. O. 1995. Saltwater fishes of Texas: a dichotomous key. Texas A&M University Sea Grant College

Program, TAMU-SG-83-607. College Station, Tex. 158 pp.

Murphy, M. D., and R. G. Taylor. 1989. Reproduction and growth of black drum, *Pogonias cromis,* in northeast Florida. *Northeast Gulf Science,* 10(2): 127–37.

———. 1990. Reproduction, growth, and mortality of red drum *Sciaenops ocellatus* in Florida waters. *Fishery Bulletin,* 88:531–42.

Pearson, J. C. 1929. Natural history and conservation of the redfish and other commercial sciaenids on the Texas coast. *Bulletin of the U.S. Bureau of Fisheries,* 54:129–214.

Perlmutter, E. 1961. *Guide to the Marine Fishes.* New York: Bramhall House. 431 pp.

Pew, P. 1966. *Food and Game Fishes of the Texas Coast.* Bulletin No. 33, Series No. IV, Marine Laboratory. Austin: Texas Parks and Wildlife Department. 68 pp.

Ponwith, B., and Q. R. Dokken. 1996. Fisheries resources. Pp. 484–543 in *Current Status and Historical Trends of the Estuarine Living Resources within the Corpus Christi Bay National Estuary Program Study Area,* ed. J. W. Tunnell Jr., Q. R. Dokken, E. H. Smith, and K. Withers. Corpus Christi Bay National Estuary Program CCBNEP-06A. Corpus Christi: Texas Natural Resource Conservation Commission.

Pulich, W., Jr. 1980. Ecology of a hypersaline lagoon: the Laguna Madre. Pp. 103–22 in *Proceedings of the Gulf of Mexico Coastal Ecosystem Workshop,* ed. P. L. Fore and R. D. Peterson. FWS/OBS 80/30. Albuquerque, N.Mex.: U.S. Fish and Wildlife Service.

Reagan, R. E. 1985. Species profiles: life histories and environmental requirements of coastal fishes and invertebrates (Gulf of Mexico): red drum. U.S. Fish and Wildlife Service Biological Report 82 (11.36). U.S. Army Corps of Engineers, TR EL-82-4. 16 pp.

Robins, C. R. 1991. *Common and Scientific Names of Fishes from the United States and Canada.* Bethesda, Md.: American Fisheries Society. 183 pp.

Robins, C. R., and G. C. Ray. 1986. *Atlantic Coast Fishes.* Peterson Field Guides. New York: Houghton Mifflin. 354 pp.

Ross, D. A. 2000. *The Fisherman's Ocean.* Mechanicsburg, Pa.: Stackpole Books. 299 pp.

Schulze-Haugen, M., T. C. Corey, and N. E. Kohler. 2003. *Guide to Sharks, Tunas, and Billfishes of the U.S. Atlantic and Gulf of Mexico.* Narragansett: Rhode Island Sea Grant and NOAA Fisheries. 118 pp.

Shipp, R. L. 1986. *Dr. Bob Shipp's Guide to Fishes of the Gulf of Mexico.* Mobile, Ala.: 20th Century Printing. 256 pp.

Simmons, E. G. 1957. An ecological survey of the upper Laguna Madre of Texas. *Publications of the Institute of Marine Science,* 4(2): 156–200.

Simmons, E. G., and H. D. Hoese. 1959. Studies on the hydrography and fish migrations of Cedar Bayou, a natural tidal inlet on the Central Texas coast. *Publications of the Institute of Marine Science,* 6:57–80.

Simmons, E. G., and J. P. Breuer. 1962. A study of redfish, *Sciaenops ocellatus* Linnaeus, and black drum, *Pogonias cromis* Linnaeus. *Publications of the Institute of Marine Science,* 8:184–211.

Smith, N. P. 1978. Intracoastal tides of upper Laguna Madre, Texas. *Texas Journal of Science,* 20:85–95.

Stokes, G. M. 1973. Life history studies of *Paralichthys lethosigma* and *P. albigutta* in the vicinity of Aransas Pass, Texas. TPWD Coastal Fisheries Division Final Report—1973. 40 pp.

Storey, M. The relation between normal range and mortality of fishes due to cold at Sanibel Island, Florida. *Ecology,* 18(1): 10–26.

Tabb, D. C. 1961. A contribution to the biology of the spotted seatrout, *Cynoscion nebulosus* (Cuvier) of east-central Florida. State of Florida Board of Conservation Technical Series No. 35. 23 pp.

Texas A&M University. 1986. Red tide in Texas: an explanation of the phenomenon. Texas A&M Sea Grant College Program Publication, College Station. 4 pp.

Texas Department of Water Resources. 1983. Laguna Madre estuary: a study of the influence of freshwater inflows. TDWR Report LP-182. Austin, Tex. 270 pp.

Texas General Land Office. *Texas Beach and Bay Access Guide.* 2nd ed. Austin: TGLO. 150 pp.

Texas Parks and Wildlife Department. 1978. *Saltwater Fishes of Texas.* Bulletin no. 52, Austin. 41 pp.

———. 1998. Red tide in Texas: from science to action. Workshop Notebook, University of Texas Marine Science Institute, Port Aransas, April 17–18, 1998. 36 pp.

———. 2000. *Texas Saltwater Fish Identification Pocket Guide.* Seattle, Wash.: Outdoor Empire Publishing. 70 pp.

———. 2002. The Texas shrimp fishery. Appendix A to *Overview of Coastal and Marine Habitat in Texas.* pp. 5–19.

Texas Parks and Wildlife Department Coastal Fisheries Branch. 1975. Information on the biology and the life history of important fish and shellfish of the Texas coast: Preliminary draft. Submitted to Coastal Management Project, General Land Office. pp. 238–45.

Tinsley, R. 1988. *Fishing Texas: An Angler's Guide.* Fredericksburg, Tex.: Shearer Publishing. 317 pp.

Tolan, J. M. 1994. Habitat selection by larval fishes immigrating into estuarine nursery grounds. MS thesis, Texas A&M University–Corpus Christi. 123 pp.

Tunnell, J. W., Jr., and S. A. Alvarado, eds. 1996. *Current Status and*

Historical Trends of the Estuarine Living Resources within the Corpus Christi Bay National Estuary Program Study Area. Vol. 4. Austin: Texas Natural Resource Conservation Commission. 298 pp.

Tunnell, J. W., Jr., and F. W. Judd, eds. 2002. *The Laguna Madre of Texas and Tamaulipas.* College Station: Texas A&M University Press. 346 pp.

Walls, J. G. 1975. *Fishes of the Northern Gulf of Mexico.* Neptune City, N.J.: T.F.H. Publications. 732 pp.

White, M. L., and M. E. Chittenden Jr. 1976. Aspects of the life history of the Atlantic croaker, *Micropogon undulatus.* Texas Agricultural Experiment Station, Department of Wildlife and Fisheries Sciences. 54 pp.

Woods Hole Oceanographic Institution. 1995. *The Ecology and Oceanography of Harmful Algal Blooms (ECOHAB): A National Research Agenda.* Woods Hole, Mass.: WHOI. 67 pp.

Zale, A. V., and S. G. Merrifield. 1989. Species profiles: life histories and environmental requirements of coastal fishes and invertebrates (south Florida): ladyfish and tarpon. U.S. Fish and Wildlife Service Biological Report 82 (11.104). U.S. Army Corps of Engineers, TR EL-82–4. 17 pp.

Index

ISBN-13: 978-1-60344-028-8
ISBN-10: 1-60344-028-3

51695

9 781603 440288